Productivity Management in Hospitality and Tourism

Edited by Nick Johns
Norwich Hotel School

CASSELL

Cassell

Wellington House   215 Park Avenue South
125 Strand   New York
London WC2R 0BB   NY 10003

British Library Cataloguing-in-Publication Data
A catalogue record for this book is available from the British Library.

Library of Congress Cataloging-in-Publication Data
Productivity management in hospitality and tourism / edited by Nick Johns.
    p. cm.
    Includes bibliographical references and index.
    ISBN 0–304–33445–6
    1. Hospitality industry – Management. 2. Tourism – Management.
I. Johns, Nick.
TX911.3.M27P76 1995
647.94′068–dc20
                                        95–22057
                                           CIP

ISBN 0–304–334456 (hardback)

Typeset by Mayhew Typesetting, Rhayader, Powys
Printed and bound in Great Britain by Redwood Books, Trowbridge, Wiltshire

CONTENTS

ABOUT THE EDITOR AND THE CONTRIBUTORS   vi

PREFACE   x

INTRODUCTION   xi

PART 1   ORGANIZATIONAL PRODUCTIVITY   1

1   Top-line productivity: a model for the hospitality and tourism industry   2
John Heap

2   Total quality: an approach to managing productivity in the hotel industry   19
Sheila Stewart and Nick Johns

3   The strategic gap: a multi-site, short break perspective   38
David Edgar

4   Macro aspects of productivity planning for the hospitality industry   55
Michael V. Conlin and Tom Baum

PART 2   THE HUMAN DIMENSION AND PRODUCTIVITY   67

5   Enhancing productivity: intervention strategies for employee turnover   68
Margaret A. Deery and Roderick D. Iverson

6   Productivity through people: the role of human resource management   96
Sandra Watson

7   Productivity in the hotel industry: a cognitive case study   115
Ian Yeoman, Tony Ingold and Sarah Peters

8   Influencing hotel productivity   141
Mark Sasse and Stephen Harwood-Richardson

PART 3   THE PRODUCTIVITY OF OPERATIONS   165

9   Perceptions and interpretations of productivity within fast-food chains: a case study of Wimpy International   166
Stephen Ball

10   Productivity measurement in food service systems   194
Mike Rimmington and John Clark

11   Traditional key ratio analysis versus data envelopment analysis: a comparison of various measurements of productivity and efficiency in restaurants   209
Tommy D. Andersson

12   Productivity and the new service paradigm, or 'servicity' and the 'neo-service paradigm'?   227
Peter L. Jones and Mike Hall

INDEX   241

ABOUT THE EDITOR
AND THE CONTRIBUTORS

Nick Johns is Reader and Director of Research in the Hotel School, City College Norwich, a Regional College of Anglia Polytechnic University. He is well known for his work on the quality and productivity of hospitality operations and has also published extensively on technical issues, such as hygiene and the environment. He has contributed to numerous conferences in the hospitality field, reflecting his wide interests. Nick is currently engaged in developing a new approach to service quality assessment in small hospitality enterprises. He is an Associate Editor of the *International Journal of Contemporary Hospitality Management* and is at present working on a book on research methods specifically for managers of service industries.

Tommy D. Andersson received his PhD from the School of Economics at the University of Göthenburg, Sweden, in 1987. He was appointed associate professor at Bodo Graduate School of Business, Norway in 1989. At present he is back in Göthenburg as a research fellow at the School of Economics, where he is conducting research mainly into hospitality and event management. He has published widely in academic books and journals. He is also a member of the board of both CHRIE and EuroCHRIE and of a number of editorial boards of academic journals.

Stephen Ball is Senior Lecturer in the Department of Food, Nutrition and Hospitality Management and Leader of the Hotel and Catering Management suite of degree courses at the University of Huddersfield. He has a wide range of industrial experience and has acted as consultant for a number of national and international hotel and catering organizations. He has published extensively on productivity in the hospitality industry and has a Master of Philosophy degree for his research into productivity and productivity management in fast-food chains. He is editor of and chief contributor to *Fast Food Operations and Their Management*.

Tom Baum is Professor of International Hotel and Tourism Management at the University of Buckingham. He has international experience of tourism planning and human resource development from work in the Caribbean, Eastern Europe and the Far East. Tom has published extensively in the human resource field, relating to tourism. He has authored and edited several influential volumes on various aspects of international tourism.

John Clark is Senior Lecturer in Hotel and Catering Management at Sheffield Hallam University. He has extensive practical operational management experience with both private and public sectors of the catering industry. John moved to Sheffield after lecturing at a number of further and higher education colleges, including Hong Kong Polytechnic. Among other responsibilities he currently holds the post of course leader for the BSc programme. For the past three years, John has been focusing his research efforts on food production management. In 1994 he received the MPhil award for his work on productivity measurement and management within the catering industry.

Michael V. Conlin is Dean of the Faculty of Business Administration and Director of the Centre for Tourism Research and Innovation at Bermuda College. Michael is a qualified barrister and holds degrees in law and business. He has published widely on human resource matters, with a particular focus on hospitality and tourism in the Caribbean area. He is co-editor (with Tom Baum) of *Island Tourism: Management Principles and Practice*.

Margaret A. Deery has an MA in Industrial Relations and Human Resources and is a lecturer in Human Resource Management in the Department of Hospitality and Tourism at Victoria University of Technology, Australia. She is known for her research interests in such human resource areas as employee turnover, job satisfaction and employee commitment within the hospitality industry, and is currently working for a PhD qualification in this field. Margaret leads a research team in this field and is the recipient of research grants to investigate labour market trends for hospitality graduates and quality control in postgraduate human resource management courses.

David A. Edgar is currently a Senior Lecturer at the Department of Hospitality and Tourism Management, Napier University, Edinburgh. His areas of research interest is the nature of organization strategic dynamics, with particular focus upon the relationships between the head offices and local units of hospitality group organizations. His main focus of interest is market structure and strategy and company performance. David is keenly interested in developments in academic communication, particularly Internet conferencing.

Mike Hall is a Principal Lecturer in the Department of Service Sector Management at the University of Brighton Business School. His main areas of interest include the history and development of UK public policy, public sector economics and the history and methodology of economic thought. He is the author of a number of journal articles and has worked as a consultant to both public and private sector organizations. He is currently writing a textbook outlining a number of economic perspectives in public sector economics.

Stephen Harwood-Richardson is the Research Manager of the Hotel and Catering Training Company (HCTC). He is responsible for a diverse and ongoing programme of research into catering and hospitality employment and training issues, fulfilling the HCTC's responsibilities as an Industry Training Organization (ITO). A graduate in economics, Stephen worked as a researcher for the Law Society for seven years before taking up his present position.

John Heap is Director of Learning Support Services at Leeds Metropolitan University. He is a Fellow of the World Academy of Productivity Science, a member of the Council of the Institute of Management Services, the Chairman of the British Standards Institution's Committee on Management Services, Chairman of the British Standards Institution's Committee on Management Services, the UK member of the International Advisory Council of the World Confederation of Productivity Science and the Functional Coordinator of International Productivity Development, a working group which is jointly sponsored by the European Federation of Productivity Services and the Internationals MTM-Directorate. John is the author of *The Management of Innovation and Design* and *Productivity Management: A Fresh Approach* and is editor of the journal *Work Study*.

Anthony Ingold graduated from the University of London, where he also gained a doctorate in physiological ecology. Trained as a medical microbiologist, he worked for several years on the development of novel chemotherapeutic treatments for chronic respiratory infections in a London hospital. More recently he has worked as a lecturer at the University of Birmingham and is now Reader and Director of Research at Birmingham College of Food. His most recent research and publication has been in the areas of productivity improvement, total quality management and human motivation.

Roderick D. Iverson obtained his initial degrees at Monash University and his PhD at Iowa, and currently lectures in human resource management at the University of Melbourne, Australia. He has published extensively in learned journals in Australia and elsewhere, his specialist fields being absenteeism, labour turnover, organizational change, organizational, union and dual commitment. He has been awarded several research grants, the most recent, from the Australian government, being to study the antecedents and consequences of employees' dual commitment to employing organizations and unions in the banking industries of Australia, New Zealand and the UK.

Peter L. Jones is Head of the Department of Service Sector Management at the University of Brighton Business School. He has worked for large multinational hospitality chains in the UK and Belgium and operated his own Brussels-based restaurant. He is the author or co-author of four key hospitality management textbooks, has written numerous influential articles and has edited an important collection of hospitality management writings. He has also presented conference papers in the UK, USA and Canada, reflecting his research interest in the performance of operational hospitality units. He holds an MBA from the London Business School and is a fellow of the HCIMA. In 1991 he was elected the first President of EuroCHRIE.

Sarah Peters gained her first degree in Hospitality Management at Bournemouth University and later a Postgraduate Diploma in Marketing. She worked as a hotel manager for several years and is currently employed as a lecturer at Birmingham College of Food. Her main teaching areas are operations management, research methods and human resource management. She is at present researching for a PhD in a project concerned with organizational behaviour and psychology, productivity and yield management. Her publications to date have been in the areas of soft systems methodology, facilitation and the group process and human resource management.

Mike Rimmington is Subject Leader for Hospitality Management in the School of Leisure and Food Management at Sheffield Hallam University. He returned to academic life in 1992, after working for Bass PLC in a variety of project and operational management positions. In 1994 he developed and launched the first hospitality management masters programme to be offered on a distance learning basis. Mike is a nominated research supervisor for the development of national occupational standards for catering, hospitality and the licensed trade. He is currently researching and publishing in the area of entrepreneurship and continues to work with John Clark investigating productivity issues within health sector catering operations.

Mark Sasse graduated in combined engineering with business studies at Coventry in 1987. Since this time he has worked in management services and business research for both the manufacturing and service sectors. Prior to joining the Hotel and Catering Training Company to work on this investigation, Mark held a research fellowship at the University of Warwick for three years, working in a consultancy role on several projects for major manufacturing companies. He is currently engaged mainly on the HCTC's productivity project

Sheila Stewart is Enterprise Development Officer at Napier University where she also lectures in the Department of Hospitality and Tourism Management. She was selected as a Fulbright Exchange Lecturer to the USA and gained extensive experience there in the teaching and practice of hospitality management. She has also held a senior position in hospitality education in Hong Kong. Recently she achieved an MBA qualification at Napier, where her research interests include total quality management and pedagogical studies.

Sandra Watson is currently Acting Head of the Department of Hospitality and Tourism Management at Napier University, Edinburgh. Her main discipline of human resource management has been built up from substantial management experience in the hotel industry and from her MSc postgraduate studies in personnel management. She has extensive lecturing experience at both undergraduate and postgraduate level and is a member of the Hotel, Catering and Institutional Management Association. Besides her well known recent studies of the industrial trend towards human resource management, Sandra is actively researching in the field of management development.

Ian Yeoman is a graduate of Sheffield City Polytechnic, with a degree in catering systems. Upon graduation he held several operational management roles with Forte Hotels. More recently he lectured in operations management at Birmingham College of Food, leaving this post in 1994 to take up a teaching post at Napier University. His most recent research and publications have been concerned with productivity, yield management and problem solving in the hospitality management field. In 1994 he received the Mike Simpson Citation from the Operations Research Society.

PREFACE

The chapters in this collection have been developed and refined from papers presented at the IAHMS Spring Conference, hosted by Norwich Hotel School at the Sprowston Manor Hotel, Norwich, England, in April 1995. They centre on the theme of hospitality productivity, which has been a subject of study at Norwich Hotel School for several years. Despite its importance, this area has produced remarkably few reviews, but since the early 1990s it has been the subject of intensive research and speculation. The 1995 IAHMS Spring Conference set out to incorporate all of this thinking and to review previous and non-hospitality work in a number of areas related to productivity. These included:

- the theoretical positioning of the productivity concept in services, particularly hospitality and tourism;
- the relationship between productivity and service quality;
- the impact of the human factor upon the productivity of services;
- new research initiatives throughout the hospitality industry;
- the measurement of productivity in services;
- the management of productivity improvement in service industries.

This book is intended for students and practitioners of hospitality and tourism management, as well as for researchers in these fields. To this end, considerable time and effort has been devoted to clarifying the language and style in which the chapters are expressed. As far as possible, each author has provided a review of extant work in his or her particular area of the productivity field. In this respect alone, the book is a valuable resource for those engaged upon projects concerned with service productivity. In addition to this, all the chapters provide new observations and results. I am particularly glad to be able to include the most up-to-date reports of the major hotel productivity project currently being jointly undertaken by the Hotel and Catering Training Company and Birmingham College of Food. However, this is in no way to denigrate the work of the other authors, all of whom have contributed significantly to our knowledge in this field.

It is impossible to prepare such a book (let alone couple it with a major conference) without incurring huge debts of gratitude. I would of course like to thank all the participants for their excellent contributions. I thank them for their patience too, and their willingness to discuss and deal with the issues that emerged as the chapters developed. In addition, I would like to thank Judith Entwistle-Baker of Cassell for her continuous support, advice and assistance with editorial and publishing matters. I must also thank Jon Bareham and Ewout Cassee of the International Association of Hotel Management Schools, for their permission to run the IAHMS conference. Many thanks are due to Professor Mike McKechnie and to my other colleagues at Norwich, particularly Sue Clark, Evie O'Hara and Darren Lee-Ross. Without them it would have been a poor conference indeed. In fact it might never have managed to get off the ground. Lastly, but probably most importantly I must thank my wife Helen and my family, who coped with me through a series of adversities, on top of which the preparation of this book must at times have seemed the last straw.

Nick Johns
April 1995

INTRODUCTION

The productivity of service industries is a source of concern in Western economies. Patterns of world industry have shifted dramatically during the past few decades, so that the developed West now finds itself in a 'post-industrial' phase of development. Manufacturing industry has been largely replaced by services, of which one of the most important is that which enjoys a general classification as 'hospitality and tourism'. However, there are good grounds for thinking that productivity in all services, and particularly in the hospitality/tourism sector, is low in comparison to that in manufacturing. There is a concern that Western economies may lag behind in an increasingly competitive world, and this fuels a growing preoccupation with service productivity.

Productivity is of course far from being a new concept. It originated during the eighteenth century, in the days of Adam Smith. Ever since that time it has been concerned with the notion of wealth generation. Hence it is firmly associated with manufacturing industry, since one cannot increase wealth without generating new possessions. The productivity concept has been successively embellished by the 'scientific management' movements of Taylor and others. It has also been extensively exploited by capitalists from Henry Ford onwards. Inevitably it has been absorbed into general economic thought and now forms part of the toolkit used by all nations to monitor and manage their economies.

Attempts to apply the productivity concept to service operations probably date back to the rise of the supermarket during the 1960s. Since then, both retail and financial services have eagerly adopted new technologies in attempts to reduce the manpower required per service transaction. In the hospitality field, the most conspicuous productivity developments have been in fast foods, which since the 1970s have pioneered the continuous production of food and the 'formularization' of service. However, the established manufacturing-based view of productivity does not sit well with the service concept. A 'good' service is not like a 'good' car, house or tractor. A service such as a financial transaction, a successful purchase or a session at the hairdresser has a degree of 'utility', but the encounter itself (for which the customer pays) has no utility, and indeed exists only in the customer's mind. Thus, in the case of services, the issue of 'wealth generation' is an arbitrary and questionable one.

Besides this problem should be set the question of *why* productivity is to be managed or measured. In the manufacturing sector, productivity provides a way of checking operational effectiveness. The primary objective of a manufacturing organization is to make goods as cheaply as possible. For a variety of reasons, simply measuring profitability may not adequately reflect whether the organization has achieved this goal. The measurement of productivity makes it possible to benchmark actual production (i.e. of material goods rather than financial turnover) against actual resources used (rather than just their cost). In service industries, productivity cannot easily measure the utility of what has been 'produced', so 'productivity' measurements tend to concentrate upon tangible aspects. This may mean measuring physical output, such as numbers of meals, beds or customers, or it can involve a comparison of the monetary values of output and input. Neither is satisfactory. The former does not measure the whole output, while the latter provides an identical result to that given by standard profitability measures, and therefore provides no basis for comparing efficiency and effectiveness.

This book is an attempt to examine this problem by examining all the aspects that comprise or influence service productivity. Each chapter deals as far as possible with just one aspect of productivity, providing both a review of that area and some original work or thought on the subject. The whole book seeks to represent a transition between the traditional manufacturing view of productivity and a body of new thought that is currently emerging from the 'soft' service sector (i.e. hospitality and tourism). However, as can be seen from the first chapter by John Heap, the manufacturing sector itself is moving away from its traditional view towards a new customer-centred approach to productivity. It is important to bear in mind that developments in our understanding of service productivity are taking place against an overall backdrop of change. This is emphasized by the final chapter: 'Productivity and the new service paradigm or "servicity" and the "neo-service Paradigm"?', in which Peter Jones and Mike Hall discuss how the concept has developed and may continue to develop in the future.

The book is divided into three parts, corresponding with the three broad aspects of productivity represented. These are *organizational/macro aspects, human dimensions* and *operational productivity*. This classification was difficult to make and is to some extent arbitrary. A number of sub-themes are spread throughout the book and overlap the sectional structure. For example, strategy features in Margaret Deery and Roderick Iverson's account of labour turnover. Human aspects are not only represented in Chapters 5 to 8 ('The human dimension and productivity') but also appear extensively in the chapters concerned with top-line productivity (John Heap) and total quality (Sheila Stewart and myself) and in Stephen Ball's account of productivity at Wimpy International. Various authors also refer to the pervasive issue of organizational culture and to the conceptual nature of service productivity.

At the time of writing this, research is an important part of the work of university departments of hospitality and tourism management. As a result there has been a definite and growing interest in research methodologies. Besides its other goals, this book attempts to illustrate a range of research styles and methodologies. Examples of discursive thought and analysis are provided in the chapters by Peter Jones and Mike Hall, and Mike Conlin and Tom Baum respectively. The chapters by John Heap and Sandra Watson place research in a practical management context. Ian Yeoman and his colleagues provide a Gestalt psychology approach to qualitative methodology, while Stephen Ball, Mark Sasse and Stephen Harwood-Richardson offer interesting examples of interview and survey research. Three different quantitative methodologies (extremely important in the investigation of productivity) are represented by the work of Margaret Deery and Roderick Iverson, Tommy Andersson, and Mike Rimmington and John Clark. It is regarded as very important to present a wide range of research approaches in the same volume, since future developments in service productivity research will probably have to bring together both qualitative and quantitative work in new ways. Clearly there are a number of problems to be solved on the research front before major progress can be made in the area of service productivity itself. Although the field is beset with problems, the rewards will be considerable in this important area.

Readers with a specific tourism focus should not be discouraged by the preponderance of articles apparently relating specifically to 'hotels' or 'restaurants'. The reason for this is quite simply that it was not possible to find any speakers in other areas. Inspection of the literature also revealed that the productivity of tourist outlets and events was even less widely researched and discussed than that of hospitality. The objective of this book is, if possible, to open up this area for discussion and study, and this aim will be served if tourism researchers note the lessons represented in this book and build upon the existing research. Apologies are of course due to any speaker in the tourism productivity field who was not made aware of the conference, or who would have liked to contribute to this volume. However, the work presented here is by no means the 'last word' on the subject. Like most fundamental research and thought it provokes many more questions than it answers and many new research directions are suggested, not least in the tourism sector. We therefore hope in this book to have drawn attention to a number of gaps in our knowledge. It will have succeeded in its purpose if it is followed by more books, more knowledge, more thought and more gaps.

PART 1
ORGANIZATIONAL PRODUCTIVITY

ONE

Top-line productivity: a model for the hospitality and tourism industry

John Heap

INTRODUCTION

This chapter introduces the concept of top-line productivity (Heap, 1992). This arises from the author's experience in manufacturing industry, where approaches to productivity measurement and improvement take a variety of forms. These forms are invariably limited in addressing the complete set of factors that the author believes should be included in the productivity ratio, and the concept of top-line productivity is an attempt to avoid such limitations and broaden the concept of productivity. It can be argued that service organizations are not fundamentally dissimilar from manufacturing organizations (Lockyer, 1986) and this chapter extends the concept of top-line productivity from its manufacturing base to the hospitality and tourism sectors.

WHY IS PRODUCTIVITY IMPORTANT?

Productivity is the key determinant of value and is closely related to all the other factors that influence value – quality, service, price and so on. At a national level it is the only means of increasing the size of the cake; most other economic and business strategies are aimed at redistributing the cake to increase the share of one section of the community. For example, companies attack productivity as a means of improving their profitability – the single most widely accepted measure of organizational well-being. Productivity offers an alternative means of measuring the well-being of an organization. Although, naturally, profitability is important, it is often a short-term indicator, and can certainly be influenced heavily over the short term by particular strategies and actions. In the UK, in particular, a company is only as good as its last quarter's profit figures. Management teams who rely only on such measures are unlikely to have a firm grasp on the reality of long-term well-being. Profitability is also affected by external factors; productivity is a much better reflector of the policies and practices of the individual organization.

Productivity may need to be addressed and measured:

- for strategic reasons, in order to compare the global performance of an organization with competitors or similar firms;
- for tactical reasons, to enable performance control of the organization or sub-units of it;
- for planning purposes, to compare the relative benefits accruing from the use of different inputs or varying proportions of the same inputs;
- for other purposes, such as collective bargaining (Teague and Eilon, 1973).

WHAT IS PRODUCTIVITY?

Productivity is both a simple and a complex concept. At its simplest level, it can be expressed as the simple ratio of output to input and is thus similar to ratios that measure efficiency or other aspects of performance. The true complexity of the concept is only realized when an attempt is made to define the components of output and input.

Because it is not a simple concept, many organizations ignore it. This is especially true of new and growing organizations, where other issues (getting and keeping 'the show on the road') either must or simply do take precedence. In fact, most organizations go through some form of 'learning curve' with respect to their attitude to productivity. Typical strategies for dealing with this are as follows:

- ignore productivity;
- concentrate on labour productivity;
- attack process efficiency (often with technology);
- review product productivity (product range, component lists, etc.);
- start again!

Of course, in manufacturing industry the concept is simpler than in service industries, since at least the product exists in a real, physical form – a car, a television, a nail or whatever. Thus (superficially at least), it is easy to measure output. The productivity of a car manufacturer can be measured (and often is) in terms of cars produced per member of the labour force.

WHAT IS TOP-LINE PRODUCTIVITY?

It is, of course, easy to count units of output but this (alone) is not what customers buy. A customer is only concerned with quantity of production in so far as it brings down the cost of manufacturing and makes the selling price lower. When someone buys a car or other product, he or she makes the purchasing decision based on a number of factors. These will vary with the particular product but could include such factors as: functionality, reliability, aesthetics, ease of use, fashion and, of course, cost. The customer weighs up these (top-line) factors and makes a judgement as to whether the purchase offers 'value for money'.

It is important to remember that productivity is a ratio and that both the numerator and the denominator are complex amalgams of a variety of factors. Many organizations claim to have productivity measurement and/or improvement programmes. Often, these are addressing only a relatively small sub-set of the total factors and thus, while perhaps being useful, may be self-limiting in the potential for success. It is very common, for example, for organizations to concentrate on addressing input factors only, i.e. attempting productivity improvement by reducing the resources going into a particular process.

Obviously, there are essentially two alternative strategies for improving productivity. The first is to improve output while keeping inputs constant (or ensuring that they rise proportionally less than output); the second is to reduce inputs while maintaining (or increasing) output. These are commonly termed expansive (increasing output) and contractive (reducing input) strategies (Johns and Wheeler, 1991).

In practice, most organizations constrain their contractive strategy on labour input alone, by measuring and attempting to improve labour productivity. This (labour productivity) is a reasonable choice of ratio if labour costs are the most significant portion of total costs. Improving labour productivity is, in fact, the basis for a whole range of productivity approaches and techniques – work study perhaps being the most common. Although they are valuable, the danger with such approaches is that effort is concentrated on reducing the ineffective time of the (direct) workers while other areas, almost certainly of greater potential, are ignored. This includes the overall 'system' of work. It is not uncommon to find situations where the direct work involved in a particular process is, say, eight hours but the overall door-to-door time for the process is, say, 40 hours. Work-in-progress lies waiting for the next part of the process. Individual operators may be highly efficient and productive but the system is ineffective and productivity is low.

Increasingly, within manufacturing, labour costs are not the most significant input. More and more capital equipment is used to reduce labour input. Any organization that changes the equipment it uses, but continues to measure productivity using only labour costs, must get a distorted view of productivity and of organizational well-being. With the introduction of capital equipment, labour productivity is almost bound to improve. If this is taken as a performance indicator for the organization, results may look impressive. But if the capital has not been spent wisely and the equipment introduced is not used effectively and efficiently, the organization will be in trouble.

This is obviously true in the hotel industry. Room rates are set partly according to market forces (what the customer will pay and the competition will allow) but partly according to the income needed to service the capital debt used to build or purchase the hotel. Powers (1992) cites a rule of thumb which suggests that the average room rate must reflect one dollar for every thousand dollars in cost per room. Thus, a hotel which cost $75,000 per room to build would need a room rate of the order of $75. If, however, this is more than the market will stand, and the hotel goes into liquidation and is subsequently bought for $50,000, the new owner will be able to survive on a rate of something like $50. Other hotel costs are based on the recovery of capital cost and are similarly fixed (e.g. for kitchen equipment), and the hotel must address (capital) productivity improvement by adding the value it adds to its capital by improving, enhancing and extending service – and increasing the rates it charges.

The concept of top-line productivity is an attempt to consider more than labour as an input to the productivity ratio but, more importantly, to recognize the importance of considering more than throughput in the numerator of the productivity ratio – the other top-line factors may have a dramatic impact on the effectiveness of an organization. Thus it is not simply an expansive strategy, since it involves consideration of not only output levels but the totality of factors that are identified as components of output. Top-line productivity is thus the amalgam of top-line factors compared to the aggregation of resource inputs (Heap, 1992).

One problem with addressing more than one factor at a time is that it is sometimes difficult to merge and/or compare figures from different sources for different resources. Combining data into some form of global measure is not easy. It can be done most simply by using some common unit of measurement, and money is by far the simplest, though not without its problems. One particular problem is the changing value of money over time and the need to make adjustments when comparing figures over different time periods. Of course, there are approaches and methods that are designed to handle this problem but they do make easy comparison of simple data problematic.

As mentioned earlier, organizations tend to address different parts of the productivity ratio and different factors at different stages of their development. There is nothing wrong in this (in fact, it is often a very wise thing to do) as long as the organization is aware of the breadth of the total picture and takes a conscious decision to concentrate on only some aspects of this total picture. Factors which may govern the principal points of attack include the external environment (the state of the market and the behaviour of competitors) and the availability of resources. For example, Britain gets 38 per cent of its overseas visitors from long-haul markets – as distinct from 12 per cent in France and 7 per cent in Italy (Medlicott, 1992). Such differences are bound to have an effect on promotion and marketing strategies, but these differences may also influence approaches to productivity improvement.

Another major factor is the location of the main thrust for productivity improvement. This can lie at corporate, central levels or at a devolved level of the organization. Where it is at the devolved level, it is almost always process-oriented – how things are done. Although this is very important, it should ideally follow an assessment of what is done, but this generally requires action at the most senior levels of the organization.

Thus the simple ratio 'productivity' is actually quite a complex expression, which hides a number of issues and a number of problems. Understanding what these issues and problems are is the first step to devising a truly effective productivity improvement programme.

Moving away from manufacturing and looking at service industries does not lessen the problems. Productivity in the service sector (in the UK, in Europe and in the USA) is less than that in manufacturing (Elfing, 1989). This suggests that it is necessary to examine new ways of measuring and improving productivity, and that the service sector is a good place to start.

TOP-LINE PRODUCTIVITY IN THE HOSPITALITY AND TOURISM SECTORS

The job of a manufacturer is to put together an acceptable mix of output factors for a target selling price as the product specification. This product specification is then translated into a manufacturing process that can deliver the right quantities of the product (to meet the marketing plan/sales forecasts) within the specification at the target cost. Controlling all the parts of the process is the job of manufacturing management.

The same principles apply within service industries. The customer 'buys' a service – but this is made up of lots of different elements which contribute to its value (Witt and Muhlemann, 1994). One obvious example is that of the 'meal out'. This can be anything from a fast-food takeaway to an expensive restaurant, and within each category, there will be a range of venue types, prices, accompaniments and embellishments.

Thus the customer could be buying such factors as food (quality of raw materials, quality of preparation), quality service (in context), atmosphere/ambience and associated entertainment. The 'value' might be dominated by one of these factors. Thus, the market price of, for example, a hamburger in a restaurant featuring roller-skating, singing waitresses might be very much higher than in a simple, fast-food outlet. The output is much more than food alone. Measuring productivity is, therefore, much more than measuring a simple factor such as meals per hour. Money taken per hour would be one simple measure but this would take no account of the fact that one establishment may have had a much greater capital investment or may need to take much more because it has significantly higher rates or a much more variable demand rate (while having the same constant supply factors). Service managers have to improve their output rates and control their resource inputs, summed up as 'Sell more, charge more and cut costs' by Michael Jolly of the Tussauds Group (Jolly, 1993).

Different customers may have different requirements, and the same customer may well have different requirements on different occasions. Any one establishment cannot provide all the variety required, so it is important that the customer knows what to expect from a particular establishment, and just as important that he or she then gets it. Managing the expectations of the customer is an important part of achieving a high value rating.

What does seem apparent is that often it is the relatively small 'additional' touches that are recognized by the customer as the factors that add particular value to a service. If one looks at the difference in service between an economy air flight and a first class flight, it is hard to understand why anyone would pay the tremendous premium for first class. The major factor is undoubtedly the additional legroom: all the rest (the better food, the slippers, eyepads, etc.) are peripheral factors (and comparatively cheap to provide); yet it is the total package that carries the first class banner, and justifies the premium.

The concept of top-line productivity recognizes that 'output' is an amalgam of a number of top-line factors, and that productivity improvement is an exercise in optimizing the mix of top-line factors for a given resource input.

A major aim of fast-food outlets is to improve productivity – this can be achieved by getting more throughput or more output (including all the other factors) or by reducing inputs. Often, addressing output factors other than throughput has a much more significant effect on the productivity ratio. If changes can be made to any of the output factors, it may be possible to charge a premium price and still retain a good value rating.

The hospitality industry has known this longer than other industries. In a hotel, for example, it is the total experience of the guest that is 'the service'. This includes not only what is done to the guest but how it is done. The physical side of the service (the size of the room, the quality of the food, the facilities available) must be 'up to scratch' but these are enhanced by the behaviour of the staff in their interactions with the guest, and it is these interactions that may shape the guest's view of the value of the service he or she receives.

Visitor management at tourist 'honeypots' is an example of an effective 'top-line strategy'. The cost of introducing visitor management increases resource inputs, but can affect both throughput of visitors and perceived quality of the visitor experience. The employment of 'town rangers' in Stratford-upon-Avon to meet, greet and guide visitors is an example.

In manufacturing, many of the top-line factors are 'designed in' to the product. The product has to be functional but it should also be designed to look good, to be reliable, to be easily manufactured, to be easily maintained and so on. In fact, one of the greatest causes of low productivity is bad design – subsequent (process) productivity improvement may only be attempts to ameliorate a bad basic design. Although in service industries there may sometimes be no tangible product, good design is just as important. Hotels, restaurants, shops, bars, museums, etc have to be functional; but it is also necessary to design in additional features to add value. Once the design is 'good', there is a potential for high productivity. That potential is turned into results by process productivity – the design of procedures and working methods that allow efficient and effective working in pursuit of serving the customers.

One important aspect of service industries (and especially the hospitality industry) is that the 'product' usually includes this interpersonal relationship between customer and service provider. Once the interaction is over, so is the service. Unlike in manufacturing industry, the 'goods' cannot be checked before being released to the customer, and a faulty product cannot be recalled. There is no stock or inventory which can be carried over for subsequent sale – if a hotel room is empty for a night, that business has been lost for ever. The concept of 'right first time, every time' really is important. That is why good design is so important. Again in manufacturing, there are two approaches to quality: quality assurance and quality control. Quality assurance is about establishing a quality specification for the product and then establishing systems, process and procedures which ensure that the product is turned out to specification. Quality control is a post-production check that it has been turned out to specification. In service industries, quality control is usually too late to avoid the dissatisfied customer.

Of course, some aspects of the total service are mechanical, and sometimes the cost-cutting approach to productivity improvement increases this mechanization and reduces the interpersonal contact – serving by vending machines, for example. Improving value may mean offering customers a choice: a low cost, mechanized service (tea and coffee making facilities in rooms) or a 'personal touch' (room service) at a premium price. Even those who don't take up some of the choices will have their perception of value increased by the existence of the choice. When the personal touch is delivered, high productivity means getting things right every time, within acceptable cost levels.

THE MEASUREMENT OF PRODUCTIVITY

If productivity (and its improvement) is valued, it follows that it needs to be measured, so that progress can be identified and targets can be set for that progress. It is dangerous to rely on simple, quantitative measures – there is always a problem of such measures being incomplete but, because they are measures, they drive behaviour. It is a general rule (and not a surprising one) that 'what you measure, you get'. Those subject to measurement will quite naturally adjust their performance to achieve better results on those factors being measured, and worry significantly less about factors that are not part of any measurement regime.

There is a natural tendency to establish measures because they are easy to measure, rather than the most appropriate. This encourages a mechanistic approach to productivity measurement and improvement which is sub-optimal (Thorpe and Horsburgh, 1984). Thus, it is vital that measures are carefully thought out and constructed. This is particularly true where longer-term attitudinal or cultural change is required; care must be taken that shorter-term aims and their quantified goals do not militate against longer-term aspirations.

Measuring productivity is not an easy task. Often the measures used are only effective as comparators – of different organizations or of the same organization over time. A single measure is meaningless. In service industries, because of the nature of the 'output', the problem is worse than in manufacturing. Of course, even in service industries, many processes are in effect 'industrial' and have obvious measures. Occupancy percentages and average room rates give a measure of hotel rooms performance, for example, and with measures of rooms servicing costs can give a direct productivity measure for that part of a hotel's business. Such figures can then be used as the basis for improving the return on investment provided by the letting of rooms (Lockwood and Jones, 1990).

As can be seen, if top-line factors are to be included, the measurement is also more complicated. Some of the top-line factors are not readily quantifiable and other means of incorporating such factors into our measures must be used. Work has been done on this using a variety of approaches and techniques (McLaughlin and Cofey, 1990). The important thing to remember about top-line factors is that whether or not the supplying organization measures them, its customers will. They may use subjective and imperfect measures, and certainly will use incomplete measures since they are concerned only with the top-line facts and not with the bottom-line ones, but they will nevertheless measure. It is important that the organization does it first!

The measures used need not necessarily be formal, quantifiable measures. If, for example, it is desired to enhance 'quality' (whatever that is!), and if the customer is the only true judge of quality, then it is necessary to have some means of measuring the customer's level of satisfaction with the service – this has to be incorporated into the overall measure. Thus the approach to establishing a useful measure is as follows:

1 *Identify the top-line factors* to be included (the criteria that influence the customer's perception of value). This would normally be done through a process of customer research. The difficulty is to establish what proportion of 'output' should be assigned to throughput. Many organizations will keep this proportion very high, at least in their initial dealings with the concept of top-line productivity.
2 *Identify the relative weightings to be assigned* to each factor (including throughput). These should be identified during the same customer research.
3 *Establish a 'scoring' system* for each factor. The precise nature of the measurement is not too important since measures are only to be used on a comparative basis over different time periods. For many factors, the scores will be based on subjective judgements (of customers); for others it may be possible to acquire reliable, quantitative measures.
4 *Establish the base (current) score* for each factor.

At some time in the future, the score for each factor can be re-established and an index for each factor can be constructed by comparing that score with the base score. The relative weights of each factor can then be used to combine all the measures into a top-line productivity index.

The process serves two main purposes: it ensures that the index includes those important factors identified as directly affecting customer perception of value, and it allows the creation of subsidiary indices for each factor. Obviously, where an organization assigns a higher weighting to non-throughput factors (i.e. to customer-derived factors), the index more strongly reflects changes in such factors. Even where the difference between a top-line index and a throughput-only index is small (because the organization has not assigned significant weighting to other factors) it does serve to remind that there is a difference, and it is worth remembering that small changes in customer perception can have a big effect on market penetration and profitability.

Although it is important to include all relevant factors in the productivity ratio, it is often necessary to establish separate measures for separate parts of an organization – or for separate activities, where these can be regarded as significantly discrete. In a hotel chain, for example, it would naturally be appropriate to measure separately the productivity of different hotels. It is also appropriate and useful to establish (additionally) separate measures on a functional or activity basis for, say, room servicing, restaurant service, bar service, etc.

Service industries often attempt to solicit customer feedback via such devices as the room questionnaire. The problem is that this is often not part of a systematic programme of measurement of guest satisfaction and, at best, will be incomplete (Jones and Lockwood, 1989). (Achieving good feedback from questionnaires is not measured – staff are therefore not driven to encourage guests to complete their questionnaires.) Remember, it is the customer's perceptions that are the most important factor, not the provider's. Thus, the measure of the efficiency with which rooms are serviced needs to be tempered with the value that the customer puts on the way in which the room is serviced. A specific technique known as 'perceptual blueprinting' has been devised to deal with such subjective measures (Randall and Senior, 1992).

The main issue is to recognize that a simple ratio of throughput to resource inputs (even if all resources are included) is an incomplete measure if it ignores all the factors that customers value in the service provided.

PRODUCTIVITY IMPROVEMENT

Productivity measurement is not an end in itself. It is used as a diagnostic tool, as a basis for measuring improvement and as a means of establishing progress towards a defined target. To be effective in such roles, measurement needs to be part of a structured programme of productivity measurement, review and management.

The fundamental questions of productivity improvement are:

- What is the aim of the activity/endeavour?
- What do the customers want?

- What are the real constraints?
- How might the aims be achieved?
- How are things done now?
- How are the same things done by others?
- How can the needs of customers best be met?
- How can things best be done?

Subsidiary questions are:

- Who is responsible for achieving specific objectives?
- When will objectives and plans be realized?

There is no simplistic approach or technique that makes the answering of these questions a formality. The questions are vital, and must continue to be asked in an iterative fashion. Almost all the questions can be followed by 'Why?' Why, for example, are things done in a particular way? This questioning approach forms the basis of many of the productivity 'techniques': work study, value analysis, organization and methods, and so on.

Whatever structure is imposed on the questioning approach of critical analysis, it is important to identify the key value and cost factors in any situation, and the sensitivity of those key factors to changes in the environment or to internal changes that might be made. For example, it may be necessary to know the effects on the profitability of a part of an operation of a 3 per cent pay rise, a 5 per cent increase in material costs or a change in technology. If the change is minor, the factor is not a key factor and too much attention should not be devoted to it; unless, although minor in impact, it is easy to accomplish, in which case it would be churlish not to take the benefit that can readily accrue. (In practice, such sensitivity analysis should be done when the productivity measurement regime is being constructed.)

Even within any one factor, it is always worth bearing in mind the Pareto rule: that 80 per cent of outcome is determined by 20 per cent of an input factor; e.g. 80 per cent of stockholding costs are normally tied up in 20 per cent of stock items. By concentration on high value or high cost items, major benefits can often be realized without the detailed effort required for complete coverage.

In addition to areas of activity, areas of non-activity must be examined. If one of the established charting techniques is used to record what goes on in a given process, and then a time estimate is assigned to each of the activities in the process, a time estimate for the overall process is obtained. However, when the process actually happens, invariably there are inefficiencies, waiting periods, corrective actions and so on which make the real time much longer. Unfortunately, much work is often sucked into such unproductive activity; recognizing this means that a process should be viewed as a complete entity, in addition to its individual components being considered.

It is important to consider productivity at all stages of activity. It has already been suggested that the greatest benefits accrue when high productivity is 'built in' at the design stage of a building, facility, system or process. In the hospitality industry the design of hotels or parts of hotels (such as kitchens) is an important determinant of productivity (Johns, 1993). If not considered at the design stage, subsequent productivity improvement is, in effect, remedial action – and almost certainly sub-optimal.

It is beneficial to consider the structure of an organization, and the parts of it under scrutiny. Few organizations review structure in a systematic way. Structures normally grow by accident: a small organization (where structure is not a major issue and certainly not a major problem) grows into a large organization; structural decisions are taken along the way but these are generally taken on pragmatic grounds. The organization is split along certain lines simply so that people can cope with responsibility or workloads. Organizations have invisible 'walls' that build up between sections and departments. These walls can militate against high productivity because communication and cooperation fail at the barrier. Obviously, organizations must have some structure but care must be taken to ensure that the structure is designed, deliberately, in order to help to provide the potential for productivity. Other things then have to be done (information and communication systems built) to help break down the barriers created (usually unwittingly) by the structure.

In large organizations, structure decisions may be based on a number of factors. Structure may be designed to aid strategic planning (breaking the organization down into manageable units with discrete business objectives), branding (breaking the organization down into units that support different markets and are differently branded, such as Forte Crest, Posthouse, etc.), the assignment of responsibility (giving key senior managers their own 'empire' to control) and so on. It is difficult to prescribe the basis on which such a decision should be made, but the decision should be made rationally for reasons that can be articulated (at least within the boardroom!). Technology gives some help. Because information can be manipulated and distributed much more quickly than in the past, it is now possible to build structures that can be supported by effective information and decision-support systems. Once, large organizations had to be decentralized because decisions had to be taken where the information was; now, it is possible (though not necessarily desirable) to build centralized, effective structures for large organizations. Structure thus becomes an important decision rather than the result of circumstance.

Structure also relates to the lower-level organization – the way in which roles and jobs are put together. Work and jobs can be designed to create roles for individuals that offer them status, variety, reward and development. This is not easy. Chambermaids, porters and kitchen-hands may have relatively low-skilled jobs but it is possible to build into their role elements that allow them some discretion, and a chance to show their commitment and concern for productivity and quality. If this is not done, it is difficult to get them to 'sign up for' any productivity programme. There is a need to respect the natural groupings of people that will form according to the work they do, and to respect the views, attitudes, concerns and feelings of these groups. It is usually necessary to build workgroups within a structure, but these should have some relation to natural, informal groups. Workgroups will be expected to contribute to the improvement of productivity – they must see that it is in their interest to do so – and they should be offered some (perhaps, small) degree of autonomy in terms of some of the decisions that have to be made about their work.

When one is considering alternative ways of doing things, it is important to start by considering as wide a variety of ideas as possible. This is best achieved by using the widest variety of people possible and by encouraging them to be creative and imaginative. It is a truism to say that ideas from those involved in the job should be considered. This is often done by implementing such approaches as suggestion schemes and other ways in which they can submit ideas. Unfortunately, ideas are time-dependent. Good ideas at the wrong time are hard to deal with. It is therefore often much better, and much simpler, to use consultative techniques at the time of specific investigations or initiatives than to attempt to have permanent idea-raising approaches. The alternative is to construct a systematic process for soliciting and dealing with ideas. The use of quality circles is one possibility – but beware of raising expectations that cannot be satisfied.

The point of using specific techniques is to systematize the process of critical questioning, to ensure that nothing is overlooked. Some people confuse the systematization of the approach to investigating the work with the systematization of the work itself. They are not necessarily linked. Systematizing the work can pay dividends – especially when the process and procedures set down are used as a means of achieving quality results with less qualified, and less expensive, staff (such as moving from the use of 'creative' chefs to the 'process kitchen' working to a limited and well-defined menu). An example is the *sous vide* process, which both renders the product less perishable and ensures that materials become a highly controllable cost (Johns *et al.*, 1992). This can be analogous to the move in manufacturing industry from craft-based production to the techniques of mass and flow production. Remember, however, that less qualified staff are often less flexible – they may be unable to cope and adapt if the system breaks down.

It is worth remembering that many of the factors involved in the productivity ratio are interdependent. When a particular factor in a productivity investigation is addressed, there is a need to be careful about the impact on other factors. Naturally, this is particularly true with regard to the relationship between bottom-line and top-line factors. Cutting costs in a specific area or activity (such as reducing the frequency of redecoration) will almost certainly have an impact on the customer's perception of quality and value. It is worth trying to 'decouple' top-line and bottom-line factors, to identify those areas which are not directly linked; for example, by first concentrating the search for cost-cutting potential on back office activity.

PEOPLE

It is apparent from what has been said so far that productivity improvement requires the entire organization to be working together, pulling in the same direction. It is also apparent that in service industries generally and in hospitality specifically, much more so than in manufacturing, top-line productivity factors are delivered and enhanced by front-line personnel. Any programme of productivity improvement must recognize the importance of the staff as the key players and must address the CREST factors:

- commitment and communication;
- respect;
- enthusiasm;
- security and support;
- training.

Commitment to productivity improvement begins at the top but must be communicated to all employees. It stems from an awareness that addressing top-line productivity is the way to deliver competitive advantage in a systematic, structured and holistic manner, and from an awareness that success is dependent on the participation and involvement of all employees. Communication depends fundamentally on a will to communicate and that comes from commitment – so they go hand in hand. But communication also requires appropriate choice of communication methods and media, and a remembrance that communication is a two-way process. Methods have to be established to seek out the views of employees on their jobs and ways in which positive changes can take place. This introduces the concept of respect – proper respect for the views of employees will pay dividends. It is necessary to understand the attitudes, beliefs and norms that form the views and feelings of employees, deal with them accordingly, accept feedback from downward communication and offer feedback to upward communication. Employees will work positively and constructively if they have self-respect: a pride in their work, in their group and in their organization. This stems from the above commitment and communication in not only what is asked of them, but also how it is asked.

Creating enthusiasm is the process of providing motivation. Motivation is not something that is done to people, but something that can be created, facilitated and promoted within them. Jobs and work roles need to be designed to offer intrinsic reward and pride, because employees have a degree of autonomy over some (however small) aspects of their own work.

If there is a desire to generate ideas and innovation from the workforce, they must be given the chance to fail. They must feel secure that what they offer will be treated with respect (that word again) and properly considered. Employees also need security of employment; this is something that may not be guaranteed but the fear of not knowing can be removed by an open and honest approach in dealings with employees and their representatives.

Support takes a number of forms. There is the physical provision and maintenance of appropriate facilities, equipment and tools to carry out the work, the provision of support services and the provision of psychological support through effective communication and respect.

Training is such an obvious support process that it should not be necessary to include it – but it is! In the UK, particularly, there appears to be an aversion to training. It seems to be assumed that employees only want training and development provided when there is a direct financial reward attached. Yet there is no evidence of this. For productivity improvement, people need to be trained to do their jobs effectively and efficiently; they should also be trained in the concepts of productivity and its improvement so that they can better assist with the process.

Employees can only be expected to give of their best when they know what is expected of them – and why – and when they are adequately prepared.

THE TOP-LINE PRODUCTIVITY IMPROVEMENT PROGRAMME

The complexity of the concepts involved in top-line productivity and the importance of ensuring that productivity is viewed in a holistic and all-embracing way mean that, in order to be effective in improving productivity, it is important to conduct a systematic, methodical programme that ensures that key issues are not omitted. It is difficult to be prescriptive about the form of such a programme but a number of key issues can be identified as guiding principles.

Ensure that a senior figure has overall responsibility for productivity measurement and improvement

This is to make sure that there is real commitment from the top – commitment that can be driven down the organization – and a focal point for information, messages, concerns and actions about productivity development.

In a large organization, it might be necessary to appoint a productivity or programme coordinator to handle the day-to-day management of activity and communication of the programme. This person would be responsible for interpreting policy decision into action and for reporting actions, progress and results to the senior executive (and colleagues). Obviously, if such a person were to have a productivity improvement background, this would be helpful; otherwise some induction and training in principles and techniques will be necessary.

Communicate!

Introduce people to the concepts of productivity and its improvement – let people know why and how things are to be changed (with their help). This might use existing communication methods and media, if they are appropriate and effective. It is worth considering the nature of 'presentation': is there to be a catchy title for the programme that can be used to help 'sell' it to the employees? As before, it is necessary to bear in mind the ability of the organization to manage the expectations of people. The programme should be launched with a blaze of publicity only when there is confidence that most people will see some action and (it is hoped) some results within a reasonable time scale – otherwise disillusionment can set in. (It might be worth considering having some key changes in mind ready to show (relatively) fast action after such a launch.) With most major initiatives, there is one chance to get it right.

As the programme continues, it is important to maintain this communication. People should be aware of what is happening and why, and they should be aware of the results being achieved. This, again, might be through some established communications method (team briefing, weekly reports or whatever) or a newsletter or some other device might be established to add weight to the whole programme. Remember, when results are communicated, they must be of interest to employees, because the results are relevant to them – this also shows respect for their concerns and views.

To aid communication, and commitment, the appointment of local coordinators or liaison officers should be considered; they will spread the message at the local level and provide feedback and input from those 'on the ground'. Naturally, these people will need some induction/orientation and training if they are to be effective in this role.

Identify key issues, key strategies and key productivity measures

This sounds simple, but actually requires much time, thought and discussion. The key is in deciding the real objectives. What is the organization most trying to change/

improve, and why? Does it want to reduce operating costs; improve its image, move upmarket; increase repeat business; attract more weekend guests? From this it should be possible to build up strategies for achieving the change and measures that will show when progress is being made. These measures may be imperfect but they must help to drive behaviour along the chosen lines. The issues, strategies and measures should involve all relevant people in their determination; common, shared ownership of the new activities is required.

In a large organization, it may also be necessary to identify priority areas for implementation of the programme. It is usually beneficial to work throughout the organization at the same time, but for logistical reasons this may not be possible. If the programme is to be phased, it is necessary to work to a strict time plan that ensures that each part of the organization knows when it comes 'on-stream'.

Identify mechanisms for participation

How are staff (as individuals and groups) to have their say, to voice their concerns and to make their contribution? Similarly, where they do make a contribution, how can it be recognized and rewarded? The programme must be made relevant, interesting and fun! Momentum must be established and maintained; people must continue to pay attention, to think and to act in support of the programme. Starting any programme is always easy; keeping it running and maintaining effectiveness is always much more difficult.

Prepare local plans

Following on from the previous step, there must be a mechanism whereby the productivity coordinator, local liaison officer and a particular workgroup can work together to install the selected measurement regime and plan measures and actions to start the process of addressing key, identified top-line and bottom-line factors in the pursuit of productivity improvement. Such plans may be a mixture of top-down and bottom-up activity but ideally the plan must be 'owned' by the local team that has to make the appropriate changes. The plan should consist of a mixture of small and large items and short- and long-term items, and may involve some issues that need external (to the working group) investment or support. Such local plans should be reported up through the structure so that an aggregated company plan can be created and overall levels of action and investment can be identified and (and it hoped) planned (recognizing that this may have some effect on timescales for certain activities).

The nature of the organization (and its culture and management style) will determine whether these local plans should be constructed according to some corporate framework; the most important thing is that local plans exist and that the local plans meet the spirit of the programme.

Get things moving!

Planning is important. Communicating is also important. Above all, results must be delivered. The high priority items of the local plans and any corporate side to the programme have to be implemented. Action must be seen to take place – and it is hoped that some quick results will flow. It is not wise to expect too much too soon, but some activities with short-term pay-backs should be selected as part of the initial portfolio of activity to give some positive feedback to all those involved in the programme.

Obviously, any results must be communicated via the chosen methods/media. It is important that communication is constant and consistent – it is no use starting a monthly newsletter that after the two first issues (when enthusiasm and momentum are high) starts to slip and become later and later. If consistency cannot be delivered, it should not be started in the first place.

The communication should form part of the feedback that is used to amend the programme. Local groups should be able to learn from the work and the results of others (there must be no 'copyright' on good ideas) and respond at their own local level, by modifying their own productivity plans.

Keep things moving!

There should be periodic 'kick-starts' to ensure the momentum is maintained. These can take a variety of forms, from particular, 'special' communications (a corporate video aimed at productivity, for example), through special events (perhaps opportunities for rewarding (via recognition) individuals or groups that have achieved spectacular results or put in special effort), to additional training sessions to introduce new techniques and approaches, or whatever. They serve to remind people that the programme is important to the company and their participation in the programme is also important.

Report

The results of the measurement regime must be reported. With changes that are designed to produce long-term, rather then short-term, benefits this can be a problem. People might feel dispirited if their efforts are not showing up in the official measurements. This means that care needs to be taken about the measures to be used, the measures reported and the ways in which they are reported. Careful choice of results can emphasize the positive aspects. At the same time, it is important not to be too patronizing in terms of filtering and censoring the information. It may be possible that some measures will get worse (while changes are taking place) before they get better. They can be reported as long as the reasons behind the figures are also reported and explained.

Review

A top-line productivity programme is concerned with the constant monitoring, review and improvement of productivity – the programme itself need to be subject to periodic and critical review. 'Mistakes' will be made; some parts of the programme will work better than others. Such things are not problems, as long as lessons are learned from them. The review process must involve all those concerned – if they are important enough to help to improve productivity, they must be important enough to help improve how it is done. Initially, at least, changes should be to application rather than to basic concept – after all, the fundamental aims of the exercise are known, and at this stage it is simply necessary to identify if there are better ways of achieving them. Deming talked about 'constancy of purpose' (Walton, 1989). Let's stick with the ends, but perhaps change the means.

CONCLUSION

Productivity is important, much more so than quality, since quality is automatically subsumed within the concept of top-line productivity. Attacking productivity in order to improve it means attacking what is done and how it is done and thinking about both the outputs and the inputs of the various processes and systems. Only by addressing both can the most complete route to productivity improvement be found; and an organization that is both effective and efficient be created.

REFERENCES

Elfing, T. (1989) 'The main features and underlying cause of the shift to services'. *Services Industries Journal*, **9**(3), 337–56.

Heap, J.P. (1992) *Productivity Management: a Fresh Approach*. London: Cassell.

Johns, N. (1993) 'Productivity management through design and operation: a case study'. *International Journal of Contemporary Hospitality Management*, **5**(2), 20–4.

Johns, N. and Wheeler, K.L. (1991) 'Productivity and performance measurement and monitoring'. In R. Teare and A. Boer (eds), *Strategic Hospitality Management*. London: Cassell, pp. 45–70.

Johns, N., Wheeler, K. and Cowe, P. (1992) 'Productivity angles on sous-vide production'. In R. Teare, D. Adams and S. Messenger (eds), *Managing Projects in Hospitality Operations*. London: Cassell, pp. 146–68.

Jolly, M. (1993) 'Increasing business profitability in the tourism industry'. *Tourism*, 79, July–September, 12–17.

Jones, P. and Lockwood, A. (1989) *The Management of Hotel Operations*. London: Cassell, pp. 164–6.

Lockwood, A. and Jones, P. (1990) 'Applying value engineering to rooms management'. *International Journal of Contemporary Hospitality Management*, **2**(1), 27–32.

Lockyer, K. (1986) 'Service – a polemic and a proposal'. *International Journal of Operations and Production Management*, **6**(3), 5–9.

McLaughlin, C.P. and Cofey, S. (1990) 'Measuring productivity in services'. *International Journal of Service Industry Management*, **1**(1), 46–64.

Medlicott, M. (1992) 'Lessons for the future'. *Tourism*, 74, May, 6–8.

Powers, T. (1992) *Introduction to Management in the Hospitality Industry*, 4th ed. New York: John Wiley & Sons.

Randall, L. and Senior, M. (1992) 'Measuring quality in hospitality services'. *International Journal of Contemporary Hospitality Management*, **4**(2), vi–viii.

Teague, J. and Eilon, S. (1973) *Productivity Measurement: a Brief Survey*. London: Imperial College of Science and Technology/Chapman and Hall.

Thorpe, R. and Horsburgh, S. (1984) 'Productivity'. In T. Bentley (ed.), *The Management Services Handbook*, 2nd ed. (ed.) London: Pitman, London, pp. 191–211.

Walton, M. (1989) *The Deming Management Method*. London: Mercury Business Books.

Witt, C.A. and Muhlemann, A.P. (1994) 'The implementation of total quality management in tourism: some guidelines'. *Tourism Management*, **15**(6), 416–24.

TWO

Total quality: an approach to managing productivity in the hotel industry

Sheila Stewart and Nick Johns

INTRODUCTION

Productivity is traditionally associated with manufacturing industries, rather than with the service sector. Manufactured products have a tangible existence as well as an economic one and the economic concept of productivity, i.e. in terms of wealth generation, is easy to grasp. By comparison, the intangible nature of services means that the traditional productivity concept is less clear. Despite this, there has been considerable interest in service sector productivity since the late 1980s, when the relatively low productivity of this sector first began to be recognized (e.g. Elfing, 1989; Medlik, 1989). The productivity of the hospitality industry has been examined in theoretical articles (e.g. Johns and Wheeler, 1991; Prihti, 1991) and also in industrial surveys (e.g. Van der Hoeven and Thurik, 1984; NEDC, 1992).

The same period has seen increasing interest in the concept of quality within the hotel industry. There have been a number of articles discussing the nature and management of service quality (see reviews by Johns, 1992a, b, 1993) and reports of hotel chains establishing quality management systems (Smith, 1991; Fender and Litteljohn, 1992) and achieving national quality awards such as BS5750 (Callan, 1992). It is likely that this interest in both the productivity and quality of hospitality services derives from the current market situation. The later 1980s were marked by steadily increasing competition as the market matured. However, this period was immediately followed by the Gulf War and a series of international terrorist incidents, while at the same time the Western world was plunged into recession (Litteljohn and Slattery, 1991). Hospitality organizations responded to these changes by downsizing their organizations (e.g. Nebel *et al.*, 1994) and by adopting a number of strategies to maximize market share. These have included company-wide initiatives designed to provide reliable services on the one hand and higher standards of customer care on the other. The present chapter examines the relationship between such quality management systems and the maximization of productivity in the hotel industry.

PRODUCTIVITY AND SERVICE QUALITY

Productivity may broadly be defined as the ratio of output to input. However, 'output' is not only a function of quantity or volume, but also of quality, since the value of what is produced depends upon both (Johns and Wheeler, 1991). The quality equation can therefore be expressed:

$$\text{productivity} = \frac{\text{volume} \times \text{quality (i.e. output)}}{\text{inputs}} \qquad (1)$$

If 'volume × quality' is accepted as being equivalent to economic value this argument applies equally to the production of both goods and services. Thus, in theory, this equation predicts three ways in which productivity can be improved:

- by improving quality without a significant fall in output volume or increase in inputs;
- by improving volume without a significant fall in quality or inputs;
- by maintaining both volume and quality while achieving a significant reduction in inputs.

Although this definition is acceptable at the macro level of national or regional economics, it is of limited use at the operational level of hospitality management. In this case, the relationship between quality and value is obscured by practical issues such as fluctuating demand, or the need to encourage repeat business. The 'instant' nature of rooms and other services means that 'value' constantly shifts as supply adjusts to demand. A further complication is that a service encounter has no independent existence of its own. Service and its quality exist only in the perceptions of the customer, further obscuring the relationship between quality and value. Furthermore, service quality is heavily dependent upon the skills and attitudes of service staff. Indeed, unlike a manufactured product, a hospitality service is not an entity, but a *process*, in which customers and staff participate. Thus service quality is fundamentally different from product quality; it is effectively the quality of the service process. A service process can, however, be seen from two viewpoints. In the customer's eyes it provides benefits, the value of which is a function of the elusive service quality characteristics. From the hospitality manager's viewpoint the service process generates income, while consuming resources. In principle, optimizing the service process should have two effects. On the one hand it should improve the quality perceived by the customer, whilst on the other it should make the conversion of inputs to outputs more efficient. Thus the productivity of a service can be regarded as a natural concomitant of service process quality, so that this argument reaches the same conclusion as that centred on equation 1. However, in theoretical terms, an integrated quality improvement approach should achieve a simultaneous improvement in productivity, whether it takes place in a manufacturing or a service industry. Quality improvement initiatives are also claimed to enhance productivity in areas such as computer engineering (Sinclair and Arthur, 1994) and motor manufacturing (Ingold and Worthington, 1994). This is noted by Deming (1984), who says: 'Improve quality [and] you automatically improve productivity, you capture the market with lower price and better quality. You stay in business, and you provide jobs. So simple.'

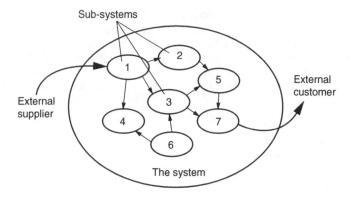

Figure 2.1. Systems model of Total Quality Management

Source: After Oakland (1988)

THE TOTAL QUALITY PHILOSOPHY

Total quality is a concept and philosophy, rather than a system or technique. It is described as 'total' because it encompasses everyone, every activity and every function in every part of the organization. The basic definition of quality is that of Feigenbaum (1983): 'fitness for purpose'. Thus total quality is about optimizing every process and output so that it fulfils the task for which it was designed, by identifying and achieving outcomes in a way that requires least cost and produces greatest value. The total quality model regards all processes as consisting of sequences of sub-systems, or transactions, in which every employee is a customer (of the previous sub-system) or supplier (of the next transaction; see Figure 2.1). As Smith (1988) notes,

> We all have a customer for our work; the department which receives our data, the next operator in the process line, the users of our service, the boss, the secretary. . . . Who the customer is depends on the transaction. But each transaction must have an identified customer. Without a customer response, we do not know whether we have added value or cost.

In this way all employees are seen as part of a chain, from external supplier through to external customer. The total quality philosophy thus emphasizes that all employees are ultimately involved in serving the final customer, so that quality matters at all stages.

In the hospitality industry, Pickworth (1987) recommends that 'quality should be defined in terms of the consumer expectations'. For example, the production of a meal and its subsequent service represent linked sub-systems, which aim to satisfy an external customer. The correct (i.e. fit for purpose) standard must be achieved by every 'supplier' for every 'customer' along the chain, from the delivery of the raw materials to the serving of the meal. Everyone from the storeman to the waiter must be committed to the overall quality of this production/service system. Any break in the chain of events from production to service may cause a product of unsuitable quality to be served, resulting in a dissatisfied customer. Oakland (1989) calls such linked subsystems the 'quality chains' of a business. The total quality philosophy attempts to increase employee commitment to the service process. It does this by focusing the attention of the workforce upon process quality, often simultaneously granting employees greater autonomy to make critical decisions at the service interface.

The total quality philosophy brings potential benefits not only in operational, but also in strategic, terms. Examples are listed by East (1993) as follows.

Operational benefits
- enhanced food safety performance;
- minimized risk of failures;
- reduced wastage;
- improved working conditions;
- lower staff turnover.

Strategic benefits
- increased ability to meet customer demands;
- improved efficiency;
- increased business opportunities;
- development of image and reputation;
- increased profit.

Thus adoption of a total quality philosophy provides an opportunity not only to create good customer relations, but also to view the management and development of a hospitality facility in a new light. It may result in a new focus upon the quality of the service process, bringing increased profitability and productivity as well as assuring the quality of the customer experience.

Arguments in favour of total quality are various, and include increased customer demand, improved staff morale and better product differentiation (Smith,1988). A number of sources imply that quality is an essential aspect to business success. Jan Carlzon, President and CEO of Scandinavian Airlines, explains that 'to be competitive and survive, one must deliver a service that supplies value, rather than one that costs less' (Carlzon, 1987). The development of better and more consistent quality services is also important in terms of customers' expectations, upon which service quality perception ultimately depends (Berry *et al.*, 1991). As Darryl Whitehead of UK accounting consultants Grant Thorton notes, 'To survive and thrive in the 1990s, the whole purpose of your organization must be performance and profitability. Failures in the quality of your product or service jeopardize these objectives' (Whitehead, 1992). The cost of quality is dependent on the type and size of a company. An interesting example of the cost of not performing 'right first time' is provided by the Department of Trade and Industry (DTI, 1991). It reports that in one major UK service organization the level of firefighting (i.e. extra work to 'fix' problems) is more than 2 hours 35 minutes per person per seven-hour day. It also estimates that failing to satisfy customers' expectations right first time costs the average company between 15 per cent and 30 per cent of sales revenue. It costs the average service organization up to 40 per cent of budget, reportedly mostly owing to weakness in management.

IMPLEMENTING THE TOTAL QUALITY PHILOSOPHY

The diverse and organic nature of organizations means that there can be no one way to embed a total quality philosophy into organizational thought and practice. However, there are some general requirements. In order to achieve a truly 'total' approach, all members of the organization need to feel a degree of ownership. This requires an organization-wide change in the shared attitudes and values that make up the work culture. Frequently it is necessary at the same time to set up new structures, and as a result the new philosophy is invariably introduced in a climate of change. Thus the implementation of the total quality philosophy usually requires the application of certain general principles, designed to motivate participants and reduce any adverse effects of change. For instance, organizations are generally recommended to refer to a 'process', rather than to a 'programme', of quality improvement. A 'process' need never end, whereas the word 'programme' implies something that will eventually finish and be superseded. Frequently the words 'continuous quality improvement' are used rather than 'total quality management' to reinforce the purpose and focus of the process (Johns and Chesterton, 1994). Top management awareness and commitment is perhaps the most crucial ingredient. East (1993) lists the attitudes and values that must be adopted at this level if a quality culture is to be achieved:

- total commitment to continuous improvement;
- the requirement to do it right first time;
- understanding the customer–supplier relationship;
- recognition that improvement of systems must be managed;
- a commitment to ongoing education and training;
- the instigation of teamwork and the improvement of communications;
- the development of a systematic approach to the implementation.

Thus a successful quality improvement process usually requires as its basic ingredients top management commitment, attitude change, continuous improvement, strengthened supervision, training and recognition (Collard, 1991). It is interesting that very similar principles are advocated by Heap (1992) for implementing productivity improvement in manufacturing organizations. They are discussed in more detail below.

Top management commitment

There should be a clear focused vision, understood by everyone, aimed at achieving the highest levels of customer service. A leader with a strong commitment to that vision will find a way to spark in others a desire to bring that vision into reality.

Attitude change

Introduction of a total quality initiative requires a major change in the attitudes and culture within organizations. Culture changes when behaviour changes; success depends mainly on the way the change is managed. Total quality requires major developments in the culture and systems of an organization, which must span a number of years before it becomes a way of life.

Continuous improvement

The creation of a climate of continuous improvement requires a managed change of employee attitudes. Quality improvement should always be at the forefront of everything that is done, continuously reinforced and developed by management through the systems and processes that make such improvements possible. Professional managers realize that bottom-line results are achieved through the company's employees. Managers must pay attention to the quality of the work, setting performance standards for both quantity and quality and managing employees in such a way that these standards are met.

Strengthened supervision

Supervision has traditionally been seen as the 'authority' within a particular department. However, in a total quality programme, supervision should be associated with facilitating and coaching, enabling a department to function more effectively.

Training

An integrated system of training programmes is one of the most effective ways to cascade the new quality culture through an organization, as it can reach a large number of staff quickly. Training provides staff with the quality principles: continuous improvement, understanding customer requirements, internal customers and teamwork. It also gives them the tools and techniques needed for problem solving. Senior management should attend exactly the same training as everyone else and be part of the training process from the very start. The learning, growth and development of people is a fundamental requirement of a flexible, efficient workforce. A conspicuous feature of most high-involvement organizations is the level of commitment to training.

Recognition

A total quality initiative should aim to maximize the involvement of all employees in the achievement of objectives, by giving them a say in how their job can be done more effectively. Thus it increases job satisfaction. Some organizations recognize significant contributions to quality improvement by means of recognition awards, usually tokens (medallions or certificates), but sometimes also financial rewards. Awards allow management to indicate to all employees that it recognizes the achievements of individuals and treats quality improvement seriously. Recognizing individual contributions to the quality improvement process reinforces the message that management is commited to quality and achieves long-term motivation of the workforce.

QUALITY MANAGEMENT IN ORGANIZATIONS

Despite the vast amount of literature and advice on the subject, there can be no single, certain approach to the implementation of a continuous quality improvement process. Organizations may adopt ideas, but they must work out the details, style and structure of the implementation according to their own specific needs. Different industries, and even different companies within the same industry, tend to find different solutions to implementation problems. These vary according to management styles, individual personalities, the type of business and so on. Yet different solutions may also vary in suitability for their particular situations. It is therefore of interest to study and compare different examples of total quality implementation.

Because continuous quality improvement is a process rather than a state of being, it cannot be observed except as a snapshot, taken at a particular moment in time. Like other management initiatives, quality management processes are very complex, since by definition they endeavour to address all aspects of the organization. The most appropriate approach for empirical study of such systems is the case study, which permits the integration of information from a range of different sources (Yin, 1989). A review of the relevant literature, together with preliminary informal interviews with personnel across a range of hotels, suggested that quality improvement strategies differ considerably between different hospitality organizations. The present study examines and compares different styles of total quality implementation at two major city hotels in southern Scotland.

METHODS

Two hotels were chosen for the present investigation. They are designated here as 'Hotel A' and 'Hotel B' for the purposes of anonymity. Both hotels were operated by prestigious international companies and offered a four-star style of service predominantly to the business market. Thus they were matched in many respects. Information gleaned during a preliminary investigation suggested that the two companies held differing views on quality management. They also appeared to be employing different implementation strategies, which made them attractive subjects for a comparative study. Both hotels agreed to cooperate with the research by permitting their staff and managers to be surveyed and interviewed. However, access to staff had to be limited, in order to minimize disruption from the hotel's point of view. This factor may have affected response rates to staff surveys. It also restricted the numbers of representatives of the management team available for interview. An alternative approach, that of a consumer survey, was rejected, since it would have brought attendant problems of access and disruption. Research techniques finally adopted were:

1   Informal introductory interviews with the personnel and training officer (responsible for the training programme) at Hotel A and the (specifically designated) quality manager at Hotel B.
2   Follow-up structured interviews with the above members of staff.
3   A questionnaire survey of 50 employees at each site.

The purpose of the informal introductory interview was to introduce the research, negotiate time for a further structured interview and discuss the administration of questionnaires. Structured interviews were conducted over a half-day and sought information and comment on the following aspects of the quality management strategy in each hotel.

• The particular approach to quality management system used (e.g. continuous quality improvement/total quality, BS5750/ISO9000, quality assurance, Investors in People).
• The quality mission statement, including its date of publication and content.
• Quality tools/techniques being used to implement the quality management system.
• Membership and structure and functions of any internal steering group overseeing the quality management strategy.
• Perceptions of the company: position of the hotel in relation to planning (short-term/long-term), management style (controlling/enabling), reaction to change (static/dynamic), company focus (inward looking/market focus).
• Appropriateness of BS5750/ISO9000 to the hospitality industry.
• Appropriateness of the total quality philosophy to the hospitality industry.
• Whether the issue of quality was likely to be increasingly important to the company.
• Views on the future plans of the company in relation to the issue of quality.

In addition to these interviews, a questionnaire, designed to provide as wide a picture as possible of employees' knowledge of quality programmes, was issued to 50 members of staff in each establishment. This included both open and closed questions, and allowed respondents to expand on their replies by supplying additional comments. In each organization, the individual responsible for quality issued ten questionnaires to staff in management positions, ten to supervisors/team leaders and 30 to operatives. This breakdown was intended to ensure that the same cross-section of employees was targeted in the two case studies. The questionnaire survey sought information on the following:

• knowledge of the hotel's quality management system;
• the meaning of doing a quality job;
• membership and attendance of a quality improvement group/team;
• encouragement and implementation of ideas for improvement;
• frequency of training;
• opportunities for taking initiative and making decisions for the sake of guest service and satisfaction;
• motivation and commitment.

The following section provides an overview of the two case studies, including the interview results, and examines the ways in which quality management approaches were being implemented. Results from the questionnaire survey are presented on a comparative basis in the subsequent section.

CASE STUDIES

Hotel A

Hotel A was operated by the UK subsidiary of an international group which had substantial holdings in the hospitality industry, and was based in south-east England. The company operated 16 hotels in the UK, Hotel A being its most prestigious unit in Scotland, located near the centre of a major city. Two years before the present study it had been refurbished at a cost of £2.5 million. Hotel A had approximately 300 rooms and employed 153 full-time staff. Facilities included two restaurants, a café, bars, conference rooms and a leisure centre, which also offered external membership. The hotel had been awarded a four-star rating by the AA, which it proudly maintained. The organization structure of Hotel A was somewhat traditional and hierarchical in nature, with clearly defined department heads, deputies and functional officers (such as the training officer interviewed in this study).

The parent company that operated Hotel A had built up a reputation as a quality-conscious company over many years. Even in the 1970s its North American operations were put forward as an example of 'quality control' in the hospitality and lodging industry. Hotel A's parent company had since built upon its reputation. It regarded service quality almost solely as a function of its front-line staff and its company literature stated that 'it takes happy employees to make happy customers'. The company was also very much committed to participatory management. These two aspects of its policy were strengthened and reaffirmed when a company-wide quality management process was introduced at all units (including Hotel A) in 1992.

The individual responsible for quality at Hotel A was the training officer. She had undergone quality training with the National Society for Quality through Teamwork (NSQT) and had acted as quality facilitator at the hotel for the first two years of the process. The company's quality mission stated: 'Our goal is simply to be the first choice provider of accommodation and services for the business traveller.' Hotel A's parent company held the view that those most able to realize this customer focus in practice were the front-line staff, who dealt with guests on an everyday basis. It was the parent company's intention to give these staff a high degree of autonomy, and their commitment to total quality had to be gained at the outset of the process. Thus a five-module training package had been introduced in 1991, which had been attended by all staff. The outline content of this package is shown in Table 2.1.

During training sessions, staff were also invited to become involved in the total quality process as members of quality circles (QCs). At Hotel A, quality circles met regularly during work time, relying upon staff commitment, with no financial incentive or reward for participation. Their objective was to effect a continuous improvement in the quality of the service, by identifying and solving problems. Techniques used for this purpose included brainstorming, paired comparison, mind mapping and cause/

Table 2.1. Structure of quality training package at Hotel A

Area	Content
Concepts	Giving an outline of the total quality concept; ensuring delegates can differentiate between successful and unsuccessful organizations; and how their actions affect the organization.
Retention of people	Explaining empowerment and the important role they have to play in total quality.
Retention of customers	Ensuring delegates understand the techniques employed to exceed customer expectations.
Profitability	Understanding that increased profitability is a vital part of total quality; determining their role in this area, and looking at tools and techniques of quality measurement.
Plan for action	Delegates' personal and practical commitment to the process.

effect analysis (Johns, 1994). Five quality circles formed at Hotel A around this period operated very successfully until 1994, when they were disbanded, owing to a shortage of resources caused by the recession.

The training officer at Hotel A identified the advantages of quality circles as:

- solving problems and improving service;
- benefiting guests;
- involving everyone in the team.

A member of a quality circle enthusiastically described an example of its work. Using brainstorming techniques, the team identified deaf guests as a particular group for whom the hotel's standard service was not satisfactory. As a result of their recommendations, Hotel A became the first hotel in Britain to have two rooms completely fitted out for the profoundly deaf. This achievement was shown on the BBC TV programme for the deaf, following which there was a large increase in demand for these facilities. As a result, 12 hotel staff were given a basic sign language course and the hotel established itself in a previously untapped market.

Top managers were the only members of staff involved in the committee that managed the quality programme at Hotel A, and they met on a monthly basis. The training officer felt that the company had an effective, long-term planning process, possessed a strong market focus and was fairly quick to react to change. The management style was an enabling one, and the training officer was very positive about the effect this had on staff morale and motivation. Managers of Hotel A were aware of the interest shown in BS5750/ISO9000 over the previous few years, but the company did not feel that it was an appropriate standard for the hotel industry. Reasons cited by the training officer were: 'too much paper-work involved; the industry is people- and service-based and not product-orientated' and (referring to the standardization of service responses) 'it is very hard to say the same things every day.' It was felt that a systematic approach to quality could be achieved, reducing wastage and increasing profitability, without the expense and bureaucracy involved in BS5750/ISO9000 certification.

The two principal reasons for implementing and maintaining the quality improvement process were felt to be rising expectations of customers and staff and the need for increased productivity/profitability in an increasingly competitive market. In addition to the benefits of increased operational and strategic efficiency, the training officer emphasized the effects on the organizational culture of the hotel, adding: 'Total quality lets the staff understand what the hotel is actually striving towards and giving the customers what they want. Staff begin to feel that quality matters.'

Hotel B

The second hotel in the study, Hotel B, was located on one of the most prestigious shopping streets in Edinburgh. It had been purpose-built at a cost of £30 million, and opened early in 1990. Hotel B had 238 rooms and employed 120 full-time staff. It was the property of a European-owned multinational group, which operated approximately 200 hotels throughout Europe, four of them in the British Isles. Hotel B offered conference facilities, two restaurants, a bar and a leisure centre with external membership. It considered its service equivalent to that of an AA four-star rating, although it was not in fact registered. Hotel B's parent company felt that a star rating was not an adequate or appropriate means of differentiating the hotel from its main competitors. The management of Hotel B considered that star ratings are mainly an indication of the facilities available, whereas in fact their hotels' main source of competitive advantage lay in the quality of service offered. Although the company professed to have a quality mission, this was not made available to the researcher for inspection (or quoting). Instead it was kept 'as part of the BS5750 paperwork'. This was in stark contrast to Hotel A, where the company mission was widely circulated and quoted. The organization structure at Hotel B also contrasted with that at Hotel A, being less hierarchical overall, with fewer layers of supervisory staff between top management and the workforce.

Hotel B's commitment to quality was illustrated by the appointment of a quality manager just after the establishment opened. Interviews with this individual indicated that although tourists are an important source of income, the main target markets were business people and conference delegates. In matters relating to quality, this market segment was felt to be more discerning than tourists. By focusing principally on the needs of business customers, the hotel believed that it could ensure that the needs of all customers would be satisfied. The quality manager's main initial aim was to achieve BS5750/ISO9000 accreditation. In order to facilitate this, the hotel began a continuous quality improvement programme in early 1991, which was regarded as a first step towards the award. Implementation of the programme was aided by the pre-existence of a suitable culture within the establishment. It was comparatively easy to set up quality teams to devise and rationalize work methods, and their existence ensured the commitment and motivation of all employees. It was also possible to take action immediately a problem was identified, and seeing instant results boosted morale.

According to the quality manager, quality is receiving an increasingly high profile at Hotel B, owing to the following key factors:

- an increasingly competitive market;
- more demanding customers;
- increased profitability/productivity;
- the impact on staff, constant awareness and taking corrective action immediately.

In principle, implementation of a total quality process should eliminate all errors and produce obvious improvements in service quality. However, service inconsistencies may exist because of a number of factors (for example, interpersonal chemistry) as well as human error. The management of Hotel B felt that by attaining BS5750/ISO9000, it would prove to its customers that it offered true quality assurance, through an externally validated system. The quality manager emphasized the importance of such accreditation as a marketing tool directed at corporate clients.

Hotel B was awarded its BS5750/ISO9000 early in 1993, and has already experienced the following benefits.

1   Managers were now subject to quality auditing, carried out by independent assessors twice a year, who looked for ways to improve services.
2   Being a quality leader in the industry has proved an advantage for sales and marketing, especially in the corporate business sector.
3   Greater success in marketing has improved sales and occupancy ratings, with consequent improvements in productivity.
4   The staff knew they were being continually assessed and the quality culture had permeated all levels. They were happiest in their work environment and teamwork was improved.
5   There was increased customer satisfaction and the hotel's reputation had been enhanced.
6   The hotel had became more united by focusing on a specific, 'physical' goal, namely BS5750/ISO9000 certification.

The quality manager's claims were supported by similar comments in the questionnaires. These referred, among other things, to increased levels of efficiency, safety and teamwork, and reductions in costs and wastage.

Unlike her counterpart at Hotel A, the quality manager at Hotel B felt that BS5750/ISO9000 was an appropriate standard for the hospitality industry, citing the above benefits as evidence. However, she intimated that in some areas the standard was incompatible with the total quality philosophy and that this problem needed further study if service industries were to adopt it more readily. An example of this was the checking of rooms after they have been cleaned. BS5750/ISO9000 was very strict about inspection by designated supervisors, but the total quality philosophy suggested that room attendants should be empowered to check their own work (the approach favoured at Hotel A). However, the quality manager noted: 'With BS5750 you can create your own systems, trying to get the balance right, [by] checking in other ways. After all, total quality is the ultimate aim of BS5750.'

Hotel B found the road to BS5750/ISO9000 a difficult one. Reasons for this stemmed from a general lack of support for the standard within the hotel industry. All aspects of implementation had to be developed locally, as it was not possible to draft in help from another organization. The national guidelines were not found to be useful in this respect, and there was a general lack of knowledge about the standard among existing employees and job applicants.

At Hotel B, top management, middle management and supervisors were all involved in the committee which manages the quality programme, meeting at least once a month. Like the parent company of Hotel A, the company took a long-term planning position with a strong market focus and felt that it reacted dynamically to environmental change. Employees perceived the management style as an enabling one, where staff were given not only the skills, but also the authority to use them. The company continued to develop quality as a way of life, and Hotel B was currently seeking Investors in People accreditation.

QUESTIONNAIRE FINDINGS

Response rates for the questionnaire survey (Hotel A 39 per cent and Hotel B 56 per cent) were encouraging. To the question, 'Do you know if your hotel operates a quality management system?', there was a 100 per cent 'yes' response at both hotels, indicating general awareness of management initiatives in this area. The question, 'What does it mean for you to do a quality job?' gave the results shown in Table 2.2. Staff at both institutions clearly felt that service quality benefited themselves and the guests, and were not simply working 'by the book'. At Hotel A there was a slightly greater focus upon the guest, while at Hotel B quality was apparently perceived slightly more as a matter of personal job satisfaction.

Responses to the question, 'Are you a member of a quality improvement team?' differed significantly between the two hotels. Only 22 per cent of staff at Hotel A responded that they were quality team members, as compared with 89 per cent at Hotel B. This confirmed the training officer's comment that quality circles had been discontinued at Hotel A. The remaining team membership was presumably at supervisory/management level. When respondents were asked about their attendance at quality team meetings, the patterns obtained were similar, as shown in Table 2.3. Attendance at quality team meetings clearly required the support of management, through an allocation of work time. The momentum of a successful quality team

Table 2.2. The meaning of doing a quality job

Question	Response rate (%)	
	Hotel A	Hotel B
Personal/job satisfaction	36	45
Meeting and exceeding guest expectations	48	37
Doing the job right first time	0	5
Meeting the requirements asked of me	5	1
Working to standards in the manual	1	2
No response	10	10

Table 2.3. Attendance at quality team meetings

Questions	Response rate (%)	
	Hotel A	Hotel B
Do you attend quality improvement meetings in work time, or in your own time?		
Work time	22	50
Own time	0	7
Both	0	32
No response	78	11

Productivity Management

Table 2.4. Frequency of training/retraining in service quality issues

Frequency	Response rate (%)	
	Hotel A	Hotel B
Weekly	0	50
Monthly	33	4
Every six months	22	14
Only on starting	11	21
Other	22	11
No response	11	0

Table 2.5. Motivation and commitment of staff at the two hotels

Question	Response rate (%)	
	Hotel A	Hotel B
Does this provide you with greater motivation for your work?		
Yes	89	100
No	0	0
No response	11	0
Would you like to have more say in the way you deal with customers?		
Yes	33	0
No	44	86
No response	23	14
Which do you consider the most important motivation factors?[a]		
Use of teams	22	36
Training and personal development	44	56
Feedback on performance	55	56
Recognition of achievements	89	68
Good communication	55	50
Clear management leadership and example	55	50

[a] Percentages total more than 100 because respondents were allowed more than one choice.

structure (as at Hotel B) evidently encouraged some individuals to give up their own time to the company's quality improvement process.

When employees at the two hotels were asked, 'Are ideas encouraged and implemented?', significant numbers replied 'yes' (Hotel A 55 per cent, Hotel B 89 per cent), and none replied 'No'. However, the numbers of staff not responding to this question were noteworthy (Hotel A 45 per cent, Hotel B 11 per cent) and presumably reflected the discontinuation of quality circles at the former hotel. Staff responses about the frequency of their quality training are shown in Table 2.4. Hotel B clearly retrained its staff more regularly than did Hotel A, although a higher proportion at the former hotel claimed that they had only received induction training.

The question, 'Are you allowed to take initiative and make decisions for the sake of guest service and satisfaction?' received a 100 per cent 'yes' response at both hotels, confirming the results of the interviews. Questions about motivation and commitment elicited the responses shown in Table 2.5. The results reflected those of the other questionnaire sections discussed above. Of interest were the numbers of respondents at Hotel A who expressed a wish to have more say in the way they dealt with customers.

Greater emphasis seemed also to be placed upon the recognition of achievements at Hotel A than at Hotel B.

DISCUSSION

The productivity of hospitality services is a complex issue, since both long- and short-term profitability are related to the quality of the service process and the environment in which it takes place. In order to examine these issues in the two subject organizations, results from the questionnaires and interviews were analysed in relation to four areas: company commitment, resources, cultural fit and the motivation and commitment of staff to the quality initiative.

Management commitment to the quality programme clearly existed, and was recognized as such by employees at both of the hotels in the study. At Hotel A it manifested itself in the well-established mission and the fact that all staff, both full- and part-time, had been involved in the training package for total quality. Management commitment at Hotel B was additionally demonstrated by the existence of a full-time quality manager dedicated to the quality improvement process. Both hotels seemed concerned to tap the knowledge of employees, so that problem solving could occur at the level most affected by the problem. By doing this, the management hoped to empower employees to solve problems independently and to make them more committed to implementing the solutions. It is noteworthy that Heap (1992) emphasizes that a productivity improvement process must begin with a top-down approach, which cascades down the organization, ensuring that all employees are geared towards the same goal. In order for this to be effective, resources must be allocated to the process.

A quality improvement initiative demands team meetings, the collection and analysis of data, presentations to management and extensive communication, all of which require a considerable input of time. At Hotel B, the appointment of a quality manager, and the regular training and retraining of staff, demonstrated management's willingness to commit resources to the strategy of service differentiation through quality. At Hotel A the commitment of resources was less clear. On the positive side, there seemed to be a commitment to training, but this was somewhat offset (as demonstrated by employees' response to the questionnaire) by the disbanding of quality circles. It seems that at least this part of the quality team structure was regarded as expendable in the face of short-term profitability problems. However, it should be noted that a lack of quality circles does not necessarily prevent individual front-line employees from suggesting and implementing service quality improvements. Both hotels have also maximized the effectiveness of their quality improvement process by concentrating upon the organizational culture.

CULTURAL FIT

Total involvement of all employees means that skills and knowledge are used to their fullest potential. Oakland (1989) states that 'total quality is concerned with moving the focus of control from outside the individual to within; the objective being to make everyone accountable for their own performance, and to get them committed to attaining quality in a highly motivated fashion.' Both Hotel A and Hotel B have approached the issue of a quality culture from the top down, signalling the message that quality is everyone's business. However, it was interesting that Hotel B seemed to have achieved this without a high-profile mission statement. Another notable development is that employees at operative level assume some managerial responsibility, by taking initiatives for the sake of guest satisfaction. Managers have adopted a supporting, facilitating role, assisting employees to overcome problems and providing them with the necessary resources. Both hotels appear to have cultures where authority and responsibility exist without blame, and employees are encouraged to try things out to find better methods of working. Thus, energy can be directed at constant improvement, and employees become more innovative as their ideas are recognized and adopted.

At Hotel B, the total quality initiative brought a simultaneous change to a flatter organizational structure. Layers of middle management became unnecessary as some of the organization and checking of work was shifted to front-line employees. This also reduced staffing costs, increasing the profitability and productivity of the unit. Hotel A has not taken this approach, retaining a rather traditional, hierarchical organization structure. This could be viewed as a 'trade-off' for the disbanded quality circles. Seddon (1989) suggests that in many organizations quality management programmes are initially received with some enthusiasm by the workforce, but that this soon wanes and disillusionment sets in. He claims that this is because of management's preoccupation with 'hard', measurable aspects of the programme such as costs, and the relative neglect of 'soft' aspects such as customer perception and employee commitment. Johns and Chesterton (1994) note that a general problem with quality improvement is the motivation of middle managers who may fall between the quality circle level (of the workforce) and the corrective action level (of senior management). Given that unit managers of affiliated hotels may be regarded as middle management, it may be that this phenomenon was ultimately responsible for the discontinuation of quality circles at Hotel A.

MOTIVATION AND COMMITMENT

Oakland (1989) argues that the assumptions a general manager must make in order to move in this direction are simply that people do not need to be coerced to perform well, and that people want to achieve, accomplish, influence activity and challenge their abilities. Despite this, it is essential that managers at all levels can motivate employees, optimizing performance and creating a happy and effective working environment. Employees in both the study hotels indicated that they wanted more recognition of their achievements. This cannot be achieved by praise alone, but generally also requires some kind of tangible reward. One approach to this is to medals, certificates or prizes to outstanding contributors to the quality programme (Johns and Chesterton, 1994). Another way is to provide financial and career development incentives (Mill, 1989). For example, Weaver (1988) proposes a simple bonus scheme based on sales–finance ratios as the best means of motivating low-paid employees in the hotel and catering industry. Another key motivation factor is training, which makes workers competent to provide a quality service and also reinforces the quality mission. Hotel A, which provided half its employees with weekly sessions, scored considerably higher in this respect than Hotel A.

If a company is going to adopt quality as a differentiation strategy, then quality improvement should be part of the corporate culture, not just an add-on programme. The crux of quality management is the use of people. They provide the service, they deal with the problems, they are even able to make poor systems work and good systems fail. Employees therefore need to believe in the cultural change and have ownership of the process. Larsen and Rapp (1993) in fact recommend that service organizations are inverted, producing an 'upside-down pyramid' in which employees take a centre stage position.

CONCLUSION

Service quality is seen as a route to competitive advantage in the hospitality industry. However, quality improvement must be managed on a holistic basis throughout the organization, as it demands the continuous assessment and development of every area. The creation of a deep and sustained commitment to quality implies fundamental organizational change. Total quality is based on a long-term view of returns and it is argued that profits, and hence productivity, follow as a result of increased sales and reduced wastage.

Both the hotels investigated in this present study took a long-term view with regard to quality, based upon reinforcing the mission and managing the organizational culture. As evidence, even the 1994 cost-cutting exercises at Hotel A did not seem to undermine staff commitment to a great extent. However, there are notable strategic differences between the two companies. Hotel B relies upon BS5750 accreditation to market itself to the business community. Hotel A, on the other hand, uses employee empowerment to generate customer commitment and repeat business. The value of formalized quality assurance system such as BS5750 in the hotel industry is still unclear, as is the way service quality should most effectively be marketed.

Of the two case studies, Hotel B appears to have paid the greatest attention to assuring a 'cultural fit', and this has been achieved by:

- creating a post for quality management;
- adopting a flatter organization structure;
- maintaining quality teams intact through the recession;
- providing frequent training and retraining.

These factors, which require investment in time and staff, demonstrate the company's commitment to the quality strategy. Hutchins (1986) suggests that companies which have a quality ethos as part of the culture of the organization also achieve productivity improvements and increased profitability. These are brought about by employees' commitment to the quality of the service process.

Lockwood (1994) notes: 'Placing the emphasis on the key elements of a quality provision should bring about three main benefits for the hospitality operation; customer satisfaction, productivity/profitability, human resources.' The present work provides some insight into the operation of quality improvement in the hospitality industry. However, like an earlier study by Steel and Lloyd (1988), it has been unable to evaluate completely the contribution to productivity made by motivation and commitment. The authors agree with Reynolds and Ingold's (1994) recommendation that a longitudinal study is needed to undertake this task satisfactorily.

REFERENCES

Berry, L.L., Parasuraman, A. and Zeithaml, A.V. (1991) 'Understanding customer expectations of service'. *Sloan Management Review*, **32**(3), 39–48.

Callan, R. (1992) 'Quality control at Avant Hotels. The debut of BS5750'. *Service Industries Journal*, **12**(1), 17–33.

Carlzon, J. (1987) *Moments of Truth*. New York: Ballinger Publishing Company.

Collard, R. (1991) *Total Quality: Success through People*. London: Institute of Personnel Management.

Deming, W. (1984) *Road Map for Change: the Deming Approach*. [Video recording]. Chicago: Encyclopaedia Britannica Educational Corp.

Department of Trade and Industry (DTI) (1991) *Total Quality Management and Effective Leadership: a Strategic Overview*. London: HMSO.

East, J. (1993) *Managing Quality in the Catering Industry*. London: Croner Publications Ltd.

Elfing, T. (1989) 'The main features and underlying causes of the shift to services'. *Service Industries Journal*, **9**(3), 337–56.

Feigenbaum, A. (1983) *Total Quality Control*. New York: McGraw-Hill.

Fender, D. and Litteljohn, D. (1992) 'Forward planning in uncertain times'. *International Journal of Contemporary Hospitality Management*, **4**(3), i–iv.

Heap, J. (1992) *Productivity Management: a Fresh Approach*. London: Cassell.

Hutchins, D. (1986) *Quality Circles Handbook*. New York: Nicholls Publishing Co.

Ingold, A. and Worthington, T. (1994) 'Extraordinary customer satisfaction: the road to success'. In R. Teare, C. Atkinson and C. Westwood (eds), *Achieving Quality Performance*. London: Cassell, pp. 111–42.

Johns, N. (1992a) 'Quality management in the hospitality industry, part 1. Definition and specification'. *International Journal of Contemporary Hospitality Management*, **4**(3), 14–20.

Johns, N. (1992b) 'Quality management in the hospitality industry, part 2: quality applications, systems and techniques'. *International Journal of Contemporary Hospitality Management*, **4**(4), 3–7.

Johns, N. (1993a) 'Quality management in the hospitality industry, part 3. Recent developments'. *International Journal of Contemporary Hospitality Management*, **5**(1), 15–16.

Johns, N. (1993b) 'Productivity management through design and operation: a case study'. *International Journal of Contemporary Hospitality Management*, **5**(2), 20–4.

Johns, N. (1994) 'Managing Quality'. In P. Jones and P. Merricks (eds), *The Management of Foodservice Operations*. London: Cassell, pp. 245–61.

Johns, N. and Chesterton, J. (1994) 'ICL: snapshot of a changing culture'. In R. Teare, C. Atkinson and C. Westwood (eds), *Achieving Quality Performance: Lessons from British Industry*. London: Cassell, pp. 79–110.

Johns, N. and Wheeler, K.L. (1991) 'Productivity and perfomance monitoring and measurement'. In R. Teare and A. Boare (eds), *Strategic Hospitality Management*. London: Cassell, pp. 45–69.

Larsen, S. and Rapp, L. (1993) 'Creating the service-driven cruise line'. *International Journal of Contemporary Hospitality Management*, 5(1), iv–vi.

Litteljohn, D. and Slattery, P. (1991) 'Macro analysis techniques: an appraisal of Europe's main hotel markets'. *International Journal of Contemporary Hospitality Management*, 3(4), 6–13.

Lockwood, A. (1994) 'Using service incidents to identify quality improvement points'. *International Journal of Contemporary Hospitality Management*, 6(1/2), 75–80.

Medlik, R. (1989) 'The main features and underlying causes of the shift to services'. *Tourism*, 61(January/February), 13–18.

Mill, R.C. (1989) *Managing for Productivity in the Hospitality Industry*. New York: Van Nostrand-Reinhold.

National Economic Development Council (NEDC) (1992) Working Party, Competitivenesss in Tourism and Leisure, Sub-Group Report. *Costs and Manpower Productivity in United Kingdom Hotels*. London: NEDC.

Nebel, E.C., Braunlich, C.G. and Zhang, Y. (1994) 'Hotel food and beverage directors' career paths in American luxury hotels'. *International Journal of Contemporary Hospitality Management*, 6(6), 3–10.

Oakland, J. (1989) *Total Quality Management*. London: Heinemann.

Pickworth, J.R. (1987) 'Minding the Ps and Qs: linking quality and productivity'. *Cornell Hotel and Restaurant Administration Quarterly*, 27, 41–44.

Prihti, A. (1991) 'Productivity and productivity management in the service sector'. *EUHOFA Congress Proceedings*, University of Helsinki.

Reynolds, S. and Ingold, A. (1994) *Evaluation of Total Quality Management Tools and Techniques in the United Kingdom Hotel Industry*. York: Young Operations Research Conference, March, University of York.

Sinclair, J. and Arthur, A. (1994) 'Campbell-Lee Computer Services: developing and maintaining a total quality work culture'. In R. Teare, C. Atkinson and C. Westwood (eds), *Achieving Quality Performance*. London: Cassell, pp. 25–52.

Smith, L.R.O. (1991) 'Achieving quality in a 5-star hotel'. *Quality Forum*, 17(4), 186–9.

Smith, S. (1988) 'Ten compelling reasons for TQM'. *The TQM Magazine*, November, 13–18.

Steel, R. and Lloyd, R. (1988) 'Cognitive, affective and behavioural outcomes of participation in quality circles: conceptual and empirical findings'. *Journal of Applied Behavioural Science*, 24(1), 1–17.

Van der Hoeven, W.H.M. and Thurik, A.R. (1984) 'Labour productivity in the hotel business'. *The Services Industries Journal*, 2(2), 161–73.

Weaver, T. (1988) 'Theory M: motivating with money'. *Cornell Hotel and Restaurant Administration Quarterly*, 29, 40–5.

Whitehead, D. (1992) 'Why quality control is worth the cost'. *The Observer*, 5 July.

Yin, R.K. (1989) *Case Study Research: Design and Methods, Applied Social Research Methods Series, Vol. 5*. London: Sage.

THREE

The strategic gap: a multi-site, short break perspective

David A. Edgar

INTRODUCTION

Productivity in the hospitality industry is difficult to define and quantify (Lee, 1991). It is similarly difficult to measure, owing to the variability of labour requirements, consistency, demand and throughput (Witt and Witt, 1989). Productivity is, however, of great importance to the welfare of individual organizations. In addition, the productivity of services in general, and of hospitality in particular, is of increasing significance to the national economies of western countries, owing to a prevailing business trend away from manufacturing industry.

Teague and Eilon (1973) argue that organizations can use the measurement of productivity in three ways. It can be used for strategic purposes, i.e. as a basis for making longer-term comparisons with competitors. Productivity measurement can also be used tactically, i.e. for controlling specific functions of an organization in order to enhance overall performance. Thirdly, productivity measurement can be used for planning purposes, as it allows management to balance and compare the different yields from a range of outputs. Jones (1990) illustrates the use of these approaches in the hospitality industry. He compares a range of food service operations, highlighting the role of productivity measurement. The analysis of sequential work processes permits the development of more efficient practices and systems. Larger quantities may be handled and thus buffers provided against fluctuating demand. The work of these and other authors (for example, Ball and Johnson, 1989) thus sheds some light upon the complex interaction between productivity (at both organizational and operational level) and the longer-term strategic concerns of businesses.

Productivity can be viewed as the relationship between the inputs and outputs of a system (Schroeder, 1985). Chew (1986) emphasizes the importance of adopting a multi-factor view of such input–output relationships. This is particularly important in the hospitality industry, owing to the structural complexity of the outputs, which possess the typical intangibility, perishability and heterogeneity characteristics of services.

Considerable attention has been paid to the relationship between productivity and the 'process' aspects of hospitality operating systems. However, few authors have considered the boundaries or direction of the hospitality 'process', that is, the ways in which organizational strategy impacts upon productivity,

In simple terms, organizational strategy can be considered as composed of two elements: (a) strategy formulation and (b) strategy implementation. Strategy formulation is essentially undertaken at corporate level by head office. It has arguably become more centralized during recent years as organizations have sought to consolidate their position in a hostile recession-based environment. Strategy implementation, on the other hand, is undertaken at unit or market level.

In many single-product or single-site firms the processes of strategy formulation and implementation are virtually synonymous, since they are undertaken by the same individual. However, for large, multi-site hospitality firms such as hotel groups, the situation is more complex. There is often a wide range of products, which impact differently upon the market at different locations. In addition, there is an inevitable gap between the perceptions and communications of managers at head office and those at local level, who are responsible for interpreting organizational policy in terms of the needs of the market place. In such situations, the coherent formulation and implementation of group strategy may be an extremely complex task. The task is further complicated where a variety of service 'products' or packages is offered. Bradley and Baron (1993), for example, have shown that the implementation of strategy in multi-product firms generally requires a range of approaches to cope with differing, and constantly shifting, local environmental conditions. Broadly speaking, the larger the range and diversity of market or operational variables, the greater the complexity of the market. In turn it becomes increasingly difficult to identify the elements of the operational environment.

As organizations become larger and more geographically scattered and offer a more diverse portfolio of services, strategy formulation and implementation also become more complex. For example, confusion or tension may arise between organizational goals and real or interpreted market needs at unit level. The result may be a considerable level of variation in performance within a group. This may in fact be greater than the productivity differences between groups (Johnson and Thomas, 1988).

Addressing these within-group variations requires extensive internal analysis of the organization's portfolio, plus strategic decision-making to enhance overall performance (and therefore productivity). It is possible, for example, to develop areas of potential synergy, in which groups of products or organizational units work together, bringing greater overall benefits than could be achieved if they operated in isolation (Ansoff, 1971; Hofer and Schendel, 1978). However, in order to provide this synergy, organizations must become increasingly complex and diversified, and this must be balanced against the benefits of the synergy itself (Prahalad, 1976). Ultimately the successful management of performance (and hence of productivity) in such situations depends upon optimizing this trade-off.

When such areas of synergy are examined, it is possible to identify similarities and differences between corporate and unit perceptions of organizational strategy. Scott and Simpson (1989) note that many companies devote valuable time to corporate planning, producing mission statements, objectives and goals. However, despite this, there may be wide gaps between the perspectives held by top and middle management of organizational direction and purpose. Thus strategies may not be implemented appropriately in terms of overall organizational direction, and poor performance (and hence productivity) may result. Banks and Wheelwright (1979) put a similar argument, highlighting disparities between the priorities of different organizational levels. Managers may be under severe pressure to produce short-term solutions that ensure a profit, yet be simultaneously bound by a commitment to long-term goals set at the corporate level of the organization. Banks and Wheelwright (1979) highlight the impact of conflicting views as to how, when and which strategy should be adopted upon organizational focus and performance.

The elements of perception and conflict are further examined by Hobbs and Heany (1977), who note that a strategy requires loyalty and understanding at all levels if it is to be successful. They emphasize the need for clear linkages between the corporal and functional levels of an organization; that is, between the formulators and implementers of strategy. The implications of this kind of analysis are that productivity results from the successful balancing of the inputs and outputs of a system. The way these elements are processed in the system determines the degree of productivity of the organization. However, the process aspect of the system is controlled and directed by organizational strategy. As such, strategy formulation and implementation are key elements of productivity management and thus important determinants of productivity. In hotel groups, strategy is generally formulated at corporate level but implemented at unit level, where it is subject to varying degrees of market complexity and organizational conflict. This may result in misunderstandings or misinterpretations of strategy between the corporate centre and the units where the strategy is operationalized. Such misunderstandings may result in a gap occurring between the intended corporate strategy and that which is actually implemented. 'Strategy gaps' of this kind lead to confusion and uncertainty of purpose and may affect productivity by reducing overall company performance.

The present work examines the short break (SB) marketing strategies of six hotel groups. Corporate perspectives of these strategies are compared with those held at operating unit level. In this way, strategic gaps are identified which can be related to the six groups' actual performance in the SB market. This allows conclusions to be drawn about the relationship between strategic gaps, organizational performance and, by extension, productivity.

THE RESEARCH CONTEXT

The present research examined the strategies used by six of the most prominent hotel groups operating in the UK SB market. The groups were coded A, B, C, D, E and F, respecting their requests to remain anonymous. Perceptions of market structure and strategy were established by interviewing key executives at the head office of each company, as well as a total of 39 general managers at unit level. Thus it was possible to determine the involvement of head office as the strategy formulator and to identify the degree of central influence over the unit-level hotels in each group. Structure gaps were then identified by examining the differences between perceived corporate structure at both head office and unit levels. Finally the strategy gap was examined, i.e. differences between the perceptions of corporate SB strategy at head office and unit level.

Strategic gaps were classified and each type was related to the hotel group's performance in the SB market. It was thus possible to determine the influence of strategic gap upon performance. The present chapter also seeks to identify possible future developments resulting from the critical role that the multi-site perspective appears to play within the strategic development of hotel groups at market level.

STRATEGY FORMULATION: THE ROLE OF HEAD OFFICE

The research first examined corporate perspectives of strategy and of the SB market structure. The six hotel groups studied had clear corporate perspectives in terms of SB strategy and structure and exhibited three prominent forms of prime strategy (i.e. the main thrust of market strategy). These were concerned with promotion, segmentation, packaging and pricing, as described below:

- *promotion* strategies were those where the emphasis was placed upon branding and distribution;
- *segmentation/packaging* strategies were those in which the packaging of short breaks formed the main method of segmenting the market and also provided additional contributions to room revenue;
- *pricing* strategies were those for which the main competitive basis was reduced pricing.

Each of these strategies offered a different degree of identified market performance depending upon the structure – strategy relationship of the hotel groups. These findings have been extensively discussed elsewhere (Edgar *et al.*, 1994a, b). Corporate perspectives of the six study hotel groups with respect to the SB market were analysed on the basis of market scope, market share and sources of competitive advantage. The results of the analysis are summarized in Table 3.1.

As Table 3.1 shows, the structural variables were clearly differentiated, with most groups indicating medium market scope (four to six market segments), high market share (ten or more rooms concentration ratio) and mixed sources of competitive advantage ('many' being five to six sources, 'few' being one to two sources). These corporate perspectives were used as a benchmark for unit comparisons and the determination of strategic gaps was based upon them.

Table 3.1. Corporate perspective summary

Group	Strategy	Market scope	Market share	Number of sources	Market performance[a] (£)
A	Promotion	Medium	High	Many	6193
B	Pricing	Medium	Low	Few	989
C	Segmentation/ packaging	Wide	High	Many	5577
D	Promotion	Medium	High	Few	1650
E	Segmentation/ packaging	Medium	Medium	Many	3210
F	Promotion	Medium	High	Few	3740

Note: [a] SB revenue per room per annum, 1991–2.

Table 3.2. Prime SB strategy formulator for hotel units 1991–2

Formulator	Percentage of hotels in hotel group					
	A	B	C	D	E	F
Hotel independently	0	0	0	60	0	15
Head office alone	42	50	50	0	0	15
Joint decision	58	50	50	40	100	70

Table 3.3. Compiler of SB packages for hotel units, 1991–2

Package compiler	Percentage of hotels in hotel group					
	A	B	C	D	E	F
Hotel independently	16	12.5	22.5	31	61	62
Specialist operator	3	10.0	3.0	23	6	3
Head office only	81	77.5	74.5	46	33	35

Table 3.2 shows the determinants of unit level strategy for the six hotel groups upon which the study was based. It can be seen that most strategies were determined by joint decision, although head office also played a key role. Hotels in group F had mixed perceptions of head office involvement, while those in group E used a joint process of strategy formulation. Hotels in group D showed considerable independence, while those in groups A, B and C seemed to have a high level head office involvement, often amounting to domination.

At first glance the influence of head office over the latter groups seemed to take the form of joint partnerships with units. However, when the key elements of SB provision (i.e. packaging, distribution, marketing, and pricing) were examined in closer focus the situation appeared different.

Packaging

Table 3.3 indicates the ways in which responsibility for compiling SB packages was distributed, for the six hotel groups. These results indicate the highly active role that head offices generally played in compiling SB packages. This was particularly striking for hotels in groups A, B and C, where over 70 per cent of packages were compiled by head office. The role of head office is questionable in this respect. Multi-site packages can lose appropriateness and flexibility in local operating environments of which head offices have only limited knowledge. Problems of communication and coordination may lead to a loss of guest satisfaction and consequently to a poorer financial performance.

Promotion

In most of the hotel groups, head offices were found to play a critical role in promoting local units. On a scale of one to five, where five was 'critical' and one was 'no role', 8 per cent of all hotels sampled indicated head office's role in promotion as being between one and three and 92 per cent indicated four or five. These results may have reflected the units' need to strive for marketing scale economies through corporate involvement. However, they also clearly highlighted the prominent role of head office in SB promotion.

Distribution

The distribution channels used by hotel units were examined, in order to determine the role of head office in distributing SBs. Hotel units identified five different methods of distribution, which they ranked in descending order of importance:

1   Hotel group brochures (most important).
2   Individual hotel group activity.
3   Destination marketing, e.g. the Edinburgh Tourist Board.
4   Short break operators such as Superbreaks or Rainbow.
5   Consortia, e.g. Best Western (least important).

In general, these results reflected the reliance of hotel units upon head office for promotion. The need to keep costs to a minimum was probably primarily responsible for the very restricted use of outlets such as SB operators, who charged around 30 per cent commission.

At a more specific level, hotel units in group D ascribed equal importance to hotel group brochures and to individual hotel activity as distribution channels. This was probably attributable to the relative independence of the hotels in this group from head office influence. Hotels in group E, on the other hand, enjoyed similar independence but indicated that the units themselves were the most important distribution channel. This probably related to their freedom in constructing SB packages within the bounds of group SB segmentation/packaging strategy. The general reliance upon individual activity and destination marketing highlighted the importance of individual locations. It also indicated a need to consider multi-site approaches, which are discussed later in this chapter. The percentages of hotel units relying on head office for 40 per cent or more of SB bookings were: A, 73; B, 50; C, 80; D, 30; E, 0; F, 45. These results may imply that head offices played a key role in administering the SB market for hotel units. Alternatively, they could mean that head offices were to some extent restricting individual units from developing and administering their own SB markets.

The reliance of so many hotel units upon bookings from head office implies that head offices felt that they had a right to impose structure and strategy perceptions on units. However, it may also mean that local market direct bookings were being minimized. This would have resulted in an excessive reliance on head office and a lethargy in seeking and developing new market opportunities at local level. These trends seemed to reflect the identified importance of the hotel group brochure and to indicate the narrow view taken by hotel units. The latter perhaps relied excessively upon their head offices to promote them, rather than seeking marketing support that might otherwise have been available from the group. In addition, the results revealed that hotel units that experienced little head office involvement in their strategy formulation were less reliant upon booking through head office.

Pricing

Even more evident than their involvement in key elements of unit SB provision was the role head offices played in influencing the price of SBs. The most popular method of pricing used by the hotel units was SB package at cost plus a margin. Since head offices influenced the packaging of SBs they also had a considerable indirect influence over price. Perhaps of more interest was the role of head office in setting prices for units in separate markets. Hotel units in most groups experienced some degree of head office involvement, and as a result there was little difference between prices at individual locations. The exceptions were the hotels in group D, which had no head office involvement, owing perhaps to greater general manager independence, a consequence of the management incentive scheme which operated within the group.

Twenty per cent of the units studied relied on trial and error as a pricing method, which in large groups such as A and F seemed surprising and inappropriate. However, a considerable (and encouraging) degree of market research took place. Forty per cent of units underpinned their pricing through research and this may indicate a trend towards more sophisticated pricing in the SB market in the future. Overall, head offices influenced the pricing of 79 per cent of the hotel units surveyed. This raised questions about the level of knowledge that head offices possessed about local market prices, and indeed whether such knowledge was perceived to be required. This might perhaps best be determined by comparing the units' average achieved SB rate with the rate indicated in the group brochure. This offers an interesting area for further potential research.

In summary, hotels in groups A, B, C and F were subject to a high degree of head office control, and strategy formulation took place almost entirely at this level. However, hotels in group D had a moderate degree of autonomy, while those in group E had the highest degree of autonomy in relation to the SB market of all those studied. Head offices were most influential in the formulation of strategy concerned with direction, packaging, promotion and distribution, but they also had considerable influence over pricing policies. This raised questions as to how appropriate such strategies were and to what extent the hotel units implemented the corporate strategy as opposed to a market-based strategy (i.e. the size of the strategic gap). It was also desirable to discover what implications this had upon the groups' overall performance. The next section identifies the strategic gaps and allows comparisons of performance. In addition it examines the value of focusing on individual locations through a multi-site market perspective when formulating SB strategy.

Strategy Implementation: The Strategic Gap

When the corporate and unit perspectives were compared with one another, the structure-strategy gaps shown in Table 3.4 emerged. In this table, the 'group level' indicates the corporate perceptions of SB direction and market structure. The 'unit level' shows the percentage of hotel units sampled in the group which agreed with the corporate perceptions. The 'gap level' indicates where the structure or strategy gaps occurred and shows their magnitude. It is clear from Table 3.4 that distinct strategy and structure gaps existed between the corporate perspective of the SB market and that of the individual hotel units.

Table 3.4. Hotel unit to corporate structure–strategy gaps

Group	Level	Scope	Share	Sources of advantage	Strategy
A	Group	Medium	High	Many	Promotion
	Unit (%)	33	17	33	42
	Gap (%)	67	83	67	58
B	Group	Medium	Low	Few	Pricing
	Unit (%)	100	0	50	50
	Gap (%)	0	100	50	50
C	Group	Wide	High	Many	Segmentation/ packaging
	Unit (%)	50	13	25	25
	Gap (%)	50	87	75	75
D	Group	Medium	High	Few	Promotion
	Unit (%)	80	60	60	0
	Gap (%)	20	40	40	100
E	Group	Medium	Medium	Many	Segmentation/ packaging
	Unit (%)	60	0	40	80
	Gap (%)	40	100	60	20
F	Group	Medium	High	Few	Promotion
	Unit (%)	29	14	29	61
	Gap (%)	71	86	71	39

Note: Figures in 'unit' rows refer to the percentages of units sharing the group structure or strategy.

The next step in the research was to examine the market structure variables of market scope, market share and sources of competitive advantage. Definitions of these areas and a full discussion of measurement validity issues may be found in the present author's previous work (Edgar *et al.*, 1994a).

Market scope

Figure 3.1 shows the size of market scope structure gaps occurring within the six hotel groups studied. It is evident that hotels in groups B and D were in good agreement with their head offices' perceptions of the degree of market segmentation within the SB market. Hotels in groups A and F, however, exhibited large market scope/structure gaps, indicating that they were not fully aware of the range of segments being targeted by head office. This may have considerable implications in terms of the consistency and hence the quality of the 'corporate' brand. It would be worthy of more detailed investigation in its own right.

Market share

In terms of the perceived market share held by hotels in the SB market, the structure gap indicates a gross misrepresentation of unit level operations. The results shown in

Productivity Management

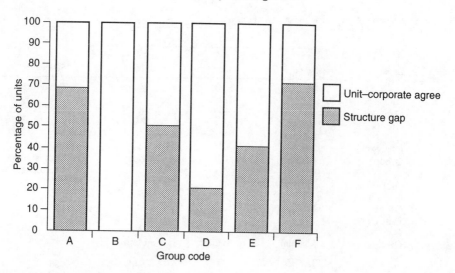

Figure 3.1. Structure gap: market scope

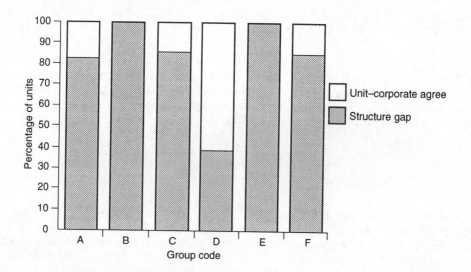

Figure 3.2. Structure gap: market share

Figure 3.2 indicate that many structure gaps occurred in the area of market share. None of the hotels in group B or E, and few in groups A, B and F, agreed with their corporate perspective of market share. This has considerable implications for strategy formulation. If head offices formulate strategy based upon their perceptions of the market share of the group and this does not match actual unit market share, strategic drift may occur, resulting in potentially poorer performance (Quinn, 1980).

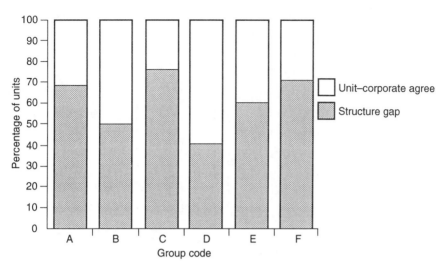

Figure 3.3. Structure gap: sources of competitive advantage

Sources of competitive advantage

The present study also examined sources of competitive advantage and therefore the potential areas for strategy development (i.e. the organizations' strategic capabilities). As shown in Figure 3.3, there were significant gaps between what hotel groups and their local hotel units perceived as their strategic capabilities. The implications of Figure 3.3 are that head offices may need to consult with their units more closely to ensure they are able to implement the centrally formulated strategy.

It can be seen that there were considerable discrepancies between corporate and unit perspectives of SB market structure. Unit level perceptions of environmental conditions were clearly different from those at corporate level. Yet no recognition was made of this by any head office and, in most cases, group SB strategy was formulated on the basis of corporate perceptions of the market structure. These were clearly not representative of the situation at unit level. This raised the question as to whether the units actually implemented the strategy formulated by head office and, if so, what the effects were upon the resulting performance.

Previous sections have established the structure gaps and the corresponding gaps in head office perceptions of the unit level operating environment. The gap between head office and unit in terms of strategy adopted is now discussed. As previously mentioned, hotels in groups A, B, C and F were under considerable influence from their head offices to follow head office SB strategies closely. However, hotels in groups D and E were given more autonomy to react to their local environments. The resulting strategy gaps are shown in Figure 3.4.

The implications of the figure are that each hotel in group D was able to develop its own strategies within the market place. Within the group there was very limited head office involvement and no hotels actively adopted the 'corporate line'. Hotels in group E, however, only exhibited a very small strategy gap. This appeared to be a conse-quence of excellent two-way communications between the units and head office. It also

Productivity Management

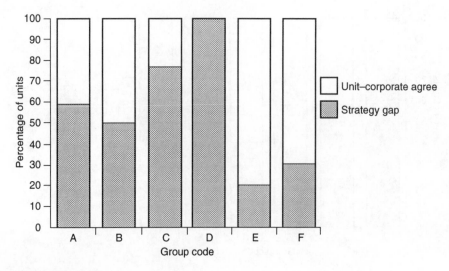

Figure 3.4. SB strategy gap

seemed be because of the adoption of 'common themes', as opposed to an all-embracing corporate SB strategy. Thus, although these hotels, like those in group D, were permitted a high level of autonomy, the outcome was very different in terms of the strategic gap. The size of the latter appeared to be influenced not only by the extent, but also by the style, of head office support.

When the strategy and structure gaps were compared it became evident that a large number of hotels did not adopt the corporate perspective of SB strategy. Given the high level of head office involvement in the packaging, promotion, distribution and pricing of SBs, this implies a considerable mismatch between the formulation and implementation of strategy. This undoubtedly affected levels of performance and hence of productivity.

COMPARATIVE PERFORMANCE

In the present study, as elsewhere in the hospitality industry, performance was measured as SB revenue per room per annum. Group performances and average unit level performance achieved by the six study groups during the year 1991–2 are shown in Table 3.5. The lowest-performing hotel units in the groups were generally found to be those which did not match the structure–strategy profile of the particular hotel group. This may have been because of high levels of head office involvement, which tended to restrict local market strategies instead of supporting unit developments.

Figure 3.5 represents the average performance of the hotel units in each group. It shows that hotels in the groups with the lowest strategy gaps performed better on average than those with larger gaps. This was essentially owing to the support provided by head office in terms of managing the SB packages and marketing them

Table 3.5. Group and unit level performance

Group	Corporate performance (£)	Unit level performance (£) Highest	Lowest	Average
A	6193	5410	712	3010
B	989	803	730	767
C	5577	3834	350	1400
D	1650	3811	183	1155
E	3210	6040	2146	3956
F	3740	4504	872	2316

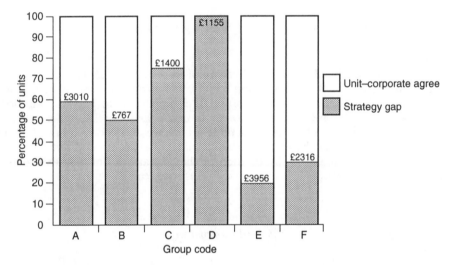

Figure 3.5. SB strategy gap and performance

locally. Such support enabled strategies developed by head offices to be implemented at unit level, with much greater focus in terms of packaging, promotion, distribution and pricing. In effect this maximized the synergy discussed earlier in the present chapter. This effect was most evident in the hotels of group E, where the head office had a limited strategy formulation role. It preferred to direct its strategy in terms of a general theme and placed more emphasis on support at local level. In this case, the head office perspective was a good reflection of unit level strategy. There was no perception among the units that central strategy had been imposed upon them.

Figure 3.5 also shows that hotels in group B performed less well than those in other groups. This was probably because of the price-cutting strategy adopted by group B, which reduced turnover and squeezed margins. It seemed to be the case that the larger the strategy gap, the poorer the overall performance. Presumably this reflected conflict between head office strategy and local market needs perceived at unit level.

IMPLICATIONS OF STRATEGIC GAPS

The occurrence of strategic gaps appeared to be directly related to the degree of control imposed by hotel groups upon their units. In order to perform well, the units needed to be 'in touch' with corporate strategy and direction. This was necessary so that they received the full benefit of strategic capability support and gained the necessary synergy. However, local market needs varied considerably and led to apparent attempts by units to develop their own strategy without the support of head office. As might be expected, this resulted in poorer average performance. The implications of these observations are that units should either ensure they are meeting corporate direction or be given greater autonomy (but at the same time supported) to develop market-led strategies. The next section examines the latter proposition, looking particularly at the influence of location upon SB strategies.

THE FUTURE: A MULTI-SITE PERSPECTIVE

This chapter has already addressed the diversity of local markets, arguing that the role of location is crucial in SB strategy formulation, which should not simply be a matter of remote decision-making from head office. It is important to examine this local geographical diversity in more detail, in order to understand more fully the nature of strategic gaps. Hotel units from the six sample groups were categorized into the three key location types identified by Slattery (1992): primary, secondary and tertiary. These categories permitted comparison by location of the SB variables of market structure, competitive strategies adopted and overall SB performance.

SB market structure

Market structure was determined in terms of market scope, market share, and the number of sources of competitive advantage. Table 3.6 shows the way these aspects varied between the different types of location.

Primary and tertiary locations predominantly exhibited wide market scope, while secondary locations were essentially medium market scope in nature. Tertiary locations had no narrow scope hotels. These findings appeared to indicate that tertiary locations were targeting a range of segments in order to encourage additional revenue, while secondary locations specialized in a medium range of niches. Primary locations provided a mix, allowing narrow market focus for specialization and wide market scope for flexibility. Thus they maintained consumer interest, return custom and fencing for different rate-paying customers. There were no high market share units in tertiary locations, but these increased in numbers up the locational scale, reaching 30 per cent in primary locations. Similarly, the size of medium share hotels increased as one moved from tertiary to primary locations, there being generally smaller units, with lower market shares, in tertiary locations. This finding agrees with those of Slattery (1992), which also link hotel size with location.

Table 3.6. SB market structure by location

Structure		Percentage of hotels		
		Primary	Secondary	Tertiary
Market scope	Wide	60	38	63
	Medium	30	52	37
	Narrow	10	10	0
Market share	High	30	19	0
	Medium	40	19	13
	Low	30	62	87
Sources of advantage	Many	20	29	38
	Average	50	38	38
	Few	30	33	24

The number of sources of competitive advantage increased along the scale from primary to tertiary locations. Thus there were fewer sources of advantage in secondary locations and average to few in primary locations. This indicated that primary and secondary locations tended to exhibit a greater degree of competition, basing their strategies upon more focused elements of the organizational structure. On the other hand, elements that would have been perceived as areas of competitive advantage in tertiary locations were the norm in primary and secondary locations and were therefore not perceived as sources of competitive advantage.

SB prime strategies

This section identifies the strategies that were adopted in each of the key location types and that presumably resulted from associated market structure variables. The three types of strategy considered were those concerned with promotion, segmentation/ packaging and pricing. Table 3.7 represents the prime strategies adopted by the different categories of location.

None of the primary site hotels used pricing strategies, an observation which probably reflected the highly competitive nature of primary locations. This enhanced contributions and improved the value of SBs to these hotels. Room rates were maintained at these locations, because SBs were not treated as a form of discounting. Hotels that adopted pricing strategies occupied secondary or tertiary locations and

Table 3.7. Prime strategies adopted by hotel units by location, 1991–2

Strategy	Location		
	Primary	Secondary	Tertiary
Promotional	50	33	25
Segmentation/packaging	50	38	25
Pricing	0	29	50

were most abundant in the latter. Segmentation/packaging strategies were used in all types of locations, but most commonly in secondary locations, while promotional strategies played a key role in primary locations. Location therefore appeared to have a considerable influence upon the type of prime SB strategy adopted.

SB performance

Average hotel performance varied considerably within and between locations, the average values being £4110.38, £2242.40 and £4162.00 at primary, secondary and tertiary sites respectively. Thus a considerable level of performance was achievable even at tertiary locations, essentially through adopting different strategies in smaller hotel units. This observation suggested a need to examine structure–strategy–performance relationships at unit level, in order to determine where performance might be enhanced. In primary locations segmentation/packaging strategies seemed to provide the greatest performance benefits. However, in secondary locations most hotels achieved their best performance by moving towards promotional strategies. This trend was also found in tertiary locations. Thus type of location appeared to have some relationship with strategy and performance. As such, it forms an alternative to head office dominance as a basis for strategy formulation.

CONCLUSIONS

The purpose of the present chapter has not been to offer any ready made solutions to enhancing productivity *per se*. However, it is clear that in a dynamic, people-oriented industry such as hospitality, the coherency of the organizational culture is an important determinant of productivity. Organizational culture is in turn dependent upon good internal communication, particularly in matters such as strategy formulation and implementation. Thus the present work has concentrated upon the enhancement of performance by reducing the strategic gap.

The SB market was a particularly suitable subject for the present study, because its scope within the six hotel groups was comparatively limited. It was therefore feasible to identify the gaps and to measure their impact upon hotel unit performance. The work showed a general failure at head office level to appreciate the complexities of multi-product, multi-site marketing, which are inherent in the nature of the SB market and hotel industry. It was also possible to provide some insights into the structure–strategy–performance relationships prevailing in the SB market, and their effect upon unit performance. The author proposes that this can be extrapolated into a perceivable link between market strategy and productivity.

The present research has also established that there was a high degree of head office intervention. Perhaps this represents an attempt to maintain control as well as to ensure a degree of longer-term planning. In some cases (most notably with hotels in group D) head office intervention appeared to cause a degree of confusion. Units were allowed to formulate SB strategies but the SB packages were then compiled almost entirely at head office. This caused inconsistency and dysfunction. It probably accounted for the poorer performance of hotels in group D and the degree of discontent shown in terms of head office communications. Clearly alternative approaches are required to strategy formulation and implementation, which take into account local market conditions as well as corporate goals, and which permit a flexible, supportive relationship between head office and local hotel units.

A key lesson of the present study is a need for autonomy in multi-site and multi-product markets, supported, rather than dominated, by head office. Clear communication of corporate direction should be matched by efficient upward communication links, by which marketing information may be communicated to strategy-makers. In all cases a multi-site perspective must be taken to strategy formulation and implementation that considers both sets of needs. Only in this way will it be possible to achieve full efficiency, and hence productivity, in this type of business environment.

REFERENCES

Ansoff, H.I. (1971) *Corporate Strategy*. New York: McGraw-Hill.

Ball, S. and Johnson, K. (1989) 'Productivity management within fast food chains: a case study of Wimpy International'. *International Journal of Hospitality Management*, **8**(4), 265–9.

Banks, R.L. and Wheelwright, S.C. (1979) 'Operations vs strategy'. *Harvard Business Review*, May/June, 127–35.

Bradley, M.D. and Baron, D.M. (1993) 'Measuring performance in a multiproduct firm: an application to the US postal service'. *Operations Research*, **41**(3), 450–8.

Chew, B.W. (1986) 'No nonsense guide to measuring productivity'. *Harvard Business Review*, **64**(1), 30–89.

Edgar, D.A., Litteljohn, D.L. and Allardyce, M.L. (1994a) 'Strategic clusters and strategic space: the case of the UK short break market'. *International Journal of Contemporary Hospitality Management*, **6**(5), 20–6.

Edgar, D.A., Litteljohn, D.L., Allardyce, M.L. and Wanhill, S.R.C. (1994b) 'Commercial short holiday breaks: market structure, competitive advantage and performance'. *Tourism State of the Art*, London: Wiley, 323–42.

Hobbs, J.M. and Heany, D.F. (1977) 'Coupling strategy to operating plans'. *Harvard Business Review*, May/June, 136–43.

Hofer, C.W. and Schendel, D.E. (1978) *Strategy Formulation: Analytical Concepts*. St Paul: Minnesota West Publishing.

Johnson, G. and Thomas, H. (1988) 'Strategic groups and financial performance: a critical examination'. *Strategic Management Journal*, **11**, 385.

Jones, P. (1990) 'Managing food service productivity in the long term: strategy, structure, and performance'. *International Journal of Hospitality Management*, **9**(2), 143–54.

Lee, J.Y. (1991) 'Measuring productivity for service firms: it's tricky but it can be done'. *Business Forum*, **16**(2), 18–22.

Prahalad, C.K. (1976) 'Strategic choices in diversified MNCs'. *Harvard Business Review*, July/August, 73–84.

Quinn, J.B. (1980) *Strategies for Change*. New York: Irwin.

Schroeder, R.G. (1985) *Operations Management: Decision Making in the Operations Function*. New York: McGraw Hill.

Scott, P.M. and Simpson, W.W. (1989) 'Connecting overall corporate planning to individual business units'. *Public Utilities Fortnightly*, **123**(12), 27–30.

Slattery, P. (1992) 'Unaffiliated hotels in the UK'. *EIU Travel & Tourism Analyst*, **1**, 90–102.

Teague, J. and Eilon, S. (1973) *Productivity Measurement: a Brief Survey*. London: Imperial College of Science and Technology.

Witt, C.A. and Witt, S.F. (1989) 'Why productivity in the hotel sector is low'. *International Journal of Contemporary Hospitality Management*, **1**(2), 28–33.

FOUR

Macro aspects of productivity planning for the hospitality industry

Michael V. Conlin and Tom Baum

INTRODUCTION

Productivity is one of the key concepts that business leaders are focusing upon in the intensely competitive global market place. This is particularly true in the international hospitality industry, where labour market and service demands are forcing a constant reappraisal of employee roles and productive output. Productivity in a general sense, however, has been an important consideration since the early days of management theory, dating back to the pre-World War I period of Frederick W. Taylor. Taylor's *The Principles of Scientific Management*, published in 1911, was (and many would argue still is) the seminal work in the development of the scientific approach to management. A key focus of that work was the continuous improvement of the productivity of workers and companies alike for their mutual maximum prosperity (Schermerhorn, 1989, p. 42). Ritzer (1993, p. 24) articulates the overall principles and consequences of scientific management as follows:

> Overall, scientific management produced a *nonhuman technology* that exerted great *control* over workers. Employers found that when workers followed Taylor's methods, they worked much more *efficiently*, everyone performed the same steps (that is their work exhibited *predictability*), and they produced a great deal more while their pay had to be increased only slightly (*calculability*). Thus Taylorism meant increased profits to those enterprises that adopted them. [authors' italics]

The features of control, efficiency, predictability and calculability are central to Ritzer's concept of McDonaldization and will be returned to at a later point in this chapter.

Productivity has continued to be a primary focus of evolving management theory throughout this century. The area of time and motion study, pioneered by Frank and

Lillian Gilbreth (Gilbreth, 1911), was and continues to be concerned with reducing work to its basic components and seeking to reduce wasted motion and improving work flow. Indeed, the work of these early theorists laid the foundations for the scientific approach to management, which continues to evolve even to this day and of which McDonaldization is just one manifestation. The issues that the Gilbreths identified and have continuing significance for management theory and the contemporary approaches to enhancing productivity have been summarized by Schermerhorn (1989, p. 44):

- the use of compensation as an incentive for increased production;
- the design of jobs, specification of work methods and identification of needed forms of supervisory support;
- the proper selection of individuals to work in these jobs once they are designed;
- the training of individuals to perform according to task requirements and to the best of their abilities;
- the use of rational and systematic approaches to solve management problems and improve performance.

Productivity continued to be the centrepiece in the work of other major classical organizational theorists, including Weber (1947) and Fayol (1949). Their focus was on structure and process designed to ensure maximum productivity. As Pugh and Hickson (1989, p. 70) state, Weber's rational-legal authority system was 'expressly designed to achieve certain goals (i.e. the organization is like a well designed machine with a certain function to perform, and every part of that machine contributes to the attainment of maximum performance of that function).' This description of the highly mechanistic approach of the classical theorists makes it clear that the early focus was on the work or task itself, with little concern about individual and group behaviour and other behavioural issues. The 1930s saw a change in approach as the influence of behaviourists began to emerge. Following World War II, some of the most important modern organizational behaviour theorists – McGregor (1985), Maslow (1974), Alderfer (1972), Herzberg (1959), McClelland (1971), Adams (1963) and Vroom (1964) – propagated theories about individual and group behaviour and its effect upon productivity. The focus of this group of management theorists was on the individual, either singly or in groups, and not on the actual work itself. Their research recognized the complexity of people and the influence that individual needs and behaviour have on the whole area of work and, accordingly, productivity. They began to talk about needs, motivation, expectations, goals, rewards, achievement, behavioural modification and equity.

These management scientists set the stage for the contemporary obsessive focus on productivity. Realizing that no single theory could explain, predict and prescribe enhanced productivity, organizational behaviour has, in its most recent metamorphosis, turned to the notion of 'contingency' or, to put it most simply, the use of whatever works. Notwithstanding the scientific cloak much of this modern thinking wears, it is essentially an integrated approach that allows managers to combine, discard and adapt whatever combination of theories suits the circumstances. It is focused on the current reality of a situation. The work of Vroom with respect to expectancy theory and the subsequent computer based models of contingency leadership styles is a good example of prescribing for the current reality (Vroom, 1964).

It is not surprising that much of the behavioural work on productivity derived from more general considerations of motivation, in that the general assumptions within these approaches appear to be that productivity or a lack of productive output are closely linked to the attitude or drive within the individual. Thus, provide the worker with the incentive (extrinsic or intrinsic) and she or he will work to better and more productive effect. Classical behaviourists, after Skinner, placed the greatest emphasis on extrinsic rewards as the means by which to motivate workers to greater productivity. Maslow and Herzberg, with their models of motivation, questioned the simplicity of this approach and postulated higher order, intrinsic motivators (Maslow) or a distinction between hygiene and true motivational factors (Herzberg). Mahesh (1994) argues strongly for the potency of intrinsic as opposed to extrinsic motivational factors in leading workers to enhanced performance and, logically, to improved productivity.

> The qualitative result of people's activities would be extremely high if they were primarily motivated by the interest, enjoyment, satisfaction and challenge of the endeavour itself. This is what psychologists refer to as 'intrinsic motivation'. Conversely, if they are applying themselves to a task due to any 'extrinsic motivation' in that they perceive the possibility of achieving other goals through accomplishment of a task – like the satisfaction of physiological, safety, belongingness or recognition needs – the quality of performance can be expected to be of a relatively inferior level. (Mahesh, 1994, p. 56)

In the context of the hospitality industry, the traditions of authoritarian management combined with an overall low skills level, limited investment in training and a transitory labour force have resulted in a motivational environment that is predominantly extrinsic in focus. This is one of the underlying problems that must be faced in considering productivity in the context of the hospitality industry.

The major focus of the chapter will be behavioural and broadly based. It will seek to respond to the generally poor image which the hospitality industry has as a career choice. It will proceed on the assumption that more productive employees are employees who are motivated, professional in their perspective and self-image, and recognized as such. Finally, it will endeavour to place productivity in the wider context of human resource management within the hospitality industry, particularly at the macro level.

WHAT IS PRODUCTIVITY?

Productivity can be thought of as something very simple or very complex. If one focuses solely on the end result, it can be quite simple. For example, the contemporary human resource management literature provides the following examples:

> In simple terms, productivity can be defined as output per hour. But this is far too simple. Productivity comes in various forms . . . some define productivity as the change in unit labor costs, or how much each item costs to produce. Others suggest that productivity is the value of production over paid hours (Anthony, Perrewe and Kacmar, 1993, 352);

Productivity is a summary measure of the quantity or quality of work performance with resource utilization considered. The traditional economic definition of productivity focuses on the ratio of product or service outputs to resource inputs. . . .

From a manager's perspective, productivity reflects a broader performance measure. It defines success or failure in producing goods and services in quantity, of quality, and with a good use of resources. Other things being equal, productivity rises in a work situation when the quantity of outputs increases, the quality of outputs increases, and/or the cost of resources utilized decreases. (Schermerhorn, 1989, p. 17)

McMahon (1994, p. 66) simplifies this in terms of a formula:

$$\text{productivity} = \frac{\text{wealth produced}}{\text{resources consumed}}$$

All these definitions focus on the ratio of inputs and outputs, or, as Schermerhorn appropriately describes it, the 'traditional economic definition', without much concern about the human side of the process used to achieve a good ratio. Schermerhorn, in his definition, does raise the notion of quality, which has become the focus of much attention in the last decade. The definition from Moorhead and Griffin (1992, p. 44) – 'Productivity is an indicator of how much an organization is creating relative to its inputs' is useful because they go on to link the definition with issues that this chapter will address:

Productivity is important for a variety of reasons. For one thing, it clearly affects an organization's ability to compete effectively. For another, it shapes the overall economic prosperity of the organization's host country. In other words, productivity created goods and services not only contribute to the home country's economic health but allow organizations to generate more revenue in the global economy. (Moorhead and Griffin, 1992, p. 44)

Moorhead and Griffin raise important concepts and issues in the world of business today:

1 The whole issue of competitiveness is tied closely to productivity.
2 The effectiveness and efficiency of firms have an effect upon the economic well-being of countries as a whole.
3 Success in the global economy demands productivity.

McMahon also ties productivity into the overall standard of living within a society.

If changes in the productive system can lead to continually growing output of goods and services, without corresponding increases in the use of resources being consumed to produce those goods and services, then a rising standard of living may be expected. (McMahon, 1994, p. 616)

These issues, as raised by Moorhead and Griffin and McMahon, will be addressed later in this chapter.

Productivity becomes increasingly complex when one examines the array of factors that face managers attempting to enhance their companies' performance. They can increase production, lower costs or develop some combination of the two. This is the simple way, focusing on the end result without much consideration for the total environment that these variables operate in. However, the role of human resources in the process of enhancing productivity can no longer be overlooked. When one factors in the human component, the concept of productivity becomes very complex indeed.

The need to consider the human factor in productivity is now firmly established: 'There is no mystery to improving productivity. A large factor in productivity increases is the proper management of human resources' (Gibson *et al.*, 1991, p. 6). MacGregor made the case strongly for moving towards a humanistic approach to management by stating that the classical, mechanistic theories were based on models of military and religious origin which are not really relevant any longer in the modern business place and that they suffered from 'ethnocentrism' by ignoring the wider political, social and economic environment (MacGregor, 1985, pp. 16–17).

Therefore, the case can be made that productivity is the objective of an integrated approach to human resource management, either at the company level or, as will be argued here, at the national or regional level. The parts are interdependent and must be considered in a systematic manner if meaningful gains are to be obtained.

PRODUCTIVITY AND THE HOSPITALITY INDUSTRY

In the hospitality industry, the need for an integrated perspective is particularly strong. The industry is very labour intensive. The overwhelming presence of people in the process of delivering the 'hospitality' product is pervasive. Gains in productivity in this industry can be obtained by the application of the mechanistic strategies of the classical theorists, but real, sustained gain must take into account the human component. The role that people play in the shaping of the product – its image, acceptability and level of customer satisfaction – is critical. Mill puts it this way:

There are several special factors that make the problem of productivity especially acute for the hospitality industry. The first of these is that the industry is in the mature stage of its life cycle . . . a second challenge for the hospitality industry is that its nature makes productivity difficult to measure, much less improve . . . a related problem is the labor intensive nature of the industry . . . a third problem is that although employees are critical to increased productivity, we have traditionally placed little emphasis on employee development and training. (Mill, 1989, pp. 1–3)

Mill believes that enhanced productivity is the key to avoiding the natural outcome of the product life cycle, namely decline. Enhanced productivity can provide the growth which the natural evolution of the product itself can no longer produce. His next point raises a major problem. How do you measure quality of service, the value of a smile and the good feeling a guest takes away from a hospitality experience? Productivity measurement has always been a key concern but its measurement in a service organization where the importance of intangibles is critical presents a major problem.

Ritzer (1993) considers the issue of productivity in the wider context of developments within the service sector, in particular, as well as society in general. For him, the demand for enhanced productivity, in the workplace, has inevitable consequences for the nature of the interaction between service providers and their customers. Ritzer argues that the process of rationalization has spawned an approach to the management of service enterprises, which he calls *McDonaldization* and which is characterized by four key elements.

Efficiency, or 'the optimum method for getting from one point to another'. In the context of productivity in the hospitality industry, efficiency means the adoption, in part, of scientific management principles and the division of all functions into their component low-skill tasks, which can then be carried out with maximum efficiency utilizing low-cost resource inputs. Ritzer illustrates this process, in some detail, by focusing on the systems employed by McDonald's, but stresses that the principles apply elsewhere in the industry and can readily be found in other hospitality operations.

Calculability or *quantificability* is a feature of McDonaldization that is designed to give the consumer the impression of high volume for low cost, creating a new sense of value which is linked to quantitative rather than qualitative criteria. From the customer perspective, McDonaldization also focuses on time factors, offering speed of service and speed of consumption that appears to be very attractive within high-pressure, time-focused societies. These factors also apply to the delivery of the service, where employees are expected to deliver high volumes of pre-specified and measured output at high speed and are judged by volume and time considerations against very limited quality criteria.

Predictability is also central to the McDonaldization process, giving the customer a sense of confidence in purchasing products or services, where any sense of adventure is also removed.

> There is great comfort in knowing that McDonald's offers no surprises, that the food we eat at one time or in one place will be identical to the food we eat at another time or in another place. We know that the next Egg McMuffin we eat will not be awful, but we also know that it will not be exceptionally delicious. The success of the McDonald's model indicates that many people have come to prefer a world in which there are no surprises. (Ritzer, 1993, p. 10)

This certainty also has implications for the manner in which work is carried out in that employees are far less likely to encounter problems and the unpredictable than is the case in a rather more fluid and unpredictable service delivery environment. As a result, with the aid of quantification, throughput in the workplace can readily be predicted and staffing levels fixed at levels to cater for this predictability. Furthermore, front-line staff are unlikely to face the unexpected and, as a result, their training needs will be less demanding. Productivity, therefore, can be expected to be greater in this environment than in the traditional hospitality context.

Control, through the *substitution of non-human for human technology*, is the final component of Ritzer's concept. This, again, has strong antecedents in scientific management. Ritzer argues that control applies both to the customers (who, in fast food restaurants, are offered, for example, limited menus and short-use seating) and to employees.

> The humans who work in fast-food restaurants are trained to do a very limited number of things in precisely the way they are told to do them. Managers and inspectors make sure that workers toe the line . . . McDonald's also controls people by using nonhuman technology to replace human workers. Human workers, no matter how well they are programmed and controlled, can foul up the operation of the system. A slow or indolent worker can make the preparation and delivery of a Big Mac inefficient. A worker who refuses to follow the rules can leave the pickles or special sauce off a hamburger, thereby making for unpredictability. And a distracted worker can put too few fries in the box, making an order of large fries seem awfully skimpy . . . technologies permit greater control over the human beings involved in the fast-food restaurant. The result is that McDonald's is able to reassure customers about the nature of the employee to be encountered and the nature of service to be obtained. (Ritzer, 1993, p. 11)

The picture that is implied by McDonaldization and that Ritzer paints has certain application across the service sector and, in particular, to the hospitality industry. In terms of productivity, it illustrates, with graphic effect, both the process and outcomes of an approach to service delivery that places maximization of employee output, through total management of both the guest experience and the work that is undertaken to provide it, at the centre of its service philosophy. However, McDonaldization has clear consequences in terms of the complexity and quality of the service that is being offered and implies that pursuing this route will, inevitably, lead to a simplification and degradation of the quality of the service offered within the hospitality industry.

Ritzer's perspective is one that is, broadly, critical of the process of McDonaldization and the pressure to increase productivity through this customer management and working culture. This, however, does not negate the need to enhance the level of productivity within the hospitality industry, possibly through other methods. McMahon (1994) argues the need to improve productivity in the hotel industry as a reality reflecting demographic pressures in developed economies. Certainly, labour market realities have dramatically altered the staffing ratios that pertain in the hotels of rapid-growth economies such as Hong Kong, Malaysia and Singapore, and the need to maintain hard earned reputations for service quality has necessitated significant increases in productive output per employee as a consequence. This, in turn, has placed attention upon the training and skills development needs of the workforce and, as a result, public and private sector investment in this area has risen significantly.

Heizer and Render (1988) have attempted to explain the generally low levels of productivity to be found in services (and within the hospitality industry by extension) to the nature of work in the sector, notably because it is typically labour intensive, frequently individually processed, often difficult to mechanize and automate, and frequently includes an intellectual task performed by professionals (not generally true of hospitality). It is, however, incomplete to consider the productive work of front-line hospitality employees as consisting solely of the tasks that they undertake at the point of service delivery. Their role within the context of relationship marketing, of particularly vital significance in the hospitality industry, means that much seemingly unproductive guest contact work may, in fact, contribute to future business and profitability in a way that is less likely to pertain in the manufacturing sector. In order to obtain a true measure of productivity in the hospitality industry, some measure of this contribution needs to be incorporated into formulae that are applied. This may lead to a reappraisal of the apparently unproductive nature of hospitality work.

PRODUCTIVITY AND THE MACRO-ENVIRONMENT

Most discussions of productivity, in the context of the hospitality, focus upon the issue in the context of the individual firm, discussing strategies that management can implement, generally, to enhance the productivity of their employees. Here, the focus of consideration, as has already been indicated, tends to be either upon scientific management/work study type approaches or upon consideration of the motivational factors which might be addressed in order to increase productivity. Consideration of productivity in the macro context tends to be the preserve of economists who attempt to assess overall productivity levels within industry sectors (although rarely hospitality), regions or countries. These tend to focus on the relationship between numbers employed and the value of their output.

Productivity, however, is also a macro-environmental consideration in the context of human resource management. Table 4.1 represents the contrast between micro and macro dimensions of productivity from a human resource perspective. The micro column includes the ground already covered in this chapter, primarily focusing on productivity in the context of the individual firm. The right-hand column, by contrast, represents the wider hospitality environment, generally at national or regional level, where productivity needs to be seen in the context of more general human resource issues affecting the sector. Baum (1993, pp. 9–10) has summarized these issues, in the context of the wider tourism industry, to include

- demography and the shrinking employment pool/labour shortages;
- the tourism industry's image as an employer;
- cultural and traditional perceptions of the industry;
- rewards and benefits/compensation;
- recruitment, retention and staff turnover;
- education and training, within both colleges and industry;
- skills shortages, especially at higher technical and management levels;
- linking human resource concerns with service and product quality;
- poor management and planning information about human resource matters in the tourism industry;
- the tendency to develop human resource policies, initiatives and remedial programmes that are reactive to what is currently happening rather than proactive to what is likely to occur.

Table 4.1. Macro aspects of productivity planning for the hospitality industry: the productivity spectrum

Type of productivity strategy	Productivity strategy perspective	
	Micro (task- or company-specific)	Macro (national, regional or industry-specific)
Mechanistic	Time and motion studies Historical production records Task planning Motion economy Workplace design	National occupational standards Apprenticeship programmes Legislation on workplace design and operating procedures
Humanistic	Organizational behaviour modification Expectancy motivation Improved communications Responsibility Recognition Team-building Corporate cultures	National tourism awareness and appreciation programmes Educational opportunities Role models and mentoring National recognition schemes Industry recognition schemes Certification schemes Concept of professionalism

These macro issues, while having clear implications for individual employers at the macro level, provide a clear agenda for, in particular, those with public sector responsibility for the planning and development of the hospitality industry. Implicit, as a remedy within this agenda, is the notion that enhanced productivity within the hospitality sector of many countries and regions, as a whole, could make a considerable contribution to overcoming the problems identified. Clearly, for example, a focus on productivity, as McMahon (1994) notes, is a logical response to a shrinking labour market in the developed world. Likewise, increasingly productive workers can, reasonably, expect to negotiate enhanced remuneration and benefits. At an industry level, however, it would be inappropriate to see this solely in terms of obtaining 'more for less', as tends to be the clarion call of individual employers when considering increased productivity. Labour shortages provide an opportunity to address related concerns, notably that of image, by upgrading the quality of the work on offer, thus seeking to attract more able recruits who, in turn, have the capacity and commitment to operate at greater levels of productivity. This is, on the one hand, the concern of individual employers. More significantly, however, there is an onus upon those responsible for the development and implementation of human resource development policies for hospitality to recognize their role in enhancing productivity and, through this, to provide responses to the identified issues.

The route to increased productivity, at a macro level, can follow a number of different routes. In Table 4.1, the options have been segmented into those which are of a mechanistic nature, concerned with measurable outcomes, and the examples given are national or regional occupational standards (such as the HOST scheme in the Caribbean) (Conlin and Titcombe, 1994), apprenticeship programmes, out of fashion in the UK but still the backbone of skills training in Germany, and legislation to enforce improvements in workplace design and operating procedures.

The outcomes of what is described as the humanistic approach to productivity gains at the macro level are, by their nature, more difficult to measure. To some extent, they involve a long-term commitment to and faith in the value of the investment. In this sense, they are compatible with arguments set out by Conlin and Baum (1994) in their discussion of human resource development in the context of sustainable tourism and

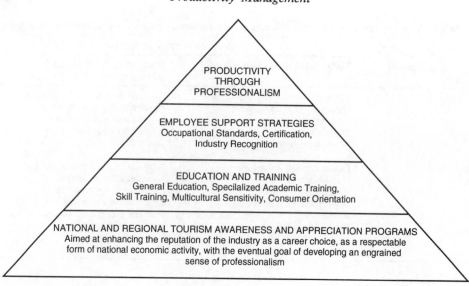

Figure 4.1. Productivity pyramid

with what Baum (1995) describes as the sustainable paradigm of human resource management for the hospitality industry, which seeks to counter traditional, short-term expediencies in the management of human resources for the industry. These measures include: national tourism awareness and appreciation programmes such as that implemented with considerable effect in Hawaii; enhancing educational opportunities as a lifelong and career-focused process rather than simply as a short-term expedient; certification for performance and existing competencies, such as that provided by National Vocational Qualifications in the UK; use of role models, mentoring and recognition schemes (national and industry-specific); and encouraging the development of professionalism at all levels, something generally absent within much of the hospitality industry worldwide.

None of these measures, in themselves, will guarantee enhanced productivity within the hospitality industry. However, a combination of attention to all the identified areas, mechanistic and humanistic, will enhance the prospects of the total workforce working with greater effect and, ultimately, achieving improved productive performance. Figure 4.1 represents a hierarchy of measures within both the mechanistic and humanistic areas, the productivity pyramid, which points to the sequencing of initiatives necessary in order to enhance overall productivity within the hospitality industry. Unless the base issues of awareness and appreciation are in place, subsequent steps through education, training and professional enhancement cannot work to full effect because the basic conditions are not in place. This is one of the existing weaknesses in attempts to enhance performance among employees in the hospitality industry. Without full acceptance of and support for the hospitality industry among the community, attempts to improve education, training and professional enhancement can only partially succeed. Primarily, the quality of those recruited into the industry will not match that of those attracted into other industries and, therefore, their potential to deliver quality and productive service will be restricted. This will be particularly true with respect to the delivery of the intangibles of service at the front-line, probably the most critical component in productivity enhancement within the hospitality industry.

In conclusion, therefore, this chapter argues that productivity in the hospitality industry needs to be seen fully in the context of its wider human resource management environment. In particular, measures to improve productivity at the level of the firm will, in the long term, be doomed to limited impact unless the wider, macro-environmental issues addressed above are taken into consideration.

This consideration has major implications at national and, in some cases, regional level and needs to be addressed in the context of wider educational and industrial development policy formulation. However, unless the industry is able to attract and retain a highly qualified and motivated workforce at all skills levels, moves to enhance worker output at anything beyond the highly mechanistic will have limited impact. However, once the industry and its educational providers focus fully upon the human resource macro-environment and devise real and effective strategies to overcome the main challenges and issues that it faces, more focused productivity measures may well have some chance of real and sustainable success.

REFERENCES

Adams, J. (1963) 'Toward an understanding of equity'. *Journal of Abnormal and Social Psychology*, November, 422–36.

Alderfer, C.P. (1972) *Existence, Relatedness and Growth*. New York: Free Press.

Anthony, W.P., Perrewe, P.L. and Kacmar, K.M. (1993) *Strategic Human Resource Management*. Fort Worth, TX: Harcourt Brace Jovanovich.

Baum, T. (1993) 'Human resources in tourism: an introduction'. In T. Baum (ed.), *Human Resource Issues in International Tourism*. Oxford: Butterworth-Heinemann.

Baum, T. (1995) *Managing Human Resources for the European Tourism and Hospitality Industry: a Strategic Approach*. London: Chapman and Hall.

Conlin, M.V. and Baum, T. (1994) 'Comprehensive human resource planning: an essential key to sustainable tourism in island settings'. In C. Cooper and A. Lockwood (eds), *Progress in Tourism, Recreation and Hospitality Management, Volume 6*. Chichester: Wiley.

Conlin, M.V. and Titcombe, A. (1995) 'Human resources: the strategic imperative for Caribbean tourism'. In M.V. Conlin and T. Baum (eds), *Island Tourism: Management Principles and Practice*. Chichester: Wiley.

Fayol, H. (1949) *General and Industrial Management*. trans. C. Storrs. London: Pitman.

Gibson, J.L., Ivancevich, J.M. and Donnelly, J.H. Jr (1991) *Organizations: Behavior, Structure, Processes*, 7th edn. Homewood, IL: Irwin.

Gilbreth, F.B. (1911) *Motion Study*. New York: Van Nostrand.

Heizer, J. and Render, B. (1988) *Productions and Operations Management*. Boston: Allyn and Bacon.

Herzberg, F., Mausner, B. and Synderman, B. (1959) *The Motivation to Work*. New York: Wiley.

MacGregor, D. (1985) *The Human Side of Enterprise*, 25th anniversary printing. New York: McGraw-Hill.

McClelland, D.C. (1971) *Motivational Trends in Society*. Morristown, NJ: General Learning Press.

McMahon, F. (1994) 'Productivity in the hotel industry'. In A. Seaton *et al.* (eds) *Tourism. The State of the Art*. Chichester: Wiley.

Mahesh, V.S. (1994) *Thresholds of Motivation*. New York: McGraw-Hill.

Maslow, A. (1954) *Motivation and Personality*. New York: Harper & Row.

Mill, R.C. (1989) *Managing for Productivity in the Hospitality Industry*. New York: Van Nostrand-Reinhold.

Moorhead, G. and Griffin, R.W. (1992). *Organizational Behavior: Managing People and Organizations*, 3rd edn. Dallas: Houghton Mifflin.

Pugh, D.S. and Hickson, D.J. (1989) *Writers on Organizations*, 4th edn. London: Penguin.

Ritzer, G. (1993) *The McDonaldization of Society. An Investigation into the Character of Contemporary Social Life*. Thousand Oaks, CA: Pine Forge Press.

Schermerhorn, J.R. Jr. (1989) *Management for Productivity*, 3rd edn. New York: Wiley.

Vroom, V.H. (1964) *Work and Motivation*. New York: Wiley.

Weber, M. (1947) *The Theory of Social and Economic Organization*. New York: Free Press.

PART 2
THE HUMAN DIMENSION AND PRODUCTIVITY

FIVE

Enhancing productivity: intervention strategies for employee turnover

Margaret A. Deery and Roderick D. Iverson

INTRODUCTION

Managing operational productivity is often one of the most difficult management tasks. Generally speaking, productivity is understood to be a measure of the output of goods and services relative to the input of labour, material and equipment (Cascio, 1992). Cascio, however, argues that 'organizations must work smarter, not harder'. rather than simply controlling resources such as time, money or people. The problem of measuring productivity in the 1990s in countries such as the USA, UK and Australia has been compounded by the change from a manufacturing economy to a service economy (Worsfold and Jameson, 1991). What the service industries are confronted by, more than ever before, is the need to improve their intangible product (Albrecht, 1992). The strategy of improved customer service, however, is only part of the formula for increased productivity. A 'bottom-line' issue is to decrease unnecessary costs; in particular, those associated with absenteeism and turnover. While the containment of these employee behaviours is critical to the survival of any industry, it is particularly crucial in the hospitality industry, where there is not only an acceptance of a high turnover rate, but also a predicted dwindling of skilled labour (Hiemstra, 1990; Johns and Wheeler, 1991).

Labour turnover is a particularly complex issue in the hospitality industry. Rates of employee turnover vary widely, and may be anywhere from 50 per cent to 270 per cent (Tourism Training Australia (TTA), 1991; Denvir and McMahon, 1992; Dienhart, 1993). These rates, however may include casual as well as permanent, full-time employees and vary according to the size of the organization. The issue of turnover is also complicated by a general acceptance of high turnover rates in the hospitality industry (Riley, 1994). Owing to the prevailing culture, labour turnover is not seen as particularly problematic or dysfunctional. It can provide management with a means of controlling the labour market, while employees may view it as a way to widen their work experience and hence employability (Denvir and McMahon, 1992). Woods and

Macauley (1989) find that while employees in most industries remain in their job for an average of 4.2 years, some hospitality organizations replace their entire workforce every four months. Complicating the issue further is the term 'hospitality', an all-encompassing word covering four identifiable segments: hotels, restaurants, licensed clubs and motels (Worland and Wilson, 1988). Within this group, restaurants are the least stable, while accommodation hotels provide the lowest rates of turnover (TTA, 1991). It is difficult to get an accurate assessment of employee turnover, since hospitality demand is generally irregular and unpredictable, making reliable workforce statistics difficult to obtain. Finally, the inclusion of the hospitality industry, at least in Australia, to wider categories (such as the Australian Bureau of Statistics (ABS) broad-band group of Recreation, Personal and Other Services), again renders specific hospitality data imprecise. Despite these problems, however, organizations generally agree that high turnover rates are harmful to staff morale and represent an avoidable cost. Research into the issue of labour turnover in the industry has produced more reliable, rigorous formulae for examining the cost of the problem. The present study argues that a more in-depth investigation into the causes and costs of turnover is warranted, in order to maintain and enhance the productivity of the hospitality industry.

The first section of the present chapter uses an adaptation of Cascio's (1991, 1994) costing of human resources formula to establish the cost of turnover, including the cost of decreased productivity. The second section examines determinants of employee turnover, using data from six large five-star hotels in Australia. The final section discusses strategies for reducing employee turnover within the hospitality industry.

THE COST OF EMPLOYEE TURNOVER TO THE HOSPITALITY INDUSTRY

One of the main issues to resolve in determining the cost of turnover in any industry is whether the turnover is functional or dysfunctional (Dalton *et al.*, 1982). As stated earlier, employee turnover can be used as a means of controlling the labour force. Clearly, involuntary turnover such as retrenchment is used as a cost-cutting exercise. Research suggests that downsizing in the hospitality industry can act as a positive force, promoting creativity, for example (Nicholls and Buergmeister, 1993). Cascio (1994) argues that this trend to downsize neither increases productivity nor, in the long run, decreases costs. However, the benefits of voluntary employee turnover are more controversial. While various studies have found that voluntary turnover can be functional in that poor performers leave the organization (Hollenbeck and Williams, 1986; Williams and Livingstone, 1994), few if any researchers have investigated the impact of excessive voluntary turnover on the organization. The financial impact of high rates of voluntary employee turnover, therefore, requires further investigation.

Little research has been conducted to determine the cost of turnover to the hospitality industry. However, Woods and Macaulay (1989) estimate that losing an hourly employee costs US$3000, although they offer no information on their method of costing the turnover. In the present study, Cascio's (1991) calculations have been used along with the measurements of lost productivity detailed by a case study of *Hotel A*. Cascio (1991) argues that separation, replacement and training costs all need to be calculated in order to gain an accurate assessment of the loss in both profitability and productivity. Woods and Macauley (1989) assert that the intangible costs of productivity losses are substantial, suggesting that an hourly employee takes as long as six months to reach full productivity. Again, however, they offer no basis for these estimates. The calculations made for *Hotel A* have been based on the decreased output of the new employee and the increased workload of experienced employees over a five-week period. Thus the calculations in the present study are extremely conservative and represent a minimum cost of labour turnover. Various estimates of the cost of turnover per employee in industries other than hospitality range from US$18,000 in the retail automobile industry to 1.5–2.5 times the annual salary in the pharmaceutical industry (Cascio, 1991). With such high rates of turnover in the hospitality industry, these figures represent an enormous and to an extent avoidable cost to the industry.

The present chapter uses two strategies for costing employee turnover. First, the formula used is an adaptation of Cascio's (1991) extensive and rigorous behavioural costing formula. Second, the formula was tested in a case study of a five-star hotel (one of those used to determine the causes of turnover, as presented later). At the time of the present study (March 1994), this unit, *Hotel A*, had a labour turnover rate of 36.7 per cent. This was, in fact, lower than the rate of 58.7 per cent recorded for 1993. The costing is based on calculations of the separation costs, the replacement costs and the training costs. While Cascio uses the weighted average pay for terminated employees, the present study costed for both permanent and casual employees from three major areas in the hotel, housekeepers, waiters and chefs, where turnover rates were 30.4, 43.6 and 100 per cent respectively. A calculation was also made of the cost of employee turnover at management level. An example of the method of calculation for the costing of a room attendant has been included in the Appendix to this chapter. The calculation was modified to suit the employment policies of the case study hotel; as a consequence, testing costs were excluded, along with minimum use of travel expenses. Cascio's (1991) unemployment tax was not applicable to this costing. An additional cost of turnover, not employed in Cascio's formula, was that of lost productivity based on calculations made by the hotel itself. Estimates of both time and expenses represent the minimum cost to the case study hotel, indicating both the level of concern for its human resources and a very conservative guide to the potential cost of employee turnover to a five-star hotel.

As can be seen from the costing methodology in the Appendix, a major area of expense lies in the loss of productivity. This is particularly so during the training period, when the employee cannot work at 100 per cent efficiency and other employees are required to work both harder and longer hours. Cascio (1992) argues that, for a learning period of 24 weeks, new managers and partners have a 75 per cent productivity loss over the first eight weeks, a 40 per cent productivity loss over the next eight weeks and a 15 per cent loss in the final learning period. When these statistics are put into conjunction with the high turnover rates within the hospitality industry, the loss of productivity is significant. Table 5.1 presents the final cost for turnover of both permanent and casual employees in housekeeping, waitering, kitchen and management. Table 5.2 shows the midpoint turnover costs for each of these areas using turnover rates for those positions provided by *Hotel A*. The total turnover cost for just those four areas amounted to over A$300,000. Table 5.2 also provides the calculation for the weighted mean cost per employee, an average used in the second part of the calculations for employee turnover.

Cascio (1994) has further developed his concept of costing employee behaviour by linking the financial impact of employee commitment to turnover, absenteeism and poor quality or service. Cascio argues that employees express their commitment to an organization by remaining in, or leaving, employment. Using Cascio's actual quit rates for those employees who stated in their survey responses that they would probably

Table 5.1. Employee turnover costing

Position	Hourly wage[a] (A$)	Permanent range[b] (A$)	Hourly wage (1.25)	Casual[c] (A$)
Room attendant	9.43	4303–5000	11.79	3955
Waiter	9.98	4575–5000	12.48	4145
Chef[d]	18.70	7197–11,739	21.00	6788
Management	24.95	9474–15,884	n.a.	–

Notes: [a] Hourly wage according to the Hotels, Resorts and Hospitality Industry Award effective July 1994.
[b] The upper ranges includes the use of an employment agency based on a percentage of the employee's annual salary. Line employee 5 per cent, middle management 10 per cent, upper management 15 per cent.
[c] Casual rates do not take into account penalty rates.
[d] Chef salary range from A$11.18 to 21.00.

Table 5.2. Hotel A calculations

Position	Midpoint[a] (A$)	Turnovers	Number employees Left×average cost
Room attendant	4651.50	21	21 × A$4651.50 = A$97,681.50
Waiter	4787.50	39	39 × A$4787.50 = A$186,712.50
Chef	9468.00	1	1 × A$9468.00 = A$9468.00
Management	12,679.00	1	1 × A$12,679.00 = A$12,679.00
		Total = 62	Total = A$306,541.00

Step 1: Calculate average cost of turnover per category of employee. Take midpoint cost from Table 5.1 of employee turnover costing (which allows for full-time, part-time and casual employees) and calculate the proportion in each category who left. Cost of turnover = A$306,541/62. Weighted mean cost of turnover per employee = A$4944.21. This average will be used in calculations for all hotels.

Note: [a] Calculation is based on midpoint of permanent employees, which corrects for penalty rates of casual employees.

Table 5.3. Costing for Hotel A

Response	Survey results		No. of employees		No. of people		Quit rate[a]		No. to quit
Probably leave	37.3	×	409	=	152.6	×	0.36	=	54.9
Possibly	11.5	×	409	=	47.0	×	0.20	=	9.4
Probably not leave	51.2	×	409	=	209.4	×	0.13	=	27.2
Totals	100		409		91.5				

Step 2: Use Cascio's (1994) worksheet for financial implications of turnover based on survey results of intent to leave (measured by a composite score of five items). Cost of turnover for Hotel A: 91.5×$4944.21 = A$452,395.21.

Note: [a] Quit rate based on Cascio (1994).

leave (36 per cent), possibly leave (20 per cent) and probably not leave (13 per cent), it is possible to calculate the total cost of turnover based on employees' intention to leave for *Hotel A* (derived from our survey results). These percentages are argued to be representative across all industries. In the education sector, Iverson (1992) finds slightly lower percentages but a similar trend. Given the high turnover rates within the hospitality industry Cascio's percentages are considered reliable measures. While the cost for *Hotel A* is nearly half a million dollars as shown in Table 5.3, the total cost

Productivity Management

Table 5.4. Costing for all hotels based on the formula (Australian dollars)

Hotel A (with 409 employees)	452,395.21
Hotel B (with 650 employees)	719,876.97
Hotel C (with 395 employees)	437,068.16
Hotel D (with 250 employees)	276,875.76
Hotel E (with 462 employees)	510,736.89
Hotel F (with 206 employees)	227,433.66
Total turnover cost for six hotels in sample	2,624,386.65

for the six hotels participating in this study is a massive A$2,624,386.65 (see Table 5.4). The question to be asked, therefore, is whether Cascio is justified in linking employee intention to leave to turnover; in other words, what are the causes of employee turnover? The next section addresses this question.

A MODEL OF EMPLOYEE TURNOVER

Turnover literature

As previously stated, research into the issue of employee turnover in the hospitality industry is limited. It has either concentrated on the relationship between job satisfaction and turnover (Mok and Finley, 1986) or has investigated strategies to reduce turnover without rigorously examining its causes (Rutter, 1988; Hendry, 1989; Woods and Macauley, 1989; TTA, 1991; Bonn and Forbringer, 1992; Ohlin and West, 1994; Reich, 1994). There is growing interest in the psychological dimensions of an employee's decision to leave a job (Riley, 1994). The present study uses some of these dimensions, such as organizational or employee commitment and job satisfaction, as the basis of an examination of turnover in the hospitality industry.

It is generally agreed that intent to leave (defined as the degree of an employee's behavioural commitment to an organization) is the single best predictor of turnover (Iverson and Roy, 1994). The literature is grounded in Ajzen and Fishbein's (1980) theory of reasoned action. This theory views a person's intentions to perform (or not to perform) a behaviour as the immediate determinant of action. The importance attached to intent to leave comes from its position in Mobley's (1977) original intermediate linkages model (i.e. between job satisfaction and turnover), and also from its link with turnover. Moreover, the two meta-analyses by Steel and Ovalle (1984) and Carsten and Spector (1987) reported intent to leave to have a strong positive relationship with turnover (0.50, and 0.47, respectively).

There are also some distinct advantages of studying intent to leave over turnover. Thompson and Terpening (1983) assert that: (a) the reasons given for leaving as indicated in an employee's report may not be true and accurate; (b) the use of archival data may not adequately distinguish between voluntary and involuntary turnover; and (c) other factors may be prevalent which are not related to the decision to leave. The preventative role of intent to leave should also not be underestimated. Managers can, after assessing the effect of certain work setting factors on an employee's intention to leave, make changes to these factors so that employees may reassess their current situation and decide to stay. Thus the present study used intent to leave as the dependent variable rather than the behavioural act of turnover.

This study seeks to replicate and modify previous turnover models (e.g. Price and Mueller, 1986; Iverson, 1992; Iverson and Roy, 1994; Mueller *et al.*, 1994). Variables such as job hazards, legitimacy, quality of students (Iverson, 1992), work unit size, physical conditions, community participation (Iverson and Roy, 1994), centralization and professionalism (Price and Mueller, 1986; Mueller *et al.*, 1994) were seen as either irrelevant to the hospitality industry or covered by other variables in the model. The present model, however, includes new variables such as turnover culture, union loyalty and job stress in dealing with the public, which were seen as pertinent and specific to the hospitality industry.

The causal model as shown in Figure 5.1 integrates structural, pre-entry, environmental, union and employee orientations that were selected from the economic, psychological and sociological perspectives of the turnover literature (see Iverson, 1992; Iverson and Roy, 1994, for more detail on the perspectives). The path diagrammatic representation of the model contains positive and negative signs to indicate the hypothesized causal relationships between the variables. If high levels of a variable are hypothesized to lead to high levels of a second variable, a positive sign appears. Similarly, if high levels of a variable are hypothesized to lead to low levels of a second variable, a negative sign appears. For example, it is hypothesized that employees who experience a high level of distributive justice will also experience a high level of job satisfaction. Definitions of the variables in the model are contained in Table 5.5.

The variables tested in previous turnover models have been numerous. For example, the employee orientated variables seen as impacting most on an employee's decision to leave are those of *job satisfaction* (Mobley *et al.*, 1978; Arnold and Feldman, 1982; Spencer *et al.*, 1983; Mok and Finley, 1986; Iverson and Roy, 1994; Mueller *et al.*, 1994), *organizational commitment* (Mowday *et al.*, 1982; Cotton and Tuttle, 1986; Price and Mueller, 1986; Mottaz, 1989) and *job search* (Mobley *et al.*, 1978; Bluedorn, 1982; Mowday *et al.*, 1982; Dalessio *et al.*, 1986; Iverson and Roy, 1994). Job satisfaction, organizational commitment and job search are expected to be produced by the structural, pre-entry, environmental and union variables. In terms of intervention strategies, both job satisfaction and organizational commitment are variables over which management has some control in dealing with employee turnover.

Other variables included in the model are those relating to the workplace, i.e. structural variables. For example, there is an abundance of literature linking *coworker support* (Martin and Hunt, 1980; Price and Mueller, 1986) and *supervisory support* (Martin and Hunt, 1980; Michaels and Spector, 1982; Williams and Hazer, 1986; Mueller *et al.*, 1994) to job satisfaction. The variables of *routinization* (Martin, 1979; Price and Mueller, 1981, 1986; Thompson and Terpening, 1983), *distributive justice* (Bluedorn, 1982; Price and Mueller, 1986; Mueller *et al.*, 1994; Iverson and Kuruvilla, 1995), *role ambiguity* (Martin, 1979; Price and Mueller, 1981, 1986; Bluedorn, 1982; Thompson and Terpening, 1983; Mueller *et al.*, 1994), *role conflict* (Keller, 1975; Parasuraman *et al.*, 1992), *work overload* (Bateman, 1980; Price and Mueller, 1986; Mueller *et al.*, 1994) and *resource inadequacy* (Clayton and Wilson, 1984; Holmes *et al.*, 1988) also come under the rubric of structural variables, the last four forming the group relating to job stress.

Other variables relating to the workplace and tested in the integrated model are *pay* (Bluedorn, 1979; Price and Mueller, 1986; Mueller *et al.*, 1994), *job security* (Gow *et al.*, 1974; Arnold and Feldman, 1982), *promotional opportunity* (Price and Mueller, 1981, 1986; Thompson and Terpening, 1983; Iverson and Roy, 1994) and *career*

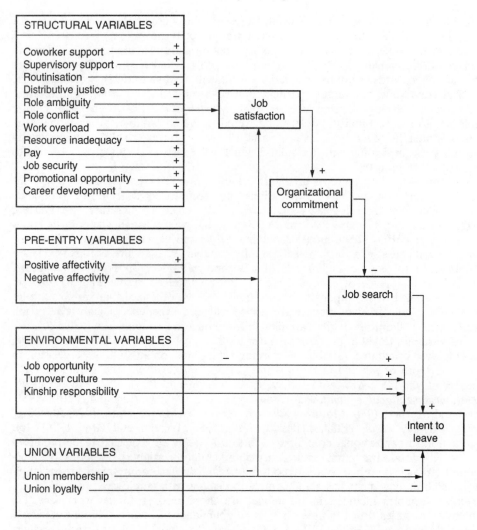

Figure 5.1. Causal model of employees intent to leave

development (Hendry, 1989; Hiemstra, 1990; Riley, 1990). These last three variables are components of an internal labour market that researchers (Hendry 1989; TTA 1991; Debrah, 1994) suggest to be important factor in the mobility and turnover of hospitality employees.

The pre-entry or personality traits argued to impact on an employee's decision to leave via job satisfaction include *positive* and *negative affectivity* (Watson *et al.*, 1987; Levin and Stokes, 1989; Agho *et al.*, 1992, 1993; Iverson and Kuruvilla, 1995), while the external environmental variables include *job opportunity* (Mobley *et al.*, 1978; Bluedorn, 1982; Price and Mueller, 1986), a new variable based on the absence literature, *turnover culture* (Ilgen and Hollenbeck, 1977; Erwin and Iverson, 1994) and *kinship responsibility* (Cotton and Tuttle, 1986; Blegen *et al.*, 1988; Mueller *et al.*,

Table 5.5. Variable definitions and source of measure

Variable	Definition and source of measure
Structural variables	
Coworker support	Degree of consideration expressed by coworkers (Blau, 1960). Modification of scale by House (1981).
Supervisory support	Degree of consideration expressed by the immediate supervisor for the subordinates (Michaels and Spector, 1982). Modification of scale by House (1981).
Routinization	Degree to which employees jobs are repetitive (Price and Mueller, 1981). Modification of scale by Price and Mueller (1981, 1986).
Distributive justice	Degree to which an organization treats employees fairly. Modification of scale by Price and Mueller (1981).
Role ambiguity	Degree to which role expectations are unclear (based on Kahn *et al.*, 1964). Modification of scale by Rizzo *et al.*, 1970).
Role conflict	Degree to which employee role expectations are incompatible (Kahn *et al.*, 1964). Modification of scale by Kahn *et al.* (1964).
Work overload	Extent to which the job performance required in a job is excessive. Modification of scale by Price and Mueller (1981).
Resource inadequacy	Extent to which employees have insufficient resources necessary to perform their jobs (Iverson, 1992). Modification of scale by Iverson (1992).
Pay	Money and its equivalents which organisations give to employees for their service (Lawler, 1971). Measured by total yearly earnings before taxes and other deductions are made.
Job security	Extent to which an organization provides stable employment for employees (Herzberg, 1968). Modification of scale by Oldham *et al.* (1986).
Promotional opportunity	Degree of movement between different status levels in an organization (Martin, 1979). Modification of scale by Price and Mueller (1981, 1986).
Career development	Degree of opportunity to develop skills and knowledge (Iverson, 1992). Modification of scale by Iverson (1992).
Pre-entry variables	
Positive affectivity	Extent to which an individual feels enthusiastic over time and across situations (Watson *et al.*, 1987). Modification of scale reported by Agho *et al.*, 1993).
Negative affectivity	Extent to which an individual experiences aversive emotional states over time and across situations (Watson *et al.*, 1987). Modification of scale reported by Agho *et al.* (1993).
Environmental variables	
Job opportunity	Availability of alternative jobs outside the organisation. Modification of scale by Price and Mueller (1981, 1986).
Turnover culture	Work group belief in the legitimacy of turnover behaviour. Modification of scale by Ilgen and Hollenbeck (1977).
Kinship responsibility	Degree of an individual's obligation to immediate relatives in the community (Iverson, 1992). Modification of scale by (Blegen *et al.*, 1988), ranging from 0 to 4.
Union variables	
Union membership	Degree of affiliation with union. Coded as 1 for union member and 0 for nonunion member.
Union loyalty	Degree of pride and instrumentality in the union (Gordon *et al.*, 1980). Modification of scale by Gordon *et al.* (1980).
Employee orientations	
Job satisfaction	Overall degree to which an individual likes his or her job (Price and Mueller, 1981). Scale developed by Price and Mueller (1981).
Organizational commitment	Degree of loyalty to the organization (Porter *et al.*, 1974). Modification of scale by Porter *et al.* (1974).
Job search	Extent to which employees intend to seek alternative employment outside the organization (Iverson, 1992). Modification of scale by Hom *et al.* (1984).

1994). Finally, the union variables of *union membership* (Freeman and Medoff, 1984) and *union loyalty* (Fukami and Larson, 1984; Iverson, 1992) have been included in the model as unions play a major role in the employment relationship in the hospitality industry.

Demographics

The demographic variables of age, tenure, education, gender, previous industry experience and employment status (i.e. either permanent or casual), although being omitted from the model, are controlled for in the analysis. This strategy is consistent with current research (Price and Mueller, 1981, 1986; Iverson and Roy, 1994; Iverson *et al.*, 1994).

Method

The data used in the research were obtained from questionnaires completed by 246 (57 per cent male and 43 per cent female) employees from six five-star hotels in the central business district of Melbourne, Australia. In relation to the employment status, 77 per cent of the sample were permanent, while 23 per cent were either part-time or casual. Around 54 per cent of the sample were union members, and 56 per cent had previously worked in the industry. The average age, tenure, and education of employees were 28.4 years (s.d. 9.2), 3.1 years (s.d. 3.9) and 12.9 years (s.d. 2.4), respectively. A multiple-item survey was administered to a random sample of 310 employees at the six hotels, the response rate being 88 per cent ($N = 272$). Following listwise deletion of missing data, a total of 246 useable questionnaires remained for the analysis. Chi-square was used to evaluate the representativeness of the sample, the results indicating that there were no differences in the demographic characteristics of gender, age and education of the respondents and the nonrespondents. Table 5.6 presents the descriptive statistics and reliability of the survey measures. Established scales were used wherever possible (see Table 5.5). With the exception of pay, kinship responsibility, and union membership, responses to all questions were measured by a five-point Likert scale ranging from 'strongly disagree' to 'strongly agree'. The reliability of each multiple-item measure was estimated using coefficient alpha (unstandardized), which indicated good internal consistency (Cronbach, 1951). The use of the statistical technique Linear Structural Relations (LISREL) controlled for attenuation in random measurement error of the variables. The measure of the dependent variable, intent to leave, was operationalized by a five-item index adapted from Iverson (1992) and Iverson and Roy (1994) and demonstrated acceptable psychometric properties.

Analysis

Multiple regression was employed to assess and support the assumptions of linearity, additivity, model specification, multicollinearity and homoscedasticity (Berry and

Table 5.6. Descriptive statistics and coefficient alpha

Determinant	Items	Mean	s.d.	α
Employee orientation				
Intent to leave	5	2.81	0.87	0.79
Job satisfaction	4	3.66	0.87	0.76
Organisational commitment	4	3.51	0.94	0.80
Job search	2	2.89	0.98	0.64[b]
Structural variables				
Coworker support	4	3.84	0.70	0.76
Supervisory support	3	3.40	0.99	0.80
Routinization	3	2.78	1.02	0.75
Distributive justice	2	2.87	0.69	0.73[b]
Role ambiguity	3	1.74	0.69	0.62
Role conflict	3	2.92	0.91	0.75
Work overload	3	3.25	0.88	0.72
Resource inadequacy	3	2.74	1.05	0.69
Pay[a]	1	20,617	6,866	–
Job security	3	3.54	0.78	0.60
Promotional opportunity	3	3.23	0.86	0.73
Career development	3	2.98	0.99	0.80
Pre-entry variables				
Positive affectivity	3	3.89	0.76	0.71
Negative affectivity	3	3.07	0.91	0.73
Environmental variables				
Job opportunity	3	3.11	0.89	0.80
Turnover culture	3	3.09	0.65	0.40
Kinship responsibility	1	1.51	1.08	–
Union variables				
Union membership	1	0.54	0.49	–
Union loyalty	3	2.59	1.01	0.91

Notes: [a] Yearly rate before taxes and deductions are made.
[b] Reliability assessed by Kuder–Richardson (KR-20).

Feldman, 1985). The statistical technique of LISREL was used to estimate the causal model. LISREL VIII produces a structural equation model and a measurement model (Jöreskog and Sörbom, 1993). Its main advantage is that it produces a statistical measure of both goodness of fit and explained variance (R-square) of the model. As the coefficients can be interpreted as standardized regression coefficients, a path analysis (decomposed into direct, indirect and total effects) can also be undertaken (Alwin and Hauser, 1975). As LISREL was the main technique used in the analysis, the measurement model had first to be validated, before we progressed to the structural model (Anderson and Gerbing, 1988). Convergent and discriminant validity of the model was supported (see Bagozzi and Yi, 1988, for the recommended process) where the normed comparative fit index (CFI) (Bentler, 1990) was an acceptable 0.90. A potential statistical power problem (i.e. the probability of rejecting a false model) might have arisen, owing to the number of parameters estimated in the model and the sample size available. Therefore a single indicator approach was used for estimating the structural model (Bagozzi and Yi, 1988). The findings of the structural model are contained in the Results section.

When one uses self-report material, such as regressing attitudes (e.g. intent to leave) on attitudes, a problem of common method variance (Campbell and Fiske, 1959;

Fiske, 1982) may occur. Podsakoff and Organ (1986) report that this problem tends to inflate the relationship between constructs. The impact of common method variance was minimized in the present work by the use of positively and negatively worded questionnaire items (Gordon and Ladd, 1990). Another way to overcome this problem is to regress actual behaviour, such as turnover on respondents attitudes. However, since behavioural data were not available, Harmans's (1967) one-factor test (Podsakoff and Organ, 1986) was employed in order to control the problem further. The results suggest that a general factor did not originate, limiting the likelihood of common method variance problems.

Results and discussion

Table 5.7 presents the LISREL VIII results used to estimate the original (hypothesized) model, which is shown in Figure 5.1. An examination of columns 1, 3, 5 and 7 of Table 5.7, indicates that the results provide general support for the model, which was then revised to give the best possible fit. The approach followed in fitting the LISREL model resembled the technique advanced by Iverson and Roy (1994) and Mueller *et al.* (1994). First, all paths in the hypothesized model were retained, even if they were non-significant after analysis. The hypothesized model was then expanded by estimation of additional paths between variables that were indicated by the LISREL modification indices and considered to be theoretically plausible. For example, the LISREL modification indices indicated that the path between career development and organizational commitment should also be estimated. It is theoretically possible to estimate this path, since career development should have a positive impact on an employee's psychological identification with the organization. The goodness-of-fit index for the revised model (χ^2 (77) = 219.39, $p<0.001$) compared to the hypothesized model (χ^2 (78) = 259.74, $p<0.001$) indicates a significant improvement in fit ($\Delta\chi^2$ (1) = 40.35, $p<0.001$), and suggests that the revised model was better able to represent the relations in the sample data. Columns 2, 4, 6 and 8 of Table 5.7 show the LISREL results used to estimate the revised model.

Discussion of the results requires an initial examination of the determinants of the four endogenous variables in the causal model: job satisfaction, organizational commitment, job search and intent to leave. After this it is appropriate to discuss the total effects of the variables on intent to leave. Intervention strategies for reducing employees' intention to leave are based on those variables with significant total effects.

Endogenous variables

Job satisfaction

Four of the variables predicted by the model had significant net impacts on the first endogenous variable, job satisfaction, after controlling for the correlates of age, tenure,

Table 5.7. LISREL (Standardized coefficients) for employee intent to leave: hypothesized and revised causal models[a]

Determinants[b]	Job satisfaction		Organizational commitment		Job search		Intent to leave	
	(1)	(2)	(3)	(4)	(5)	(6)	(7)	(8)
Structural variables								
Coworker support	-0.07	-0.07						
Supervisory support	0.08	0.07						
Routinization	-0.48*	-0.49*						
Distributive justice	-0.00	0.00						
Role ambiguity	-0.09	-0.09						
Role conflict	-0.21*	-0.21*						
Work overload	0.13†	0.14†						
Resource inadequacy	0.04	0.04						
Pay	0.06	0.06						
Job security	0.06	0.05						
Promotional opportunity	0.23*	0.24*						
Career development	0.07	0.02	–	0.41*				
Pre-entry variables								
Positive affectivity	0.03	0.03						
Negative affectivity	-0.13*	-0.14*						
Environmental variables								
Job opportunity	0.00	0.01					0.26*	0.26*
Turnover culture						0.41*	0.41*	
Kinship responsibility						0.09	0.08	
Union variables								
Union membership	0.01	0.01				0.06	0.06	
Union loyalty			0.16*	0.14*			-0.15*	-0.15*
Employee orientations								
Job satisfaction			0.65*	0.45*				
Organizational commitment					-0.43*	-0.43*		
Job search							0.39*	0.39*
R^2	0.62	0.63	0.46	0.55	0.19	0.19	0.65	0.66

Notes: [a] $N=246$; the results of the hypothesized and revised models are contained in the odd and even numbered columns respectively. Chi-square values: hypothesized model χ^2 (78)=259.74 ($p<0.001$), revised model χ^2 (77)=219.39 ($p<0.001$). Goodness of fit: hypothesized model = 0.937, revised model = 0.945.
[b] Age, tenure, education, gender, industry, previous jobs and status were controlled.
† Not significant at $p<0.05$ one-tail test in hypothesized direction.
* $p<0.05$, one-tailed test.

education, gender, previous industry experience, and employment status (see column 2 of Table 5.7). The structural variables routinization (Price and Mueller, 1981, 1986), role conflict (Parasuraman *et al.*, 1992) and promotional opportunity (Iverson and Roy, 1994) and the pre-entry variable of negative affectivity (Levin and Stokes, 1989) had significant impacts on job satisfaction. Job satisfaction was increased when employees had greater variety in their work, compatible role expectations and advancement opportunities, and did not display a negative mood disposition. Although work overload had an impact on job satisfaction in the opposite direction from that hypothesized, it had a significant, negative zero-order correlation with job satisfaction. Overall, 63 per cent of the job satisfaction variance was explained by the variables in the model.

Organizational commitment

In addition to the employee orientation of job satisfaction originally hypothesized (Iverson and Roy, 1994) and the union variable, union loyalty (Iverson, 1992), the structural variable career development was found to have a positive effect on organizational commitment (see column 4 of Table 5.7). These variables explained 55 per cent of the variance in organizational commitment. The model predicted that organizational commitment should be increased when employees like their jobs and have pride in the union. The finding that career development also increased loyalty to the organizations is plausible given that it forms part of the internal labour market of organizations.

Job search

Organizational commitment had a significant net impact on the third endogenous variable, job search (Iverson and Roy, 1994) (see column 6 of Table 5.7), which was increased when employees had low loyalty to the organization. Nineteen per cent of the variance in job search was explained by organizational commitment.

Intent to leave

Sixty-six per cent of the variance of the intent to leave variable was explained by four statistically significant variables (see column 8 of Table 5.7). As expected, the environmental variable of turnover culture (Leslie, 1991) had the strongest influence, followed by the employee orientation job search (Iverson and Roy, 1994), the environmental variable job opportunity (Price and Mueller, 1986) and the union variable union loyalty (Fukami and Larson, 1984). These results were consistent with the proposed model. Hence, employees who believe in the legitimacy of turnover behaviour engage in job search behaviour, do not have pride in the union and are more likely to leave if there are many alternative jobs in the labour market. The correlates of age and gender also had significant negative and positive effects on intent to leave, respectively. Younger employees had a higher propensity to leave than older ones, and males were less likely to stay than females.

Total effects

A simplified causal model ($\chi^2(26)$ = 114.71, $p<0.001$; GFI = 0.93, CFI = 0.90 is presented in Figure 5.2. This model retained only those variables significantly related to intent to leave in Table 5.7 (see Brooke and Price, 1989; Iverson *et al.*, 1994, 1995, for a review of this strategy). All paths were statistically significant and in the hypothesized direction. The decomposition of direct, indirect and total effects of the determinants of intent to leave (see Table 5.8) is based on the simplified model. In

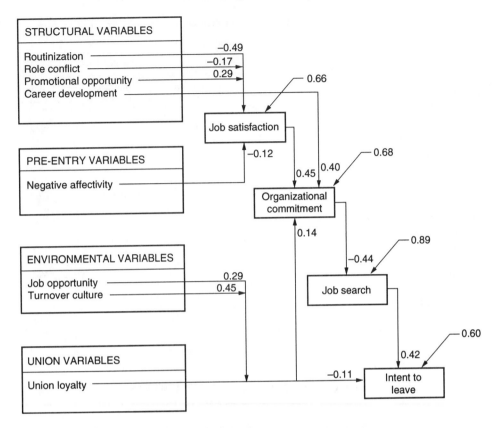

Figure 5.2. Simplified model of employee intent to leave

relation to the significant total effects of the variables on intent to leave, the rank order of the variables is as follows:

1	Turnover culture	(0.45)
2	Job search	(0.42)
3	Job opportunity	(0.29)
4	Organizational commitment	(−0.18)
5	Union loyalty	(−0.14)
6	Job satisfaction	(−0.08)
7	Career development	(−0.07)
8	Routinization	(0.04)
9	Promotional opportunity	(−0.02)
10	Role conflict	(0.01)
11	Negative affectivity	(0.01)

Productivity Management

Table 5.8. Decomposed direct, indirect and total effects of determinants on employee intent to leave

Determinant	Direct effects	Indirect effects via			Total indirect causal effects
		Job search	Organizational commitment and job search	Job satisfaction, organizational commitment and job search	
Employee orientation					
Job satisfaction			−0.08		−0.08
Organizational commitment		−0.18			−0.18
Job search	0.42				
Structural variables					
Routinization				0.04*	0.04*
Role conflict				0.01*	0.01*
Promotional opportunity				−0.02	−0.02*
Career development			−0.07		−0.07
Pre-entry variables					
Negative affectivity				0.01	0.01
Environmental variables					
Job opportunity	0.29				
Turnover culture	0.45				
Union variables					
Union loyalty	−0.11		−0.03		−0.03

INTERVENTION STRATEGIES FOR REDUCING EMPLOYEE TURNOVER

The results discussed above indicate general support for the causal model of intent to leave in the hospitality industry. Findings suggest that the employee orientations (job search, organizational commitment and job satisfaction) are important determinants of an employee's intent to leave an organization. As Figure 5.2 indicates, these are in turn influenced by the structural variables (career development, routinization, promotional opportunity and role conflict). The model is also borne out in terms of the proposed pre-entry variable (negative affectivity), environmental variables (turnover culture and job opportunity) and the union variable (union loyalty). While some of these causes of turnover, such as job satisfaction (Mok and Finley, 1986) and the internal labour market (Debrah, 1994), have been investigated specifically within the hospitality industry, the impact of many of the determinants, notably turnover culture, organizational commitment, routinization, negative affectivity, role conflict and union loyalty, has been underrated.

Past research into intervention strategies for the high turnover rates in the hospitality industry has frequently revolved around the issue of pay. Hiemstra (1990), for example, recommends higher wages and improved fringe benefits in order to retain good employees. Bonn and Forbringer (1992) suggest a range of monetary incentives as an employee retention strategy. Interestingly, however, pay was not a significant determinant of turnover in the present study. A major reason for this result may lie in the centralized wage fixing system of Australia, where neither the employee nor the employer has a great deal of control over wages. In a review of the literature concerning the effects of fringe benefits on employee turnover, Ohlin and West (1994) include performance bonuses and rewards such as flexible staffing arrangements, health care insurance and child care facilities for the children of hotel workers as possible strategies. However, many of these responses appear to be 'impetuous and ill-conceived practices' (Denvir and McMahon, 1992, p. 152) because of lack of research into the causes of turnover.

The most important variable in the simplified model is the environmental variable *turnover culture*. This finding is notable in that, while absence culture has been a well researched determinant of absenteeism (Ilgen and Hollenbeck, 1977; Steers and Rhodes, 1978; Erwin and Iverson, 1994), turnover culture has, until this study, been largely untested as a determinant of employee turnover. While it is possible to attribute a turnover culture to a casual or part-time workforce, there was no difference between the responses of permanent, casual and part-time workers in the present study. The conclusion to be drawn is that employees enter the hospitality industry with the expectation of working for a minimum amount of time in any one organization. In addition, the hospitality industry has created a turnover culture, in which there is a normative belief among workers that turnover behaviour is quite acceptable. Krackhardt and Porter (1986) found, in their examination of the quitting behaviour of adolescent workers in the fast-food industry, that employees were more likely to leave if they saw their peers quitting. Clegg (1983) further observed that new employees may not accurately perceive the work culture of an organization that has ineffective socialization processes. The challenge to the hospitality industry is to change this turnover culture to one of employee retention.

The research reported above suggests that employers should deal with sub-groups, rather than the workforce as a whole, in order to stop the spread of a turnover culture (Krackhardt and Porter, 1986). The key to this strategy is improving the communication within organizations by addressing both work and social issues of groups within the workforce. Another strategy directed at reducing the growth of a turnover culture may lie in more comprehensive and strategically placed induction programmes highlighting the organization's aim for long-term employment (Clegg, 1983). As can be seen from the earlier costing exercise, financial commitment to induction programmes is minimal in some hotels. Denvir and McMahon (1992), for example, found that hotels which spent more time and money on their induction programmes retained their employees longer at both operative and management level. Other research suggests that if the organization's espoused culture of employee retention is not consistent with the operating culture, the employees' performance is impaired and ultimately they may leave (Tidball, 1988). It is therefore also important to ensure that the long-term employment culture is matched by employee job security (i.e. by long-term contracts and permanency). Ohlin and West (1994) report that the fringe benefits impacting negatively on turnover were those that valued the employee and offered a long-term association. More specifically, they found that retirement plans, for example, reduced turnover.

The employee orientation variable *job search*, the second most important determinant of the intent to leave, has received consistent support in the literature (Mobley *et al.*, 1978; Bluedorn, 1982; Mowday *et al.*, 1982; Dalessio *et al.*, 1986; Iverson and Roy, 1994). For example, Mattila (1974, p. 235) found that 'at least 50 to 60 percent of all workers line up their new jobs before quitting and leaving their old jobs'. Hence, job search is an important precursor to intent to leave in the turnover process of employees. Job search can also be linked to the third most important variable, *job opportunity*. Although job opportunity was posited to have both direct and indirect effects on intent to leave via job satisfaction, all of its impact was direct. The greater the availability of jobs in the labour market, the greater the employees' propensity to leave (Thompson and Terpening, 1983; Price and Mueller, 1986; Iverson and Roy, 1994).

Intervention strategies for the variables of job search and job opportunity are limited, except, of course, to make the job and the organization as competitive as possible. Research by Ohlin and West (1994) observed that most hotels offer inducements such as paid vacations, free or discounted rooms and meals, and some form of life insurance. In Herzberg's (1968) terms, these inducements have become hygiene factors; that is, they prevent employees from being dissatisfied, but do not serve to motivate and retain employees. Motivators to stay were the provision of child care facilities (offered by some hotels) but aspects such as health care schemes. Organizations therefore need to be very selective in their retention strategies, as some fringe benefit schemes are not only costly but also ineffective (Ohlin and West, 1994).

Consistently with current research, the employee orientation variable of *organizational commitment* was found to be a better predictor of intent to leave than job satisfaction (Bluedorn, 1982; Mowday *et al.*, 1982; Stumpf and Hartman, 1984). Employees with high organizational commitment are more in tune with the goals and values of the organization. They may be willing to put in extra effort on behalf of the organization and display a strong desire to remain in their employment. All of organizational commitment's impact was indirect, through job search (Arnold and Feldman, 1982; Dalessio *et al.*, 1986). An increase in loyalty to the organization produces a decrease in job search, leading to employees' increased intention to stay. Interestingly, the fifth most important determinant, the union variable *union loyalty*, had a negative impact on intent to leave (Fukami and Larson, 1984; Iverson, 1992).

Intervention strategies for gaining organizational commitment in the hospitality industry require a combination of activities. For example, the findings from this research suggest that the development of career paths within each hotel would reduce employee turnover. Some of the more progressive hotels have incorporated all-staff salary and multi-skilling into the conditions of their employment contracts. The latter enables staff to gain training and accreditation for their skills and so improve their careers. As stated previously, the components of an internal labour market affect an employee's intention to leave an organization. There is evidence that internal labour markets also promote employee commitment in the Singapore hotel industry (Debrah, 1994). The impact of union loyalty on organizational commitment also suggests an interesting strategy for the management of dual commitment (e.g. Deery *et al.*, 1994). The greater the loyalty to the union and organization, the more likely employees are to stay. This is consistent with Larson and Fukami (1984, p. 24), who reported that employees with a strong loyalty to both the union and organization displayed 'fewer incidents of unexcused absenteeism'. Hence, conversely to what is generally believed, having employees who are loyal to the union may actually assist an organization's human resource planning.

The employee orientation variable of *job satisfaction* was also an important determinant of intent to leave in the simplified causal model. It had an indirect effect on intent to leave via organizational commitment and job search (Arnold and Feldman, 1982; Spencer *et al.*, 1983; Iverson and Roy, 1994). Thus, the higher the job satisfaction of employees, the higher their propensity to stay. Job satisfaction was determined by the structural variables routinization, role conflict and promotional opportunity.

Intervention strategies to increase job satisfaction, and therefore reduce employee turnover, include providing greater variety in employees' work. This can be achieved by multi-skilling employees and allowing them a greater range of work activities. This strategy is also linked with the variable of career development and underlines the importance of training (Debrah, 1994). Again, the issue of the lack of a career path through a dearth of promotional opportunity can be addressed by continuous training. Job satisfaction can also be increased by reducing role conflict. As it is important to have compatible job demands, there is a need for explicit, accurate job descriptions and clear reporting policies. Precise job descriptions should be compiled by the incumbent, by line management and by the human resource department. Such participation by the three areas should ensure accurate job descriptions, leading to greater role clarity and increased staff retention.

Career development was negatively related to the intent to leave (Hendry, 1989; Riley, 1990). Along with job security and promotional opportunity, it is regarded as forming part of an internal labour market. The total causal impact of career development was indirect, via organizational commitment and job search. Hence, providing for the career development of employees increases their loyalty to the organization, a finding consistent with current strategies for reducing turnover in the hospitality industry (Hendry, 1989; Hiemstra, 1990; Riley, 1990; TTA, 1991). Woods and Macauley (1989, p. 88) note that hotels and restaurants which have developed supervisory and management career-path programmes, along with a 'hire-from-within' policy, have reduced turnover. Debrah (1994) argues that internal labour markets provide a constant supply of trained and qualified workers, but in return for this stability employers give up some flexibility (e.g. temporal) in managing employees. Managers of hotels must choose between a stable or flexible workforce, but given the cost of a more flexible work force estimated earlier, stability and therefore lower employee turnover is important.

The structural variables of *routinization, promotional opportunity* and *role conflict*, and the pre-entry variable of *negative affectivity* had total causal effects less than 0.05 and are therefore discussed together. As hypothesized, routinization had an indirect effect on intent to leave via job satisfaction (Martin, 1979; Price and Mueller, 1981, 1986; Thompson and Terpening, 1983). The greater the variety in employees' work, the more likely they were to stay with the organization. Like routinization, promotional opportunity exerted its total causal effect indirectly via job satisfaction (Price and Mueller, 1981, 1986; Thompson and Terpening, 1983; Iverson and Roy, 1994). Thus increases in promotional opportunity decreased the propensity of employees to leave. The indirect impact of role conflict on intent to leave through job satisfaction is supported in the literature (Keller, 1975; Parasuraman *et al.*, 1992). This highlights the stressful environment existing within the industry, where incompatible role expectations increased employees' likelihood of leaving. The finding that negative affectivity was a determinant of the intent to leave via job satisfaction confirms research by Levin and Stokes (1989). Moreover, it indicates that employees enter organizations with personality traits that affect their attitudes and behaviour (Iverson and Kuruvilla, 1995).

Intervention strategies have already been addressed for all but one of the variables studied. Results for this one, *negative affectivity*, were consistent with Bonn and Forbinger's (1992) research into the relationship between recruitment and selection procedures and turnover. The issue might best be managed by employing a variety of recruitment and selection methods, including a formal referral system, the hiring of minorities, elderly and disabled people, more rigorous interviewing procedures, realistic job previews, biodata collection and finally personality tests. The use of personality testing has become much more widespread and provides a means for management to select those employees who display greater job satisfaction, and consequently are more likely to stay. While the use of such testing procedures presents a cost in the initial stages of recruitment, the present authors' finding of negative affectivity suggests that this expenditure is cost-effective. However, the use of personality tests in the recruitment and selection strategies of organizations does raise important legal and social questions (Davis-Blake and Pfeffer, 1989).

CONCLUSION

In this chapter we have examined the high cost of labour turnover in the hospitality industry and the resulting loss in productivity. Cascio's (1991) costing of employee turnover has been extended to calculate the productivity loss in an actual hotel. An estimated total loss of over A$2 million for the six hotels studied represented a substantial overall loss in productivity. A model of employee turnover has been developed which considers the determinants of the intent to leave an organization, but at the same time introduces more industry specific variables. The variables turnover culture, organizational commitment, job satisfaction, union loyalty, career development, promotional opportunity, routinization, role conflict and negative affectivity were all determinants over which organizations have control. The variables job search and job opportunity can alert management to potentially higher turnover rates. As a consequence of these findings from the causal model, a series of intervention strategies are proposed. These include multi-skilling staff, providing longer-term employment contracts, developing internal labour markets to retain good staff and using personality tests to establish those employees most suited to the hospitality industry. While many of these strategies have been suggested previously, they have generally been presented in an *ad hoc* way, with little substantiating evidence as to the causes of labour turnover.

The findings from the present study also highlight the need for further research into employee attitudes. For example, the new variable of turnover culture clearly requires serious and urgent attention from the hospitality industry. Further investigation into the gaining of employee commitment and job satisfaction is also warranted. Although research into these variables has occurred in other industries, they have received little attention in the hospitality industry. Advances in combating the causes of turnover outlined in this chapter will surely enhance the productivity of the hospitality industry.

APPENDIX

Measuring separation costs

Cost element		Formula				
Exit interview (S₁)	= cost of interviewer's time	= time required prior to interview	+ time required for interview during period	× interviewer's pay rate during period	× number of turnovers	
		= 0.25	+ 0.50	25	× 21	= $393.75
	cost of terminating employee's time	= time required for the interview	× weighted average pay rate for terminated employees	× number of turnovers during period		
		= 0.25	× 9.43	× 21		= $49.50
Administrative functions related to termination (S₂)	= time required by personnel department for administrative functions related to termination	× average personnel department employee's pay rate	× number of turnovers during period			
	= 0.75	× 15.5	× 21			= $244.12
Separation pay (S₃)	= amount of separation pay per employee terminated	× number of turnovers during period				
	= 38×9.43 (existing employee) 38×9.43 (new employee)	× 21				= $15,050.28
					Total	= $15,737.65

Source: Adapted from Cascio, W.F. (1991), *Costing Human Resources* (3rd edn), Boston, PWS-Kent.

Measuring replacement costs

Cost element	Formula						
Communicating job availability (R₁)	= advertising and employment agency fees per termination $1400	+ time required communicating job availability (2	× personnel department employee's pay rate 50)	× number of turnovers replaced during period 21			= $31,500.00
Preemployment administrative functions (R₂)	= time required by personnel department for pre-employment administrative functions 1	× average personnel employee's pay rate 13	× number of applicants during period 21				= $273.00
Entrance interview (R₃)	= time required for interview 0.5	× interviewer's rate 25	× number of interviews during period 5				= $62.50
Staff meeting (R₄)	= time required meeting 1	× personnel department employees' pay rate 25	+ department representatives' pay rate 25	× number of meetings during period 3			= $150.00
Travel/moving expenses (R₅)[a]	= average travel cost per applicant (only occasionally)	× number of applicants	+ average moving cost per new hire	× number of new hires			= $300.00
Post-employment acquisition and dissemination of information (R₆)[a]	= time required for acquiring disseminating information 0.5 + 0.5	× average personnel department employee's pay rate 25 × 13	× number of turnovers replaced during 21 × 21				= $399.00
Contracted medical examinations (R₇)	= rate per examination 18.30	× number of turnovers replaced during period 21					= $385.00
						Total	= $33,069.50

Note: [a] Costed by hotel management.

Source: Adapted from Cascio, W.F. (1991), *Costing Human Resources* (3rd edn), Boston, PWS-Kent.

Measuring training costs

Cost element	Formula	Result
Information literature (T_1)	= cost of informational package × number of replacements during period = 10 × 21	= $210.00
Instruction in a formal training programme (T_2)	= length of training programme × average pay rate of trainer(s) × number of programmes conducted × proportion of training costs attributed to replacements = 10 × 11.75 × 1 × 0.5	= $58.75
	+ average pay rate per trainee × total number replacements training during period × length of training programme = 9.43 × 21 × 10	= $1980.30
Instruction by employee assignment (T_3)	= number of hours required for instruction × average rate of experienced employee × proportional reduction in productivity due to training × number of experienced employees assigned to on-the-job training + new employee's pay rate × number of instructions during period = 38 × 11.75 × 0.5 × 21 + 9.43 × 21	= $12,213.39
	Total	= $14,462.44

Source: Adapted from Cascio, W.F. (1991), *Costing Human Resources* (3rd ed.), Boston, PWS-Kent.

Loss of productivity

Cost element					
Substandard performance of new employee	50%	2 weeks	=	$358.50	
	70%	2 weeks	=	$215.00	
	80%	1 week	=	$71.60	
Extra work for others	50%	2 weeks	=	$358.50	
	30%	2 weeks	=	$215.00	
	20%	1 week	=	$71.60	
				$1,290.20 × 21	
	Total			$27,094.20	

Total costing

Separation costs	=	$15,737.65
Replacement costs	=	$33,069.50
Training cost	=	$14,462.44
Productivity cost	=	$27,094.20
Total		$90,363.79
Cost per employee (room attendant)	=	$90,363.79 ÷ 21
	=	$4,303.00

REFERENCES

Agho, O.A., Mueller, C.W. and Price, J.L. (1992) 'Discriminant validity of measures of job satisfaction, positive affectivity and negative affectivity'. *Journal of Occupational and Organizational Psychology*, **65**, 185–96.

Agho, O.A., Mueller, C.W. and Price, J.L.(1993) 'Determinants of employee job satisfaction: an empirical test of a causal model'. *Human Relations*, **46**, 1007–27.

Ajzen, I. and Fishbein, M. (1980) *Understanding Attitudes and Predicting Social Behaviour*. Sydney: Prentice Hall.

Albrecht, K. (1992) *The Only Things that Matter: Bringing the Power of the Customer into the Center of Your Business*. New York: Harper.

Alwin, D.F. and Hauser, R.M. (1975) 'The decomposition of effects in path analysis'. *American Sociological Review*, **40**, 37–47.

Anderson, J.C. and Gerbing, D.W. (1988) 'Structural equation modeling in practice: a review and recommended two-step approach'. *Psychological Bulletin*, **103**, 411–23.

Arnold, H.J. and Feldman, D.C. (1982) 'A multivariate analysis of the determinants of job turnover'. *Journal of Applied Psychology*, **67**, 350–60.

Bagozzi, R.P. and Yi, Y. (1988) 'On the evaluation of structural equation models'. *Academy of Marketing Science*. **16**, 74–94.

Bateman, T.S. (1980) 'A longitudinal investigation of role overload and its relationships with work behavior and job satisfaction'. PhD Thesis, Indiana University.

Bentler, P.M. (1980) 'Multivariate analysis with latent variables: causal modelling'. *Annual Review of Psychology*, **31**, 419–517.

Bentler, P.M. (1990) 'Comparative fit indexes in structural models'. *Psychological Bulletin*, **107**, 238–46.

Berry, W. and Feldman, S. (1985) *Multiple Regression in Practice*. Beverly Hills, CA: Sage.

Blau, P.M. (1960) 'A theory of social integration'. *American Journal of Sociology*, **65**, 545–56.

Blegen, M.A., Mueller, C.W. and Price, J.L. (1988) 'Measurement of kinship responsibility for organizational research'. *Journal of Applied Psychology*, **73**, 402–9.

Bluedorn, A.C. (1979) 'Structure, environment and satisfaction: toward a causal model of turnover from military organizations'. *Journal of Political and Military Sociology*, **7**, 181–207.

Bluedorn, A.C. (1982) 'A unified model of turnover from organizations'. *Human Relations*, **35**, 135–53.

Bonn, M.A. and Forbringer, L.R. (1992) 'Reducing turnover in the hospitality industry: an overview of recruitment, selection and retention'. *International Journal of Hospitality Management*, **11**, 47–63.

Brooke, P.P. and Price, J.L. (1989) 'The determinants of employee absenteeism: an empirical test of a causal model'. *Journal of Occupational Psychology*, **62**, 1–19.

Bureau of Tourism Research (1990) *Hospitality Industry Labour Force Survey, 1988*. Canberra: Bureau of Tourism Research.

Campbell, D.T. and Fiske, D.W. (1959) 'Convergent and discriminant validation by the multitrait-multimethod matrix'. *Psychological Bulletin*, **56**, 81–105.

Carsten, J.M. and Spector, P.E. (1987) 'Unemployment, job satisfaction, and employee turnover: a meta-analytical test of the Muchinsky model'. *Journal of Applied Psychology*, **72**, 374–31.

Cascio, W.F. (1991) *Costing Human Resources: the Financial Impact of Behaviour in Organizations*, 3rd edn. Boston: PWS-Kent.

Cascio, W.F. (1992) *Managing Human Resources: Productivity, Quality of Work Life, Profits,* 3rd edn. New York: McGraw-Hill.

Cascio, W.F. (1994) 'The role of human resources in gaining and sustaining competitive advantage'. National Seminar Series, Australian Human Resources Institute, Melbourne.

Clayton, W.D. and Wilson, E.S. (1984) 'Nonreturning first year teachers: a profile'. Paper presented at Ninth Annual Conference of the National Council of States on Inservice Education.

Clegg, C.W. (1983) 'Psychology of employee lateness, absence, and turnover: a methodological critique and empirical study'. *Journal of Applied Psychology,* **68**, 88–101.

Cotton, J.L. and Tuttle, J.M. (1986) 'Employee turnover: a meta-analysis and review with implications for research'. *Academy of Management Review,* **11**, 55–70.

Cronbach, L.J. (1951) 'Coefficient alpha and the internal structure of tests'. *Psychometrika,* **16**, 297–334.

Dalessio, A., Silverman, W.H. and Schuck, J.R. (1986) 'Paths to turnover: a re-analysis and review of existing data on the Mobley, Horner and Hollingsworth turnover model'. *Human Relations,* **39**, 245–63.

Dalton, D.R., Todor, W.D. and Krackhardt, D.M. (1982) 'Turnover overstated: the functional taxonomy'. *Academy of Management Review,* **7**, 117–23.

Davis-Blake, A. and Pfeffer, J. (1989) 'Just a mirage: the search for dispositional effects in organizational research'. *Academy of Management Review,* **14**, 385–400.

Debrah, Y.A. (1994) 'Management of operative staff in a labour-scarce economy: the views of human resource managers in the hotel industry in Singapore'. *Asia Pacific Journal of Human Resources,* **32**, 41–60.

Deery, S.J., Iverson, R.D. and Erwin, P.J. (1994) 'Predicting organizational and union commitment: the effect of industrial relations climate'. *British Journal of Industrial Relations,* **32**, 581–97.

Denvir, A. and McMahon, F. (1992) 'Labour turnover in London hotels and the cost effectiveness of preventative measures'. *International Journal of Hospitality Management,* **11**, 143–54.

Dienhart, J.R. (1993) 'Retention of fast-food restaurant employees'. *Hospitality and Tourism Educator,* **5**, 31–5.

Erwin, P.J. and Iverson, R.D. (1994) 'Strategies in absence management'. *Asia Pacific Journal of Human Resources,* **32**(3), 13–32.

Fiske, D.W. (1982) 'Convergent-discriminant validation in measurements and research strategies'. In D. Brinberg and L. Kidder (eds), *New Directions for Methodology of Social and Behavioral Science: Forms of Validity in Research,* pp. 77–92. San Francisco: Jossey-Bass.

Freeman, R.B. and Medoff, J.L. (1984) *What Do Unions Do?* New York: Basic Books.

Fukami, C.V. and Larson, E. (1984.) 'Commitment to company and union: parallel models'. *Journal of Applied Psychology,* **69**, 367–71.

Gordon, M.E. and Ladd, R.T. (1990) 'Dual allegiance: renewal, reconsideration, and recantation'. *Personnel Psychology,* **43**, 37–69.

Gordon, M.E., Philpot, J.W., Burt, R.E., Thompson, C.A. and Spiller, W.E. (1980) 'Commitment to the union: development of a measure and an examination of its correlates'. *Journal of Applied Psychology,* **65**, 479–99.

Gow, J.S., Clark, A.W. and Dossett, G.S. (1974) 'A path analysis of variables influencing labor turnover'. *Human Relations,* **27**, 703–19.

Harman, H.H. (1967) *Modern Factor Analysis.* Chicago: University of Chicago Press.

Hendry, P. (1989) 'The feasibility of reducing labour turnover in the hotel industry'. Honours thesis, University of New South Wales.

Herzberg, F. (1968) *Work and the Nature of Man*. London: Granada.

Hiemstra, S. (1990) 'Employment policies and practices in the lodging industry'. *International Journal of Hospitality Management*, **9**, 207–21.

Hollenbeck, J.R. and Williams, C.R. (1986) 'Turnover functionality versus turnover frequency: a note on work attitudes and organizational effectiveness'. *Journal of Applied Psychology*, **71**, 606–11.

Holmes, D. H., Impink-Hernandez, V. and Terrell, J. (1988) *Study of DCPS Teacher Attrition (Dropout) Patterns*. Washington, DC: District of Columbia Public Schools.

Hom, P.W., Griffeth, R.W. and Sellaro, C.L. (1984) 'The validity of Mobley's (1977) model of employee turnover'. *Organizational Behavior and Human Performance*, **34**, 141–74.

House, J.S. (1981) *Work Stress and Social Support*. Reading, MA: Addison-Wesley.

Ilgen, D. and Hollenbeck, J.H. (1977) 'The role of job satisfaction in absence behavior'. *Organizational Behavior and Human Performance*, **19**, 148–61.

Iverson, R.D. (1992) 'Employee intent to stay: an empirical test of a revision of the Price and Mueller model', PhD thesis, University of Iowa.

Iverson, R.D., Deery, S.J. and Erwin, P.J. (1994) 'Absenteeism among health care workers: causes and intervention strategies'. Paper presented at the 54th Annual Academy of Management Meetings, Dallas, Texas.

Iverson, R.D., Deery, S.J. and Erwin, P.J. (1995) 'Absenteeism in the health services sector: a causal model and intervention strategies'. In P. Riedel and A. Preston (eds), *Managing Absenteeism: Analysing and Preventing Labour Absence*. Canberra: AGPS.

Iverson, R.D. and Kuruvilla, S. (in press) 'Antecedents of union loyalty: the influence of individual dispositions and organizational context'. *Journal of Organizational Behavior*.

Iverson, R.D. and Roy, P. (1994) 'A causal model of behavioural commitment: evidence from a study of Australian blue-collar employees'. *Journal of Management*, **20**(1), 15–41.

Johns, N. and Wheeler, K. (1991) 'Productivity and performance measurement and monitoring'. In R. Teare and A. Boer (eds), *Strategic Hospitality Management. Theory and Practice for the 1990s*, pp. 45–71. London: Cassell.

Jöreskog, K.G. and Sörbom, D. (1993) *LISREL 8: Structural Equation Modeling with the SIMPLIS Command Language*. Chicago: Scientific Software, International.

Kahn, R.L., Wolfe, D.M., Quinn, R.P., Snoek, J.D. and Rosenthal, R.A. (1964) *Organizational Stress: Studies in Role Conflict and Ambiguity*. New York: Wiley.

Keller, R.T. (1975) 'Role conflict and ambiguity: correlates with job satisfaction and values'. *Personnel Psychology*, **28**, 57–64.

Krackhardt, D. and Porter, L. (1986) 'The snowball effect: turnover embedded in communication networks'. *Journal of Applied Psychology*, **71**, 51–5.

Larson, E.W. and Fukami, C.V. (1984) 'Relationships between worker behaviour and commitment to the organization and union'. *Proceedings of the 44th Annual Meeting of the Academy of Management*, pp. 222–6.

Lawler, E.E. (1971) *Pay and Organizational Effectiveness*. New York: McGraw-Hill.

Leslie, D. (1991) 'The hospitality industry, industrial placement and personnel management'. *The Services Industries Journal*, **11**(1), 63–74.

Levin, I. and Stokes, J.P. (1989) 'Dispositional approach to job satisfaction: role of negative affectivity'. *Journal of Applied Psychology*, **74**, 752–8.

Martin, T.N. (1979) 'A contextual model of employee turnover intentions'. *Academy of Management Journal*, **22**, 313–24.

Martin, T.N. and Hunt, J.G. (1980) 'Social influence and intent to leave: a path-analytic process model'. *Personnel Psychology*, **33**, 505–28.

Mattila, J.P. (1974) 'Job quitting and frictional unemployment'. *American Economic Review*, **64**, 235–9.

Michaels, C.E. and Spector, P.E. (1982) 'Causes of employee turnover: a test of the Mobley, Griffeth, Hand and Meglino model'. *Journal of Applied Psychology*, **67**, 53–9.

Mobley, W.H. (1982) *Employee Turnover: Causes, Consequences and Control.* Reading, MA: Addison-Wesley.

Mobley, W.H. (1977) 'Intermediate linkages in the relationship between job satisfaction and employee turnover'. *Journal of Applied Psychology*, **62**, 237–40.

Mobley, W.H., Horner, S.O. and Hollingsworth, A.T. (1978) 'An evaluation of cursors of hospital employee turnover'. *Journal of Applied Psychology*, **63**, 408–14.

Mok, C. and Finley, D. (1986) 'Job satisfaction and its relationship to demographics and turnover of hotel food service workers in Hong Kong'. *International Journal of Hospitality Management*, **5**, 71–8.

Mottaz, C.J. (1989) 'An analysis of the relationships between attitudinal commitment and behavioral commitment'. *The Sociological Quarterly*, **30**, 143–58.

Mowday, R.T., Porter, L.W. and Steers, R.M. (1982) *Employee–Organization Linkages: the Psychology of Commitment, Absenteeism and Turnover.* New York: Academic Press.

Mueller, C.W., Boyer, E.M., Price, J.L. and Iverson, R.D. (1994) 'Employee attachment and noncoercive conditions of work: the case of dental hygienists'. *Work and Occupations*, **21**(2), 179–212.

Nicholls, L.L. and Buergmeister, J.J. (1993) 'Retrenchment as a force for achieving creativity in hospitality education'. *Hospitality and Tourism Educator*, **5**, 11–15.

Ohlin, J.B. and West, J.J. (1994) 'An analysis of the effect of the fringe benefit offerings on the turnover of hourly housekeeping workers in the hotel industry'. *International Journal of Hospitality Management*, **12**, 323–36.

Oldham, G.R., Kulik, C.T., Stepina, L.P. and Ambrose, M.L. (1986) 'Relations between situational factors and the comparative referents used by employees'. *Academy of Management Journal*, **29**, 599–608.

Parasuraman, S., Greenhaus, J. and Granrose, C. (1992) 'Role stressors, social support, and well-being among two-career couples'. *Journal of Organizational Behaviour*, **13**, 339–56.

Podsakoff, P. and Organ, D. (1986) 'Self-reports in organizational research: problems and prospects'. *Journal of Management*, **12**, 531–44.

Porter, L.W., Steers, R.M., Mowday, R.T. and Boulian, P.V. (1974) 'Organizational commitment, job satisfaction and turnover among psychiatric technicians'. *Journal of Applied Psychology*, **59**, 603–9.

Price, J.L. and Mueller, C.W. (1981) *Professional Turnover: the Case of Nurses.* New York: SP Medical and Scientific.

Price, J.L. and Mueller, C.W. (1986) *Absenteeism and Turnover of Hospital Employees.* Greenwich, CT: JAI Press.

Reich, A.Z. (1994) 'Applied economics of hospitality production: reducing costs and improving the quality of decisions through economic analysis'. *International Journal of Hospitality Management*, **12**, 337–52.

Riley, M. (1990) 'The labour retention strategies of UK hotel managers'. *The Service Industries Journal*, **10**, 614–18.

Riley, M. (1994) 'Labour turnover: time for a new paradigm?' *International Journal of Contemporary Hospitality Management*, **5**, i–iii.

Rizzo, J.R., House, R.J. and Litzman, S.I. (1970) 'Role conflict and ambiguity in complex organizations'. *Administrative Science Quarterly*, **15**, 150–63.

Rutter, D. (1988) 'Chance to cut staff turnover'. *Caterer and Hotelkeeper*. July.

Spencer, D.G., Steers, R.M. and Mowday, R.T. (1983) 'An empirical test of the inclusion of job search linkages into Mobley's model of turnover decision process'. *Journal of Occupational Psychology*, **56**, 137–44.

Steel, R.P. and Ovalle, N.K. (1984) 'A review and meta-analysis of research on the relationship between behavioral intentions and employee turnover.' *Journal of Applied Psychology*, **69**, 673–86.

Steers, R.M. and Rhodes, S.R. (1978) 'Major influences on employee attendance: a process model'. *Journal of Applied Psychology*, **63**, 391–407.

Stumpf, S.A. and Hartman, K. (1984) 'Individual exploration to organizational commitment or withdrawal'. *Academy of Management Journal*, **27**, 308–29.

Thompson, K.R. and Terpening, W.D. (1983) 'Job-type variations and antecedents to intention to leave: a content approach to turnover'. *Human Relations*, **36**, 655–82.

Tidball, K.H. (1988) 'Creating a culture that builds your bottom line'. *The Cornell Hotel and Restaurant Administration Quarterly*, **5**, 63–9.

Tourism Training Australia (1991) *The Tourism Labour Market – Constraints and Attitudes*. Melbourne: KPMG Peat Marwick Consultants.

Watson, D., Pennebaker, J.W. and Folger, R. (1987) 'Beyond negative affectivity: measuring stress and satisfaction in the workplace'. *Journal of Organizational Behavior Management*, **8**, 141–57.

Williams, L.J. and Hazer, J.T. (1986) 'Antecedents and consequences of satisfaction and commitment in turnover models: a reanalysis using latent variable structural equation methods'. *Journal of Applied Psychology*, **71**, 219–31.

Williams, C.R. and Livingstone, L.P. (1994) 'Another look at the relationship between performance and voluntary turnover'. *Academy of Management Journal*, **37**, 269–98.

Woods, R.H. and Macauley, J.F. (1989) 'R for turnover: retention programs that work'. *The Cornell Hotel and Restaurant Administration Quarterly*, **30**, 79–90.

Worland, D. and Wilson, K. (1988) 'Employment and labour costs in the hospitality industry: evidence from Victoria'. *International Journal of Hospitality Management*, **7**, 363–7.

Worsfold, P. and Jameson, S. (1991) 'Human resource management: a response to change in the 1990's'. In R.Teare and A. Boer (eds), *Strategic Hospitality Management: Theory and Practice for the 1990s*, pp. 99–119. London: Cassell.

SIX

Productivity through people: the role of human resource management

Sandra Watson

INTRODUCTION

Over the past 25 years the UK has seen a dramatic shift in the balance of the economy, with the proportion of those employed in manufacturing industry declining. There has been a corresponding growth in the service sector, which is now the UK's largest employment sector accounting for over two-thirds of the workforce. Within the service sector, the hospitality industry is now considered to be a significant contributor to the UK economy, and currently employs approximately two million people. As the hospitality industry matures, it is clear that productivity is becoming a major issue. Reasons for this industrial focus include the increasingly competitive market environment, demographic changes and the progressive sophistication of demand (Johns, 1995). Although profitability may be increased in the short term by improved operational effectiveness, sustained growth can only come from improvements in productivity.

The fact that the hospitality industry provides a distinctive combination of tangible and intangible products and services makes productivity a complex area in terms of measurement and improvement. An additional complicating issue is the labour-intensive nature of the hospitality industry. Service demands human input and productivity gains can often only be achieved by increasing the productivity of individuals. By contrast, more product-oriented industries might rely upon automation or technology to achieve a more productive operation. Although employees are critical to increased productivity, the hospitality industry has traditionally placed little emphasis on the treatment and development of the workforce. Money spent on employees is rarely seen as an investment, but often viewed as a cost. The transient nature of the hospitality labour force, with its prevalent high labour turnover, is often cited as the reason for this attitude towards employees.

This chapter proposes that there is a need for a fundamental change in the industry's approach to people management, in order to realize a long overdue improvement in productivity. It examines the nature of productivity and suggests that productivity must be viewed as an aggregate concept encompassing four distinct functional levels. It argues that hospitality organizations need to adopt a human resource management approach to people management in order to develop a holistic attitude to productivity.

THE NATURE OF PRODUCTIVITY

The complex nature of productivity in the service sector has been noted by a number of writers, including Jones and Lockwood (1989) and Witt and Witt (1989). Researchers have established that the features and characteristics of service have limited the evolution of a universally accepted definition of productivity. The commonly cited aspects of service which influence the complexity of productivity are as follows:

- *intangibility*, referring to the problem of being able objectively to define and measure the service being provided;
- *perishability*, relating to the issue of the immediacy of consumption of the service/product, which makes storage difficult or impossible;
- *simultaneity*, concerned with the issue of the consumer and service provider's interaction, with production and consumption occurring at the same time;
- *heterogeneity*, i.e. the variety of service encounters that can be experienced by the consumer, owing to the variety of features that can affect the service.

These features are not separate in nature, but can be seen to exist concurrently within most services. For example, a consumer in a fast-food restaurant may experience features of 'perishability', as the food provided must be consumed within a short period of time. The service encounter is characterized by simultaneity and to a lesser degree by heterogeneity, as standardization is likely to be an issue in fast-food restaurants. These features of service make it difficult to find an acceptable definition difficult.

A further aspect, service quality, must be considered as a dimension of productivity. The British Standards Institute (1987) defines quality as 'the totality of features and characteristics of a product or service that bear on its ability to satisfy stated or implied needs'. This definition highlights the consumer orientation of quality and focuses on the provision of products and services which meet consumers' needs. It also implies that suppliers need to take both a technical and a behavioural perspective in addressing the management of quality. Quality is based on the customer's perception of service, rather than the service itself. The nature of a service industry is such that quality is influenced not only by physical or material aspects, but also by interaction with staff. Both of these components can be either tangible or intangible in nature. For example, the provision of a drink in a bar can be viewed as providing a tangible product, but the environment and design of the surroundings will provide a degree of intangibility. The social interaction aspect of the staff involved in pouring and serving the drink is tangible in terms of the technical skills used, but intangible in relation to the manner and attitude adopted during the process. The relationship between productivity and quality in the service industry is highly integrated, because qualitative aspects play a significant role in service productivity.

Productivity at an organizational level is characterized not only by understanding the complexities discussed above, but also by external and internal variables. These are summarized in Figure 6.1, derived from a model proposed by Pickworth (1994, p. 277). The figure shows the numerous factors which affect productivity, divided into 'environmental' and 'organizational' variables, according to whether they emanate from outside or from within the business organization. Further sub-divisions are made in relation either to discipline base or to the level at which the variables affect organizational productivity. Pickworth's framework is similar to other productivity models in that it encourages a focus on specific variables of productivity, rather than the development of a 'holistic' approach to productivity. Much of the research in this area to date has focused on either one or a few aspects of productivity, e.g. labour productivity, productivity control or operational productivity. Pickworth (1994) suggests that a 'reconceptionalizing of productivity' is needed, moving away from the historical, disciplinary-based approach towards a holistic one that considers 'all inputs and all outputs'. To this end, a hierarchical model of the components in organizational productivity is presented in Figure 6.2, which shows productivity as an aggregate concept.

Within the context of this model, human resource management (HRM) is likely to have a key role in improving productivity. It can focus attention on all factors affecting productivity, at all levels of the organization, and can consider both external and internal variables. Thus it permits the development of a holistic view of productivity. Human resource management influences productivity not only at the operational and individual productivity levels, but also in strategic terms. However, before this argument can be developed it is necessary to provide a definition of HRM.

PHILOSOPHY OF HRM

The concept of HRM has largely emerged since the 1980s (e.g. Guest, 1987; Farnham and Pimlott, 1990). Its distinction from traditional personnel management is made most clearly by Torrington and Hall (1991). They regard personnel management as workforce centred and directed mainly at the organization's employees. It includes finding and training staff, arranging for them to be paid, explaining management's expectations, justifying management's actions, satisfying employees' work-related needs, dealing with their problems and seeking to modify management action that could produce unwelcome employee responses. HRM, on the other hand, is resource-centred, directed mainly at management's need to provide and deploy human resources (not necessarily employees). There is a greater emphasis on planning, monitoring and control, as opposed to mediation. HRM can therefore be seen to be a proactive, strategic and coherent approach to the management of an organizations workforce.

Armstrong (1993, p. 13) identifies the main areas of emphasis within human resource management as:

- the interests of management;
- the adaptation of a strategic approach;

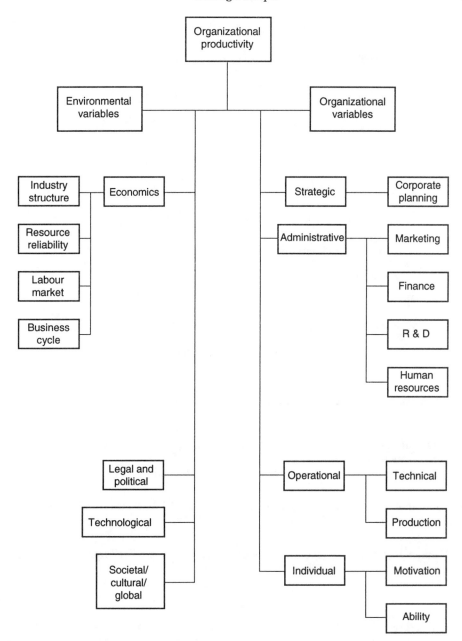

Figure 6.1. Variables influencing organizational productivity

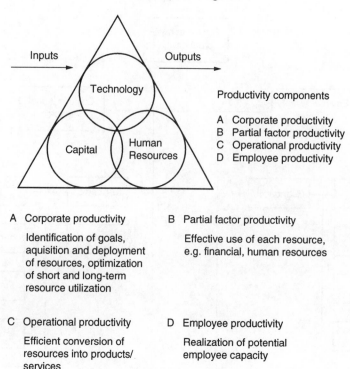

A Corporate productivity

Identification of goals,
aquisition and deployment
of resources, optimization
of short and long-term
resource utilization

B Partial factor productivity

Effective use of each resource,
e.g. financial, human resources

C Operational productivity

Efficient conversion of
resources into products/
services

D Employee productivity

Realization of potential
employee capacity

Figure 6.2. Hierarchy of organizational productivity

- obtaining added value from employees through human resource development and performance management;
- gaining commitment to organizational objectives and values.

He notes that as a style of people management HRM has four fundamental philosophical principles:

1 Human resources are recognized as the organization's most important asset, their effective management being the key to its success.
2 Organizational success is most likely to be achieved if the personnel policies are closely linked with, and make a major contribution to, the achievement of corporate objectives and strategic plans.
3 Corporate culture and values, the organizational climate and the managerial behaviour that emanate from that culture exert a major influence on the achievement of excellence.
4 Continuous effort is required to achieve integration, getting all members of the organization involved and working together with a sense of common purpose.

Storey (1992) makes a further distinction between 'hard' and 'soft' versions of HRM. In the 'hard' version, employees are treated as just another part of the organization's input–output equation. Strategies are concerned with improving employee utilization and getting them to accept that their interests coincide with those of the organization (unitarist approach). Resourcing strategies and practices aim to recruit and develop employees who 'fit' the organization's culture. Employees are involved in the improvement of quality and productivity, but not in business decision-making. Organizations in the hospitality industry which currently fit this model include McDonald's and Disneyworld. This 'hard' version therefore stresses the management aspect of an HRM approach.

The 'soft' version of HRM emphasizes communication, motivation and leadership. It is concerned with developing what Handy (1986) refers to as a 'culture of consent' and recognizes that employees cannot be treated just like any other resource. Because people feel and react there should be more emphasis on strategies for gaining employee commitment. Thus employees are informed about the company's mission, values and plans; they are involved in the organization of work, and are often grouped into self-managing teams. A pluralistic view is taken, which recognizes that the needs of employees will not always coincide with those of the organization, and care is taken to balance the respective needs, as far as this is possible. Hospitality organizations currently adopting a 'soft' version of HRM include Marriott Hotels and Sheraton Hotels.

Although much has been written on the subject of HRM as a distinct approach to the management of employees, there are two conflicting opinions on the extent to which it is being implemented in practice. The first proposes that the apparent increase in the number of human resource managers is in name only and that in reality approaches have remained the same. The second view is that HRM-inspired employment practices are radically different and can be seen to be more 'sophisticated and strategically integrated' (Storey, 1992), encompassing the philosophies outlined previously. The present author concurs with this latter view and proposes that the aims of HRM are more strategic in nature, focusing on both the development of the individual and the business requirements of the organization. However, within the hospitality industry the extent to which organizations are developing HRM approaches is limited. It might be expected that organizational restructuring undergone by the industry during the early 1990s (Johns, 1995) would result in companies moving towards the adoption of an HRM philosophy. Umbreit (1987) concurs with this view and proposes that organizations will need to develop systematic human resource policies in order to maintain operational quality. However, Wood (1994) argues that 'The development of high quality human resource strategies is perhaps antithetical to the pursuit of the low wage policies that typify the industry, and is reflected in the hiring of large numbers of part-time and casual workers.'

HRM AND PRODUCTIVITY

Much research has focused upon labour productivity, particularly upon such factors as experience and training, motivation and incentives, employee participation, team-working and job design. Although these issues are important, the main focus of interest is the broader, conceptual relationship between HRM and productivity. Philosophical links between HRM and productivity can be perceived by examining characteristics of successful companies. For example, Peters and Waterman (1982, p. 239) identified nine major attributes which are found in 'excellent' companies.

These excellence factors include aspects such as 'productivity through people', which are fundamental to the philosophy of HRM. They encompass the belief that people are an organization's most important asset and must be developed to their total ability, with commitment to organizational beliefs and values being encouraged, through the development of a 'soft' or 'hard' dimension to their management.

HRM is a strategic approach, inherently integrated into business policy and development. Productivity is affected because business needs become the focus for all individuals within the organization, with a strong emphasis on customer requirements. This not only influences the focus of work, but also ensures that employment practices reflect this philosophy in terms of the structure and nature of the workforce. There is now a growing appreciation in industry that competitive advantage is achieved through employees, who are the implementors of corporate plans and must be managed effectively in order to achieve business success (e.g. Johns and Chesterton, 1994; Handy, 1994). Productivity is an important aspect of competitive success. Economic and business trends of the late 1980s and early 1990s include increased global competition, increased complexity and size of organizations, technological change and changing values and structures within the workforce (Olsen, 1989). Together, these have resulted in more attention being paid to productivity (e.g. Heap, 1992; Ingold and Worthington, 1994). Guest (1989) states that 'HRM is an attractive option to managements driven by market pressures to seek improved quality, greater flexibility and constant innovation'. HRM can therefore be viewed as means of managing people to achieve competitive advantage, by maintaining a business orientation and concentrating on gaining added value from all employees.

Conceptual models of HRM and productivity are only of use if practical aspects of HRM are considered in relation to their influence on productivity improvements within the hospitality industry. As previously discussed, differences between personnel management and HRM can be seen as 'a matter of emphasis and approach rather than one of substance' (Armstrong, 1993, pp. 15–16). However, it is useful to identify HRM approaches through a range of operational features, before discussing their influence on productivity. Storey (1992) offers a range of dimensions which can be used to compare personnel and HRM approaches. From these, key HRM characteristics can be extrapolated under four main headings of *'beliefs and assumptions'*, *'strategic aspects'*, *'line managers'* and *'key levers'*. These are shown in Table 6.1.

The characteristics identified in Storey's model affect productivity at four different levels: *corporate, partial factor, operational productivity* or *employee productivity*. Variables appearing under the headings of beliefs and assumptions and strategic aspects respectively can be seen as impacting upon corporate and partial factor productivity, while those appearing within line management and key levers will have more effect upon the lower levels of the hierarchy, i.e. operational and employee productivity. However, it can also be argued that these variables and characteristics influence productivity at all levels within the hierarchy. Thus a holistic view must be taken to both the management of people and productivity in today's competitive business environment. The following discussion focuses on the integrative nature of the key HRM characteristics and highlights how these can influence productivity at the four levels of Pickworth's (1994) model. Productivity is often viewed as a functional role in management, but the concept of HRM provides a consistent and mutually reinforcing system to the integration of all operational activities.

Table 6.1. Human resource dimensions

Dimension	HRM
Beliefs and options	
Contract	Aim to go 'beyond contract'
Rules	'Can do' outlook, impatience with 'rule'
Guide to management action	'Business need', management flexibility, commitment
Behaviour referent	Values, mission
Managerial task *vis-à-vis* labour	Nurturing
Nature of relations	Unitarist
Conflict	De-emphasized
Standardization	Low (e.g. 'parity' not seen as relevant)
Strategic aspects	
Key relations	Business customer
Initiatives	Integrated
Corporate plan	Central to
Speed of decision	Fast
Line management	
Management role	Transformational leadership
Key managers	General, business, line managers
Prized management skills	Facilitation
Key levers	
Foci of attention for intervention strategies	Wide-ranging cultural, structural and personnel
Selection	Integrated key task
Pay	Performance-related, few if any grades
Conditions	Harmonization
Labour management	Towards individual contracts
Communication	Increased flow, direct
Job design	Teamwork
Conflict handling	Manage climate and culture
Training and development	Learning companies

HRM AND CORPORATE PRODUCTIVITY

Corporate productivity is often seen as the most important component within the hierarchy of productivity. It is related to the effectiveness of corporate or organizational objectives and the efficient deployment of organizational resources. In addition, it is concerned with the productive strategic management of the organization. An HRM approach has greater influence at the strategic level of the organization than a traditional personnel focus, as it involves a broader view of the management of people, where strategies are closely linked to corporate objectives and plans.

HRM strategies encompass both resourcing and performance within an organization. Resourcing strategies highlight both skills and performance standards and are therefore linked with performance management. Performance management provides a basis not only for improving individual through to corporate performance, but also for rewarding people. Thus the major activities within HRM impinge on performance levels and are closely linked to the management of productivity. Although employees can be considered the most important organizational asset in the labour-intensive hospitality industry, few hospitality organizations are taking this strategic approach to the management of human resources. This could be one of the fundamental reasons why productivity was found to be relatively low in a survey of the UK hotel sector compared with both France and Germany (NEDC, 1992).

A few companies do take this approach to their employees. For example, TGI Friday's Restaurants use highly developed and sophisticated resourcing strategies to ensure the correct selection of staff. Productivity-based performance management systems and a heavy investment in training and development of all staff indicate an HRM approach to people management (King-Taylor, 1993, pp. 142–52).

The recent economic environment of greater competition, recession and a more sophisticated demand for services has resulted in many hospitality organizations redefining objectives and changing management styles in an attempt to increase productivity. Typical examples are Forte Hotels, Holiday Inns and Hilton Hotels (Watson and D'Annunzio-Green, 1994). This attention to productivity is likely to continue during the 1990s, with pressure deriving from external factors such as new employment practices, new legislation, changing economic and political boundaries and changing consumer trends (Jones & Lockwood, 1989). These external factors have resulted in a physical restructuring of many organizations, e.g. in the form of delayering and redeployment. The notion put forward by Peters and Waterman (1982) that excellent companies are 'people-driven' and have 'loose and tight' properties has encouraged organizations to examine their beliefs and values. Within the hospitality industry, companies like Harvester Restaurants are moving from a 'control' to a 'trust-oriented' culture, in order to accommodate the customer-driven aspect of service and the need to develop appropriate attitudes and behaviour in employees (Sternberg, 1992).

HRM emphasizes the importance of involving senior management in the development of organizational culture (Bowen and Basch, 1992). Effective human resource strategies are essential for the evolution of the culture, ensuring that there is an emergent 'vision' driving the organization forward. Within the hospitality industry, Disneyworld and McDonald's are often cited as 'excellent companies' (Peters and Waterman, 1982; Ritzer, 1992). Both have clear visions, which are widely understood by employees. However, one aspect of this excellence which is often understated is that both organizations have highly developed human resource strategies, policies and processes to support understanding of and convergence to the organization's vision. This ensures that the vision is seen as being pivotal to the business and that culture is managed in a way that integrates beliefs and values throughout the organization. Human resource strategies should be designed and implemented to support the beliefs and attitudes inherent in the vision. For example, TGI Friday's focus on customer service impinges on all aspects of the business (King-Taylor, 1993, pp. 145–52).

The recent economic climate has forced organizations to address the role of the customer in business development. It could be argued that this has been realized as a result of the total quality management (TQM) focus of the 1980s, but the cynical may view it as a response to market forces. The important issue is that human resource strategies lead to the development of procedures and policies relating to employee resourcing, utilization and development. These undoubtedly support the organization and ensure that the customer remains the focal point for the business. Human resource strategies may provide all employees with a sense of common purpose through an ability to focus on customers' service needs. Team-working strategies that are currently used to achieve this include TGI Friday's 'self-managed groups' (Guerrier and Pye, 1994), Scandic Crown Hotels' quality teams (Maxwell, 1993) and multi-skilling in Forte Hotels (Watson and D'Annunzio-Green, 1994). The important feature of these are that they aim to increase productivity by focusing on meeting customer's needs. Very often these are associated with performance-related pay related linked to productivity improvement.

Resourcing and development strategies are designed to encourage a nurturing approach as opposed to a monitoring approach to the management of staff. In some instances this has required a reprofiling of management positions, with increased emphasis on facilitation as a key management skill. Forte Hotels, for example, is currently paying more attention to the acquisition of transformational leaders. Transformational leadership can be defined as charismatic leadership that inspires subordinates to levels of motivation considerably higher than are objectively required to complete their duties (Bennett, 1992). Bass (1990) suggests that 'fostering of transformational leadership through policies of recruitment, selection, promotion, training and development will pay off in the healthy well-being and effective performance of today's organizations'. It is through the deployment of strategies of this nature that hospitality organizations will be able to develop a culture that is conducive to increasing productivity at the corporate level.

HRM AND PARTIAL FACTOR PRODUCTIVITY

The next level of the hierarchy to examine is 'partial factor productivity', which is concerned with the effective use of each separate resource. Johns and Wheeler (1991) propose that productivity strategies generally fall into two categories. 'Contractive strategies' are those concerned with minimizing inputs, while 'expansive strategies' deal with maximizing outputs. Both strategies can be implemented concurrently. Contractive strategies in relation to human resources include increased automation and technology, in order to decrease the number of individuals required to produce the output. This approach has been used across many sectors of the industry and includes the use of cook–chill technology in food production areas (Johns *et al.*, 1992) and of computerized reservations and reception systems in the hotel sector (Barker *et al.*, 1994). There are numerous other examples that could be cited of contractive strategies in terms of automation and technology, but the important issue is that an HRM perspective ensures that these are implemented proactively at a strategic level. There has been a general move towards a contract culture during the past few years, with organizations reducing numbers of core workers and using a range of alternative contractual relationships. This process can be viewed as one of the most important recent contractive strategies and is often referred to as numerical flexibility.

Expansive strategies encompass a range of approaches designed to increase employee productivity in terms of both quantity and quality of output. Numerical flexibility can be realized through the increased use of part-time workers and sub-contractors. Sub-contracting of work is also becoming increasingly prevalent in the hospitality industry. For example, many hotel organizations have contracted out such functions as laundry, maintenance and auditing, and there is increasing interest in contract facilities management (Parry and Collins, 1993). In the contract catering sector, Gardner Merchant has reduced employee numbers in design and planning and in information technology, buying in extra specialists to meet business requirements.

Numerical flexibility is used extensively in the hospitality industry, because fluctuating demand makes it an ideal strategy for maximizing staff deployment. However, human resource strategies need to address both the resourcing and development of appropriate support mechanisms, to ensure that productivity levels are maintained. Forte Heritage Hotels now employs most staff on 20-hour contracts, but has had to implement new training strategies, promotion policies and communication procedures. Some commentators (e.g. Heap, 1992; Pickworth, 1994; Wood, 1994) argue that the interactive nature of hospitality service makes numerical flexibility an inappropriate productivity improvement strategy. Although there may be short-term financial benefits, the long-term effect will be a decline in standards. This could be the case if support policies are not introduced to ensure the maintenance of the quality and quantity of outputs.

The 'flexible working practices' approach (Atkinson, 1984) has been adopted by many hospitality organizations to increase productivity. Atkinson advocates three forms of flexibility: numerical, functional and financial. A study carried out by the Advisory, Conciliation and Arbitration Service (1988) found that the majority of employers were seeking to introduce flexible working practices with a view to increasing productivity and reducing the cost of labour. Functional flexibility, also referred to as multi-skilling, is increasing the scope of workers' skills. Multi-skilling has been used in the hospitality industry in an *ad hoc* manner for many years, but there are now moves to use structured multi-skilling in many hotel groups, such as Hyatt, Holiday Inn and Queen's Moat House (Watson and D'Annunzio-Green, 1994; Yeoman, 1995). However, multi-skilling depends to some extent upon the nature of the product/service mix and therefore does have some limitations in the hospitality industry. Multi-skilling is incorporated into training programmes by the provision of staff training in a number of departments, enabling them to gain skills and widen promotion opportunities. The process also enables staff to understand what is expected of other departments, including the pressures and problems involved. This assists teamwork in problem resolution, as staff morale can be improved and turnover is often reduced. It does, however, involve organizations in the costs of training and retraining. Sheraton Hotels has used multi-skilling between reception and reservations departments with a view to increasing productivity.

Financial flexibility is the third dimension of the Atkinson model that impacts upon productivity. HRM may help to achieve it through such aspects as individual contracts and performance-related pay. Researchers including McFarlane (1982) and Wood (1992) note that the hospitality industry is rife with 'individual contracts' owing to the prevailing industrial relations environment. Lack of unionization and a generally unitary perspective on the management of industrial relations encourage the use of individual contracts. However, there is a tendency for these to feature at the supervisory or managerial level only, owing to the poor bargaining power of the largely unskilled workforce.

Performance-related pay has been a feature of the hospitality industry predominantly at managerial level, with many receiving bonus payments based on performance targets. Some companies (e.g. Forte Hotels, McDonald's and Harvester Restaurants) use performance payments that are linked into productivity at all levels of the organization. TGI Friday's employees are paid on a commission basis, related to sales and performance (King-Taylor, 1993, pp. 145–52). Flexible working practices currently in use encompass both 'contractive' and 'expansive' strategies. They are often operated concurrently; for example, the introduction of multi-skilling often occurs at the same time as a reduction in the employees, so that both numerical and functional flexibility approaches are used together.

Other HRM dimensions influencing productivity at this level include the predominant values and missions that are used as a reference within the organization. These influence the procedures used to implement strategies and thus affect the way an organization operates on a day-to-day basis. The HRM approach emphasizes the importance of *managed* values and missions, rather than *ad hoc* custom and practice. The author believes that a general drift towards this approach is presently occurring within the industry. It can be observed in companies such as Inter-Continental Hotels, where attention is being focused on the management of organizational culture so that beliefs and values are understood throughout the organization. For example, the vision statement of the Intercontinental George Hotel in Edinburgh is 'Service with no excuse' (King-Taylor, 1993, pp. 177–85). Policies are designed to ensure that this vision is clear to all staff and becomes the reference point for operational behaviour. This involves not only ensuring that operating procedures have sufficient flexibility for this to occur, but also aligning employee resourcing, development and deployment strategies to achieve this goal.

In the hospitality industry the importance of the customer has always been considered to be fundamental to business success. However, centralized service procedures may impede the ability to meet customers' needs. For example, complaint procedures normally revolved around a decision-making hierarchy at either unit or head office level. This delays the process and loses 'the moment of truth' (Carlzon, 1987).

However, increased awareness of the importance of customer care, through TQM, Investors in People initiatives and customer care training, has pushed customer orientation to the forefront of business philosophy. Organizations demonstrate this through a range of strategies and approaches. For example, Forte Hotels places 'professional customer image' and 'anticipative service' at the top of departmental managers' job description and job profile, demonstrating the importance of the customer to the organization (Watson and D'Annunzio-Green, 1994). The use of well-defined customer complaint procedures, with complaints and problems being addressed quickly through empowerment and flexibility, is further evidence of this philosophy. For the past five years, Sheraton Hotels has conducted integrated measurements of managerial effectiveness, encompassing financial performance, customer satisfaction and employee satisfaction. External measurement and auditing of these areas at both unit and departmental level is carried out at three- and six-monthly intervals. The Sheraton approach highlights a move towards the adaptation of the 'internal customer' philosophy (Simms et al., 1988) which is expressed in total quality management literature (Oakland, 1989; Collard, 1991). As well as being fundamental in team-building and team-working, it is important for the successful and productive delivery of products and services. Intercontinental Hotels also regularly conducts an employee opinion survey, which is used as a feedback mechanism for management (King-Taylor, 1993, pp. 177–85). These initiatives focus on the importance of employees and could eventually become benchmarks within the industry.

Employee empowerment is the process of decentralizing decision-making in an organization, so that front-line employees are given maximum discretion and autonomy (Brymer, 1991). It helps employees to meet the needs of customers and is therefore often seen as the key to providing good customer care. It is also used as a tool to increase employee commitment to organizations. However, it cannot be developed in isolation. It requires the development of procedures to ensure speedy problem resolution, and various aspects of organizational culture are fundamental to its success. These include:

- commitment of strategic management and the philosophy of leadership that is prevalent in the organization;
- practices, procedures and an authority hierarchy that are conducive to empowerment;
- clear definition of the latitudinal terms of empowerment strategies;
- trust in employees' capabilities, which may involve a change in management style;
- training provision for front-line employees in terms of social skills, decision-making, communication skills and operational implications.

TGI Friday's represents a good example of empowerment implementation within the hospitality industry. This company has addressed all the above aspects within an extremely strong organizational culture focused on sustaining customer service (King-Taylor, 1993, pp. 145–52). More importantly for this discussion, there is a concurrent focus on productivity. However, there are many organizations which have neither the appropriate culture nor the management style for the effective implementation of employee empowerment.

HRM AND OPERATIONAL PRODUCTIVITY

Operational productivity is concerned with the efficient conversion of resources into products and services. Pickworth (1994) identifies three broad approaches which can be taken to improve operational productivity level. These are 'problem-oriented' and centre on the identification of the problem and the manner in which obstacles can be overcome to increase productivity. 'Systems-oriented' approaches involve investigating the ways in which service delivery systems can be optimized, while 'capacity-oriented' approaches are designed to help to align supply to demand. The contribution of HRM is to instil in all employees the need for continuous productivity improvement. The fundamental philosophy of HRM engenders a change of focus within operations, ultimately resulting in all three approaches being addressed. HRM requires an organization to identify operational problems related to structural, financial or human resource issues. The focus on customer and business needs results in alternative approaches being developed to alleviate the problem and increase productivity. However, this idealized view can only be realized if a holistic approach to both HRM and productivity is taken and HRM strategies are closely linked to corporate goals and objectives. Without this, both HRM and productivity will continue to be viewed from a functional perspective only.

Organizations like Sheraton Hotels and Intercontinental Hotels use sophisticated guest and employee satisfaction measurement techniques which assist in the identification of problem areas. The results are used to identify improvement strategies. For example, the Edinburgh Sheraton Grand Hotel identified from a guest satisfaction index that there were problems in not being able to meet the guest's expectations in terms of room provision. This produced dissatisfied customers and often resulted in a reduction in the room rate being offered. The problem was identified as being two-fold: at one level, reservation clerks lacked knowledge in relation to the availability of non-standard rooms; second, they were unaware of the impact of a false promise on receptionists and on the financial performance of the unit. The problem was overcome by cross-training reservation clerks in both reception and housekeeping, and the result was measurable as an improved score in the guest satisfaction index.

Systems-oriented approaches focus upon service delivery systems, requiring organizations to examine both behavioural and scientific approaches to improve productivity. These include greater emphasis on team-building, motivational factors, group dynamics and employee participation. The complex nature of the service industry, discussed previously, has resulted in many organizations focusing productivity improvements on the tangible aspects of service, with little attention being given to the intangible customer-interactive components. Attempts to address this have often involved the development of routine responses; for example, standardization of the way a telephonist answers the telephone. However, this may result in a perceived insincerity and depersonalization of the service being delivered. TGI Friday's has adopted a very different approach by selecting staff through an 'audition', with a strong emphasis on personality and uniqueness. An element of entertainment is incorporated into the service delivery system within laid-down operating procedures. Team-building and employee commitment are managed through highly sophisticated systems of 'shift meetings', 'communications' and 'recognition' systems.

In HRM terms, capacity-oriented approaches involve the deployment of staff, through, for example, flexible working practices, increased training in sales techniques and the increased use of empowerment to make decisions that influence demand. These aspects have been discussed earlier in the chapter. The main issue is that there should be an understanding at all organizational levels that human resource strategies influence individuals' behaviour and hence capacity-oriented productivity.

HRM AND INDIVIDUAL PRODUCTIVITY

The final level of Pickworth's model is concerned with the realization of the potential productivity of the individual employee. An HRM approach to people management aims to develop an organizational climate in which employees are seen as the organization's most important asset. It would thus seem likely to increase employee productivity. Key HRM policies are those concerned with selection, training, development, performance and feedback. Organizations that employ an HRM approach tend to view selection, training, development, performance and recognition procedures as fundamental, integrated tasks of key managers. For example, Forte Hotels has restructured its personnel activities so as to place them within the control of operational managers (Watson and D'Annunzio-Green, 1994). This is evidence that people are seen as a key operational resource and must be managed and developed like any other resource within a manager's control. TGI Friday's also demonstrably regards its employees as its most important asset, viewing selection, training and development as an investment on which considerable time is lavished (King-Taylor, 1993, pp. 145–52).

A fundamental principle of HRM is that of the nurturing organization, in which development and training are seen as the keys to success. Employees are thus continuously encouraged to undertake self-development. Recently, more attention has been paid to training and development within the hospitality industry, although this may not always be because of the adoption of a HRM approach. Other influences are the competitive business environment and government initiatives such as NVQs and Investors in People. Hospitality organizations are focusing more attention on these integrated aspects of HRM (Goss-Turner, 1994). Incorporation of these aspects within the scope of operational managers brings a need to ensure that managers have the skills and abilities to optimize individual productivity fully. Thus it is necessary to address management styles. Traditionally, hospitality managers are viewed as 'authoritarian, dictatorial, and heavy handed and hold a unitary view of managerial and leadership relationships' (Wood, 1994, p. 126). Clearly they need to adopt a more nurturing perspective, considering the development of staff and their care and nurturing as part of their role (Guerrier and Lockwood, 1989). This is not going to be an easy transition, as fundamental beliefs and attitudes must be addressed.

In the author's view a move in this direction is currently occurring in some hospitality organizations. There is increasing use of employee satisfaction measurements and labour turnover figures as performance criteria for managers, linked to financial incentive schemes. This has helped to focus managers' attention on the care and nurturing of individuals and their productivity. This is a necessary shift in focus owing to both the external labour market and the internal restructuring which has taken place in industry. Some researchers, including Heap (1992), propose that a 'hybrid' manager will be required to manage productivity with a wide range of skills and experience, including information technology. HRM approaches will ensure that skills, abilities, processes and individuals all influence productivity. It is the integration of a strategic approach to the total business as well as a focus on the abilities and skills of managers that will have maximum impact on productivity.

Structurally oriented approaches to individual productivity are concerned with the improvement of the working environment. This is normally associated with job design. McDonald's employs work procedures and methods that optimize and maximize productivity, and this can be viewed as a 'hard' approach to job design. However, other organizations within the industry adopt a 'soft' approach to improving the work environment, focusing on teamwork plus the development of wider skills and responsibilities.

Employee productivity can also be addressed through gain-sharing approaches designed to distribute the benefits of increased productivity. Such systems align employees' goals closer to those of the organization. In this context, HRM advocates the increased use of performance-related pay and incentive schemes, as well as management of the organizational climate and culture. The role of training and development in this area cannot be overstated. The world expert in relation to 'bringing employee goals closer to those of the organization' in the hospitality industry must be Disneyworld. Extensive training and development enables the individual employee to be 'Disneyfied' in a short period of time (Pizam, 1993). This should not be seen as a criticism of the company, but something to be envied by other hospitality providers. However, there appears to be little use of incentive payments or performance-related pay schemes at Disney.

Very sophisticated performance-related pay schemes are now being used in the hospitality industry. For example, McDonald's 'observation checklist system' (OCS) involves the observation of work procedures and includes both physical tasks and knowledge. Employees are rated against each component of the job and OCS is incorporated into a review process where the total scores across the range of operational procedures are tallied. If an employee achieves an overall score of 90 to 95 per cent, an additional hourly payment is awarded. This is coupled with a gold star recognition scheme, based on customer service and length of service in recognition of increased performance (Lashley, 1993). Harvester Restaurants uses a system of job performance recognition in which employees work towards gaining a silver badge. The focus is on job competence and achievement of a silver badge results in an additional hourly rate. To develop individuals' expertise further there may be an additional payment for taking on a wider responsibility within a work team. A further dimension to this incentive scheme is the development of a 'team expert', who takes over responsibility for training, again receiving additional payments. In addition, the 'team expert' gains a share of bonuses if the team surpasses agreed levels of productivity (Ashness and Lashley, 1995).

Participation-oriented approaches focus on fostering employee contributions and commitment by initiatives such as empowerment, self-managed teams and quality circles. Examples of all these approaches can be found in the hospitality industry in organizations like Harvester Restaurants (Ashness and Lashley, 1995), TGI Friday's (King-Taylor, 1993, pp. 145–52) and Scandic Crown Hotels (Maxwell, 1993). Participatory schemes can improve productivity and product quality while reducing conflict. Problem-solving exercises are more likely to be successful if they involve employees: the solution is more likely to work as they have been involved in the process. Quality circles are an example of participatory management that has contributed to increased productivity, mainly through cost savings. Empowerment is another participative technique that enhances productivity through individuals' ability to make on-the-spot decisions to meet customers' expectations.

The success of any initiative designed to increase employee productivity depends not only on commitment from top management but also on the approach taken to manage human resources. Some writers would suggest that the optimization of productivity can only be achieved if the industry addresses the fundamentals of people management, including appropriate payment levels, good working conditions, the provision of training and an appreciative management style. The present author concurs with this view, but suggests that the above issues alone are not sufficient. What is actually required is the development of a strategic approach to people management encompassing the philosophies of the HRM movement.

CONCLUSION

This chapter highlights the importance of people to productivity within the hospitality industry. Traditionally, productivity approaches by both industry and researchers have involved short-term, *ad hoc* personnel 'fixes'. Both have focused on functional operational aspects, with an emphasis on the economic context. This chapter shifts the focus to a more holistic, longer-term, conceptual approach. It highlights the importance of a strategic perspective to the management of 'productivity through people'. The HRM philosophy proposed aims to address all inputs and all outputs (i.e. an aggregate concept of productivity). It is with this emphasis on 'productivity through people' that increased productivity will be realized in the hospitality industry. The conceptualization of productivity forms the framework for the integrative implementation of productivity improvements through the adoption of an HRM approach. This chapter does not intend to simplify the complex issue of productivity, but to highlight the behavioural and attitudinal shift that the industry needs if it is to realize the goal of 'productivity through people'.

REFERENCES

Advisory, Consultation and Arbitration Services (ACAS) (1988) *Labour Flexibility in Britain*. London: ACAS.

Armstrong, M. (1987) 'Human resource management: a case of the emperor's new clothes?'. *Personnel Management*, **14**(8), 30–5.

Armstrong, M. (1991) *A Handbook of Personnel Management Practice*, 4th edn. New York: Kogan Page.

Armstrong, M. (1993) *HRM Strategy and Action*. New York: Kogan Page.

Ashness, D. and Lashley, C. (1995) 'Employee empowerment in Harvester Restaurants'. Paper presented at the CHME HRM Conference, February, London.

Atkinson, J. (1984) 'Flexibility, uncertainty and manpower management'. IMS Report No. 89, Brighton.

Baker, S., Bradley, P. and Huyton, J. (1984) *Principles of Hotel Front Office Operations*. London: Cassell.

Bass, B. (1992) 'From transaction to transformational leadership: learning to share the vision'. *Organizational Dynamics*, Winter, 19–31.

Bennett, R. (1992) *Dictionary of Personnel and Human Resource Management*. London: Pitman.

Bowen, J. and Basch, T. (1992) 'Strategies for creating customer-oriented organizations'. In R. Teare and M. Olsen (eds), *International Hospitality Management: Corporate Strategy in Action*. pp. 199–219, London: Pitman

British Standards Institute (1987) *BS4778, Quality Vocabulary*. London: BSI.

Brymer, R.A. (1991) 'Employee empowerment: a ghost-driven leadership strategy'. *Cornell Hotel and Restaurant Administration Quarterly*, **32**, 59.

Carlzon, J. (1987) *Moments of Truth*. New York: Harper & Row.

Collard, R. (1991) *Total Quality: Success through People*. London: Institute of Personnel Management.

Farnham, D. and Pimlott, J. (1990) *Understanding Industrial Relations*, 4th edn. London: Cassell.

Goss-Turner, S. (1994) 'Human resources and line management: a changing relationship'. Paper presented at CHME HRM Conference, February, London.

Guerrier, Y. and Lockwood, A. (1989) 'Core and peripheral employees in hotel operations'. *Personnel Review*, **18**, 9–13.

Guerrier, Y. and Pye, G. (1994) 'Managing human resources in restaurant and catering outlets'. In B. Davies and A. Lockwood (eds), *Food and Beverage Management*, pp. 161–70. Oxford: Butterworth-Heinemann.

Guest, D.E. (1987) 'HRM and industrial relations'. *Journal of Management Studies*, **24**(5), 503–21.

Guest, D.E. (1989) 'HRM, its implications for industrial relations'. In J. Storey (ed.), *New Perspectives on Human Resource Management*, pp. 41–55. London: Routledge.

Handy, C. (1986) *Understanding Organizations*. Harmondsworth: Penguin.

Handy, C. (1994) *The Empty Raincoat: Making Sense of the Future*. London: Hutchinson.

Heap, J. (1992) *Productivity Management: a Fresh Approach*. London: Cassell.

Ingold, A. and Worthington, T. (1994) 'Extraordinary customer satisfaction: the road to success'. In R. Teare *et al.* (eds), *Achieving Quality Performance*, pp. 111–42. London: Cassell.

Johns, N. (1995) 'Development of quality management in the hospitality industry'. In R. Teare (ed.), *Quality Management in the Hospitality Industry*. London: Cassell.

Johns, N. and Chesterton, J. (1994) 'ICL Kidsgrove: snapshot of a changing culture'. In R. Teare *et al.* (eds), *Achieving Quality Performance: Lessons from British Industry*, pp. 79–110. London: Cassell.

Johns, N. and Wheeler, K.L. (1991) 'Productivity and perfomance monitoring and measurement'. In R. Teare (ed.), *Strategic Hospitality Management*. London: Cassell.

Johns, N., Wheeler, K.L. and Cowe, P. (1992) 'Productivity angles on *sous vide* production'. In R. Teare, S. Adams and S. Messenger (eds), *Managing Projects in Hospitality Organizations*. London: Cassell, pp. 146–68.

Jones, P. (1988) 'Quality, capacity and productivity in service industries'. *International Journal of Hospitality Management*, 7(2), 104–12.

Jones, P. (1990) 'Managing foodservice productivity in the long term: strategy, structure and performance'. *International Journal of Hospitality Management*, 9(2), 143–54.

Jones, P. and Lockwood, A. (1989) *The Management of Hotel Operations*. London: Cassell.

Jones, P. and Lockwood, A. (1990) 'Productivity and the product life cycle in hospitality firms'. *International Journal of Contemporary Hospitality Management* Launch Conference, Dorset Institute, Bournemouth.

Kelliher, C. and Johnston, K. (1987) 'Personnel management in hotels – some empirical observations'. *International Journal of Hospitality Management*, 6(2), 103–8.

King-Taylor, L. (1993) *Quality: Sustaining Customer Service*. London: Century Business.

Lashley, C. (1993) 'Consultancy work for McDonald's'. Private communication to the author.

McFarlane, A. (1982) 'Trade union growth the employer and the hotel and restaurant industry: a case study'. *Industrial Relations Journal*, 13(4), 29–42.

Maxwell, G. (1993) 'Service quality: the HRM dimension strategy'. Paper presented at the IAHMS Spring Conference.

National Economic Development Council (NEDC) (1992) *Working Party on Competitiveness in Tourism and Leisure, Sub-Group Report: Costs and Manpower Productivity in UK Hotels*. London: HMSO.

Oakland, J. (1989) *Total Quality Management*. London: Heinemann.

Olsen, M.C. (1989) 'Issues facing multi-unit hospitality organizations in a maturing market'. *Journal of Contemporary Hospitality Management*, 1(2), 3–6.

Parry, B. and Collins, B. (1993) 'Where is facilities management going?'. *International Journal of Contemporary Hospitality Management*, 5(2), 36–40.

Peters, T.J. and Waterman, R.H. (1982) *In Search of Excellence: Lessons from America's Best Run Companies*. New York: Harper & Row.

Pickworth, J. (1994) 'Framework of the main variables influencing organization productivity'. In B. Davis and A. Lockwood (eds), *Food and Beverage Management*, pp. 277–83. Oxford: Butterworth-Heinemann.

Pizam, A. (1993) 'Managing cross-cultural hospitality enterprises'. In P. Jones and A. Pizam (eds), *The International Hospitality Industry: Organizational and Operational Issues*, pp. 205–23. London: Pitman.

Price, L. (1994) 'Poor personnel practice in the hospitality industry: does it matter?' *Human Resource Management Journal*, 4(4), 44–62.

Ritzer, G. (1992) *The McDonaldization of Society*. London: Pine Forge Press.

Sternberg, L.E. (1992) 'Empowerment: trust versus control'. *The Cornell Hotel and Restaurant Administration Quarterly*, 33(1), 69–72.

Storey, J. (1992) 'HRM in action: the truth is out at last'. *Personnel Management*, April, 28–31.

Torrington, D. and Hall, L. (1991) *Personnel Management: a New Approach*, 2nd edn. Englewood Cliffs, NJ: Prentice Hall.

Umbreit, W.T. (1987) 'When will the hospitality industry pay attention to effective personnel practices?' *Hospitality Education and Research Journal*, **11**, 3–14.

Watson, S. and D'Annunzio-Green, N. (1994) 'The influence of organizational structure on personnel management: a move towards HRM'. Paper presented at the CHME Research Conference, April, Napier University, Edinburgh.

Witt, C.A. and Witt, S.F. (1989) 'Why productivity in the hotel sector is low'. *International Journal of Contemporary Hospitality Management*, **1**(2), 28–33.

Wood, R.C. (1992) *Working in Hotels and Catering*. London: Routledge.

Wood, R.C. (1994) *Organizational Behaviour for Hospitality Management*. Oxford: Butterworth-Heinemann.

Yeoman, I. (1995) Private communication to the author.

SEVEN

Productivity in the hotel industry: a cognitive case study

Ian Yeoman, Tony Ingold and Sarah Peters

INTRODUCTION

This chapter examines the dimensions of productivity through the eyes of hotel managers, using the process of cognitive mapping. The results provide insight into management attitudes towards productivity. They also permit an analysis of the relationship between quality, organizational type and size, training, personnel policies and management roles.

The complexity of the productivity concept can be seen from the diversity of available definitions. *Chambers' Dictionary* defines productivity as 'the rate of or efficiency of work, especially in industrial production', but Heap (1992. p. 3) comments that 'most people when faced with the term have some understanding of its use but would be hard pressed to offer a definition'. Medlik (1989) relates the term virtually solely to labour productivity (e.g. number of covers, number of guest visits) per work hour. Prokopenko (1987), on the other hand, argues that productivity 'means different things to different people. However, the basic concept is always the ratio of output to input, a simple equation of resource conversion.' At the operational level there is some disagreement and confusion over the meaning of productivity in service systems, owing to inherent service dimensions of intangibility, perishability, heterogeneity and simultaneity (Mahoney, 1988). McLaughlin and Coffey (1990) argue, however, that these characteristics should not be considered a reason to avoid measurement of service productivity. They suggest that operations managers should be trained to recognize and use productivity measures inherent in services, i.e. those based on customization, complexity and the degree of aggregation.

PRODUCTIVITY AND THE HOTEL INDUSTRY

Medlik (1988) notes that productivity in the hospitality industry declined by 0.7 per cent per annum between 1979 and 1985, while Ball (1994) finds it to have been only two-thirds that of the manufacturing sector in the early 1990s. Reasons for this difference are examined by Witt and Witt (1989). They conclude that a major problem for managers seeking to control productivity is that of *ceteris paribus*, i.e. the need to hold other influences constant when examining the impact of a particular factor. Hospitality productivity is affected by numerous factors, including labour, grade and type of hotel, product/service mix, nature of the technical systems and remuneration. These tend to be highly interdependent, making it very difficult to identify the effect of one particular influence.

However, several studies have attempted to examine the effects of individual factors. For example, Van der Hoeven and Thurik (1984) studied productivity in European hotels using an operations research model. They concluded that productivity was influenced by advanced booking, which enabled hotel managers to plan and to match supply to demand. In addition, economies of scale could be obtained for larger, affiliated hotels because of their purchasing power and the advantages of inventory management systems. The National Institute of Economics and Social Research (1989) undertook a comparative study of hotels in Great Britain and Germany. The research concluded that the main factor affecting hotel performance in the two countries was the level of qualified manpower. A survey by the National Economic Development Council (NEDC) (1992) found that British hoteliers had a general ignorance of labour productivity measures, coupled with a poor understanding of productivity management techniques. Witt and Clark (1990) surveyed hotel managers, finding that 40 per cent of respondents were aware of productivity management techniques such as activity sampling, classification coding, critical path analysis and time study. Lee-Ross and Ingold (1994) regard the knowledge and understanding of productivity of managers in small hotels as questionable. They point out that previous studies of productivity within the hotel industry have not taken into account hotels of fewer than 20 bedrooms, which make up some 80 per cent of the UK hotel industry.

DIMENSIONS OF HOTEL PRODUCTIVITY

Customization

Lovelock (1991) notes that because services are created as they are consumed, and because the customer is often actually involved in the production process, there is far more scope for tailoring the service to meet the individual needs of the consumer. He proposes the model shown in Table 7.1, which relates the degree of customization to: (a) how much the characteristics of the service and its delivery system incline it towards customization; and (b) how much judgement customer-contact personnel are able to exercise in defining the nature of the service received by individual customers.

The customization of service has profound implications for productivity because there is conflict between the addition of product value and the reduction of costs

Table 7.1. Customization and judgement in service delivery

Extent to which customer contact personnel exercise judgement in meeting individual customer needs	Extent to which service characteristics are customized	
	High	Low
High	Legal services Health care/surgery Architectural design Real estate agency Taxi service Beautician Plumber Education (tutorials)	Education (large classes) Preventive health programmes
Low	Telephone service Hotel services Retail banking (excluding major loans) Good restaurant	Public transportation Routine appliance repair Fast-food restaurant Movie theatre Spectator sports

Source: Lovelock (1991, p. 30).

through standardization. Processes of price–value trade-off and competitive positioning are fundamental to customization. For example, the Forte Hotel Group undertook a rebranding exercise to focus its property portfolio towards its various customer segments (Connell, 1992), making it easier for customers to choose between the type of hotel they needed. Forte, the largest single player in the United Kingdom accommodation market, divided its hotels into three brands, three collections and four branded products. Branded hotels had comparatively well defined service characteristics, i.e. low-customization and judgement in service delivery according to Lovelock's (1991) matrix (Table 7.1). For example, hotels within the brand of Posthouse and Travelodge were product-oriented, with a high element of standardization. Each Forte product brand defined what it offered its customers, establishing a level of service appropriate to its market segment. Consolidation of the customer focus in this way enabled the Forte group to examine the issue of productivity in service delivery. For example, there is a set, standard cleaning servicing time of 15 minutes for a Travelodge bedroom. This type of standardization also allows a degree of productivity measurement. Slattery (1991) examines the development of branding and the implications for the hotel industry in the 1990s, noting that 'branding will remain a dominant feature in the international hospitality industry. Hotel brands will achieve higher productivity through economies of scale, underpinned by the use of reservation systems and marketing.'

The role of quality

The acceptable quality level (AQL) of a product or service is defined as the poorest level of quality the producer and consumer are willing to accept (Heizer and Render,

1993). This target or tolerance level is in effect a balance between productivity and quality. The role of the operations manager is thus to deliver a quality service at least cost (and hence at the right price). AQL is a tactical decision process involving the assessment of risk to both consumer and producer. Jones and Lockwood (1989) define quality in terms of fitness for purpose, moving the emphasis away from the producer to the consumer. Hotel managers thus do not need to produce the best but the best at the price the customer is prepared to pay. In this context a suitable definition of quality is that of the British Standards Institute (1983): 'The totality of features and characteristics of a product or service that bear on its ability to satisfy a given need.'

Quality and productivity are inextricably linked, but the relationship is nebulous, even in the manufacturing sector. For example, Ingold and Worthington (1994) note in their study of Land Rover that continuous quality improvement (CQI) had a very positive effect on the productivity of the company, although the specific links proved elusive and difficult to quantify. Reynolds and Ingold (1994) note that there have been relatively few documented examples of successfully implemented CQI programmes in the service industries and very few in the hospitality sector. They cite as examples the Ritz-Carlton Group in the United States, which in 1993 received the Malcolm Baldridge Award. The Marriott Corporation is also well known for its commitment to total quality management (TQM).

Two sets of criteria may be used to evaluate the productivity benefits of CQI/TQM programmes. There are direct impacts which arise from such activities as problem-solving, and indirect effects from aspects such as reduced employee absenteeism, lower accident rates and improved relationships between employees at all levels in the company. One major drawback in most research in this area seems to be the lack of *a priori* measures. Many CQI/TQM programmes seem to have been introduced without the establishment of measures for productivity. This makes it impossible later to measure any improvements that have come about as a result of the implemented programmes. Measurement of the indirect effects of CQI/TQM programmes may involve the collection of attitudinal data. Hutchins (1986) refers to the indirect impact of such programmes as the 'magic dust effect'. Productivity improvements seem to occur by a conscious or unconscious concerted effort of the workforce, owing to enhanced feelings of trust, personal satisfaction and self-esteem, pride in job performance and in the organization. Together these lead to greater cooperation and care for the customer.

The role of management

Kast and Rosenzweig (1985) describe the managerial function in terms of the achievement of organizational purpose. At the core it involves making decisions that maintain the balance that is necessary to achieve organizational performance objectives. The management function involves goal-setting, planning, assembling resources, organizing, implementing and controlling, although these may take place in an informal, integrated way. Hotel managers are central to the interactive processes that maintain the equilibrium between customer needs and organizational goals.

Stewart (1982) describes the manager's role as composed of constraints, choices and demands and comments. Arnaldo (1981) surveyed 194 American hotel general managers who indicated their activities in the terms of Mintzberg's (1973) ten managerial roles. They also indicated the amount of time and importance assigned to each role. Arnaldo suggests that the activities of leader, monitor, disseminator and entrepreneur are the most critical factors. Lee-Ross (1993) relates management styles in seasonal seaside hotels to the job satisfaction of employees. He notes that management styles fell into two main categories: 'hands-on', where managers tended to work alongside operatives undertaking similar tasks, and coordinative, where managers delegated tasks to operatives for most of the time.

Heap (1992) suggests that a successful strategy of productivity improvement should involve all the functions and personnel within an organization. This style of productivity improvement initiative is not about finding faults and imposing solutions on an unwilling or uncooperative workforce. Instead, management must build an organization that treats all employees with respect and uses their enthusiasm to identify and solve productivity problems. A similar approach appears in quality improvement programmes of the TQM/CQI type, which are also claimed to have a beneficial effect upon productivity (Ingold and Worthington, 1994; Johns and Chesterton, 1994).

Watson and D'Annunzio-Green (1994) consider the implications of organizational structure for management productivity within a major hotel group. Their study examined a shift from a traditional personnel management function towards a human resource management approach. The group's strategy was to remove personnel managers from the units, replacing them with regional personnel and training services. This emphasized the role of personnel and training in the hotels. Regional managers were based away from the units and therefore not distracted by operational concerns. Unit and departmental managers moved towards general management competencies, rather than emphasizing technical skills.

Boyatzis (1982) defines management competencies as 'determined by types of actions and their place in the system and sequence of behaviour and what the results or effects were, and what the intent or meaning of the actions and results were'. Schroder (1989) defines competencies in the context of organizational effectiveness. Managerial competencies are personal effectiveness skills, and at the lowest level include 'entry competencies' (the abilities and skills personnel bring to the organization). Competencies are also the consequences of socialization and education. Broadly speaking, basic competencies are task-related personal effectiveness skills. Higher competencies are a relatively stable set of behaviours which produce significantly superior workgroup performance in organizational environments.

Baum (1989) studied general managers' perceptions of the competencies required by potential hotel managers, and his results emphasize a 'soft' approach to management. Technical skills were not seen as essential because they were often included in company training programmes. This 'soft' approach to management is also discussed by Pickworth (1994), who stresses that higher productivity in the long term can only be achieved by means of a 'softer' or behavioural approach.

Employee productivity

Lee-Ross and Ingold (1994) identify the importance of multi-skilling to productivity in the small hotel sector. Multi-skilling involves cross-training staff in a number of different task areas, and is a way of matching available labour to the peaks and troughs of service demand. Multi-skilled staff have been common for many years in small hotel operations, and larger hotel organizations have recently moved towards this concept in order to increase labour productivity and flexibility (Johns, 1993). In TGI Friday's restaurants (Guerrier and Pye, 1994), operatives progress from kitchen to restaurant to bar. At Little Chef, progression is from food service operative to chef. Both these examples are part of the trend towards softening the boundaries between back-of-house and front-of-house staff. This results in decreased departmental conflict, better team spirit and flexibility of labour.

Multi-skilling uses the principle of job design to bring the outputs of a business into line with the organizational structure and enables hotels to develop a flexible strategy towards productivity improvement. Bagguley (1990) also suggests that research into labour policies for the hospitality industry has developed because of flexible labour demand. Flexibility is considered an operational management strategy by Atkinson (1985) who defines four different types:

1   Functional flexibility, concerned with the flexibility of employees and their competence to handle different tasks and move between jobs.
2   Numerical flexibility, related to the capacity to accommodate the number of employees' hours in answer to shifts in demand.
3   Pay flexibility, concerned with reward methods that encourage functional flexibility.
4   Distancing strategies, concerned with contracting out operations to shift burdens of hazard or uncertainty elsewhere.

Atkinson's (1985) strategies of job flexibility are central to the role of operations managers in the hotel industry. Job flexibility techniques are also highlighted by Watson and D'Annunzio-Green (1994) in their study. Movement towards a flatter organizational structure within hotels leads to better team effectiveness and improved communication within hotels. Team effectiveness (Russell, 1991) allows higher productivity in hotels, shared goals, reduced conflict and the opportunity for team members to solve problems through their own initiative.

The relationship between employee motivation and productivity improvement has been widely discussed (e.g. Jones and Lockwood, 1989). Sornchai (1986) mentions motivation factors in terms of intrinsic and extrinsic outcomes. This classification enables hotel managers to examine the job of hotel operatives in the contexts of job enlargement, job rotation and job enrichment. Jones and Lockwood (1989) stress the importance of motivation in job design in order to achieve efficient fulfilment of the task at an equitable rate of return. A survey of a number of successful companies by Peters and Waterman (1982) identifies several crucial business themes relevant to hospitality organizations. These include:

1   Inclination for activity, where companies had a disposition towards open channels and unhindered communication.
2   Importance of the customer as a means of increasing revenue rather than a focus upon cutting costs.
3   Entrepreneurship, i.e. the competence to grow large while retaining the high performance characteristics of a small operation.
4   People focus, i.e. an emphasis on results through people.
5   Beliefs to stand by; in other words a commitment to communicate values to customers and to stick to them.

6　Stick to what you know; in other words successful operations expand only into areas related to their basic expertise.

7　Simple and clear structure; this forces authority downward through the company and permits the empowerment of front-line employees.

8　Advancing individual employees within the context of company objectives.

Mills (1989) notes that a corporate culture which has these characteristics facilitates productivity improvement. Conversely, Glover (1987) identifies cultural characteristics that may impede productivity. These include lack of standards, unbalanced accountability, ineffective communications, lack of recognition, treating symptoms not causes, inadequate or absent teamwork, recriminations and an absence of managerial effectiveness.

Training is a key means of increasing productivity in the workplace (Jewell, 1993). It conveys the productivity mission (or message) and also provides employees with the special skills needed to achieve productivity improvement. Training is thus a key element in organizational effectiveness. Barker (1989) highlights the importance of training for successful hospitality operations and notes the need for managers to devise a strategy to use training effectively. Ranfti (1984) examines the relationship between productivity and training, finding that managers place a strong emphasis upon training for personal productivity in relation to Maslow's (1943) needs of esteem and self-actualization. Delivery of training in the workplace can also be achieved by the use of National Vocational Qualifications (NVQs). These represent part of a UK government strategy to improve training in the workplace. Russell (1991) describes the use of an NVQ programme to improve standards and productivity in the hospitality industry.

Physical layout and design

Mills (1989) notes that productivity is affected by the interaction between employees and their work environment. Efficient layout is important to profitable and productive operation (Beer, 1987). Kirk (1994) discusses the importance of task scheduling, ergonomic analysis and work study for productive design. Poor design can lead to unproductive and wasted work effort. Johns (1994) discusses the impact of kitchen layout upon productivity and notes elsewhere (Johns, 1993) that kitchen space represents an opportunity cost in hotel design. The basis of kitchen design is ergonomic efficiency, defined as the best use of human movement in the workplace. Johns (1994) discusses the techniques that can be used to minimize the unnecessary movement of kitchen staff. According to Brown (1995), 20 per cent of hotels are purpose-built. Johns (1993) notes that in the purpose-built Marriott Courtyard brand productivity is promoted through services, bedroom equipment and better energy management. Thus a purpose-built unit permits output to be maximized while minimizing operating costs.

Other factors

Slattery (1992) notes that the labour productivity of small, unaffiliated hotels depends partly upon the work contribution of family members. This formula is productive in itself, as it often leads to lower than average rates of pay. However, unaffiliated hotels offer their employees jobs, rather than career structures, and provide only limited training. They attract fewer graduates, pay lower salaries and offer fewer organizational benefits than affiliated establishments. According to Brown (1994), budgetary control in the hospitality industry depends on the following criteria:

1 Objectives must be clearly defined.
2 The output must be measurable.
3 A predictive model is required.
4 It must be possible to take remedial action when actual performance deviates from that budgeted.

Discussions thus far have examined hospitality productivity in terms of isolated inputs and outputs. A holistic picture can only be obtained by examining perceptions of productivity.

Perception and attitude

The human environment, and hence the senses, are continually bombarded with stimuli of all kinds. *Perception* is the process of organizing, processing and interpreting them. The perceptual process follows the sequence: stimulus, attention, organization, interpretation and response (McKenna, 1987), the latter depending upon interpreting stimuli and 'reading' a situation or event. *Attitude* is defined (Second and Backman, 1969) as: 'certain regularities of an individual's feelings, thoughts and predispositions to act toward some aspect of his environment'. According to Arnold *et al.* (1991), an attitude consists of three components: an affective aspect (i.e. feelings), a cognitive aspect (thoughts), and a behavioural aspect (i.e. the predisposition to do something). Attitudes are judgemental, reflecting an inclination to feel, think or behave towards objects in a particular way. The affective component of an attitude is reflected in a person's physiological responses and the intentions expressed about the object of the attitude. The cognitive component is reflected in thoughts and beliefs expressed about the object. The behavioural component is reflected by observed and expressed behaviour towards the object. Thus, for the purposes of the present study, individuals' feelings about, perceptions of and actions towards productivity may be assessed from an analysis of their comments and behaviour.

Cognitive mapping

One way to represent and analyse perceptual attitudes is through cognitive maps. Such maps may be produced by interviewing subjects and then transcribing and linking the concepts they express on a chart. Cognitive mapping was selected for the present research because it allowed the concepts surrounding productivity to be considered in a holistic way. It was adopted as an attempt to overcome the *ceteris paribus* limitation of previous work. The technique may be explained as follows. Cognitions are the belief systems that people use to interpret events around them (Swan and Newell, 1994). To make sense of the world in this way requires 'models' (also known as 'constructs') that represent concepts and relationships and facilitate predictions about possible future events. Cognitive maps make it possible to investigate the ways in which people organize and interrelate their cognitions in a visual and practical form (Eden *et al.*, 1983).

Cognitive mapping provides valuable clues to how a problem owner perceives a given problem (Ackermann *et al.*, 1994). A picture of the problem situation is built up by capturing the chains of argument in interview and linking the insights together. Aims and objectives can be identified and explored and options examined to see which are the most beneficial and whether more details need to be considered. Dilemmas, feedback loops and conflicts can be quickly identified, explored and resolved. In the present study, cognitive maps were used to identify and represent managerial cognitions of productivity in the hotel industry. The research described here was part of a larger study on productivity within the industry, undertaken jointly by the Research Department of Birmingham College of Food, Tourism and Creative Studies, and the Hotel and Catering Training Company (HCTC). Target interviewees were hotel general managers, or their appropriate nominees.

RESEARCH DESIGN

A restricted random sample was taken at several levels: country level (i.e. England, Scotland and Wales), area level (e.g. city centre, countryside and seaside resort hotels) and number of bedrooms. The sampling frame selected was the 1993 *Automobile Association Hotel and Restaurant Guide*. The sample was as follows:

AA star rating	Number of hotels
No star hotel	5
One star hotel	0
Two star hotel	10
Three star hotel	5
Four star hotel	5
Five star hotel	3

The research technique principally used was the semi-structured interview. It was intended that all interviews would be comparable in terms of content, but would allow interviewees to express themselves more fully on each point. Interviews, which averaged 1.5 hours, were conducted by a team of carefully briefed interviewers, in order to ensure comparability of results. They produced a mixture of quantitative and subjective information, together with some anecdotal evidence.

The recorded interviews were transcribed and results analysed using the cognitive mapping software *Graphics Cope* (Moriarty and Jones, 1992). Several types of analysis were used. Domain analysis (Eden & Ackerman, 1992) provided a measure of the local complexity of issues but not of the overall complexity. It allowed exploration of the richness of meaning of each particular concept and also provided a means of identifying the main concepts from cognitive maps. Since a very large amount of qualitative data was collected, only the ten most mentioned concepts were examined from each cognitive map at the domain analysis level.

Central analysis (Eden and Ackermann, 1992) was used to examine the concept of productivity from a broader perspective. It permitted the evaluation of relationships at a more indirect level, providing insight into the centrality of concepts within the whole model. Here again, only the ten most frequently mentioned concepts were analysed. Cognitive maps produce a very large amount of qualitative data, and when several maps were merged into one strategic map, the data sometimes appeared irrelevant because individuality was lost. Cognitive maps that showed a high proportion of common concepts were subjected to further path analysis in order to extract further qualitative information.

DOMAIN ANALYSIS RESULTS

Domain analysis of the cognitive maps produced the top ten concepts shown in Table 7.2. Local analysis of each cognitive concept revealed both positive (i.e. helpful) and negative (i.e. hindering) associations between them.

Role of the manager was perceived to have the largest influence on productivity (score 194) and this was associated with related management verbs of *measurement* (score 68) and *standards* (score 60). *Importance of management* was also associated with *management competencies* (score 36) but only barely with *management development training* (score 6). In general staff terms, *training* was perceived to have a significant relationship with *productivity* (score 144) but *National Vocational Qualifications (NVQs)* received a neutral output, (score 10 positive, but 8 negative), reflecting indifferent views towards NVQs. This indifference was also more or less apparent for *qualifications* (score 17 positive, but 8 negative). However, the concept of *multi-skilling* was quite strongly associated with *productivity* (score 32). The importance of *staff* to *productivity* was generally recognized (score 90), as one might expect in a labour intensive industry. Although *staff* scored highly, *teams* only scored 4.

Quality had a perceived relationship with *productivity* (score 84) and was associated positively with *measurement* (score 68), *standards* (score 60), *product* (score 14) and *consistency* (score 12). *Quality* was negatively associated with *measurement* (score 6) and the *balance between profit and the customer* (score 4). The importance of accounting procedures to *productivity* was highlighted with a score of 74 in terms of *cost centres, budgets and control*. Accounting terms were generally associated with productivity; for example, *measurement* (score 68), *forecasting* (score 44) and *profit* (score 20). Dimensions such as the *role of the manager, training, staff, quality, cost centres, budgets and control, measurement* and *standards* collectively represented a score of 654. *Building design* was less strongly linked with *productivity* (score 4), demonstrating that the concept was not seen as a primary influence.

CENTRAL ANALYSIS RESULTS

Central analysis was conducted by scoring the top ten concepts from the 28 maps according to their interconnective links with other cognitive perceptions. The results of this phase of the analysis are shown in Table 7.3.

Table 7.2. Domain analysis: perceived impact of productivity in hotels

Concept		Score
1	Role of the manager	194
2	Training	144
3	Staff	90
4	Quality	84
5	Cost centres/budgets/control	74
6	Measurement	68
7	Standards	60
8	Forecasting	44
9	Management competencies	36
10	Motivation/reward/effort	32
10	Multi-skilling	32
12	Profit	20
13	Organizational structure	16
15	Motivation	16
16	Product	14
17	Consistency	12
17	Qualifications (+)	12
17	Efficiency	12
20	Purchasing	10
21	NVQs (+)	10
21	Customer	10
23	Market	9
24	NVQs (−)	8
24	Qualifications (−)	8
24	Team	8
27	Capital finance	6
27	Planning	6
27	Rate of pay	6
27	Measurement (−)	6
27	Completion	6
32	Management development	5
33	Career structure (−)	4
33	Balance between profit and customer	4
33	Building design	4
34	Entrepreneurship	4

Table 7.3. Central analysis: perceived impact of productivity in hotels

Concept		Score
1	Training	217
2	Role of the manager	215
3	Measurement	149
4	Quality	99
5	Staff	92
6	Flat organization	64
7	Building design and layout	63
8	Don't understand the term productivity	39
9	Marketing	39
10	Service level	35
11	Cost of labour	31
12	Reward/motivation/effort	31
13	Customer	30
14	Multi-skilling	29
15	Information technology	28
16	Purchasing	26
17	Standards	25
18	Efficiency	23
19	Staff development	23
20	Team	23
21	Motivation	20
22	Qualifications	19
23	Role of personnel and training manager	17
24	Quality versus quantity	17
25	Top-down management	16
26	Planning	16
27	Product	16
28	Culture	15
29	Gross profit margins	15
30	Weather	15
31	Staff (−)	15
32	BS5750 (−)	15
33	Guest satisfaction	14
34	Fear of getting it wrong	14
35	Control	14
36	Cost	13
37	Sales	13
38	Recession	13
39	Duty managers	12
40	Management competencies	12
41	Flexibility	11
42	Systems and procedures	10
43	Head office (−)	10
44	Competition	10
45	Targets	9
46	Forecasting	6
47	Atmosphere	6
48	Best use of resources	6

The most important perceived influence was *training* (score 217), which showed a direct connection with most other concepts in hotel managers' perceptions of *productivity*. The *role of the manager* (score 215), was perceived as the second most important influence upon productivity and central analysis indicated this concept to be a shaper of productivity within the overall cognitive structure. Significantly, it was linked to almost all the other concepts, on all the cognitive maps. *Measurement* (score 149) was seen as a key dimension of successful productivity implementation, related to *quality* (score 99), *training* (score 217), *staff* (92) *reward, motivation and effort* (score 31) and numerous others. Successful *utilization of staff* scored 99 against *productivity*. The fundamental aspects of productivity were found to be *training, the role of manager, measurement, quality* and *staff,* which scored 680 between them.

Some concepts received significantly higher scores in central analysis than in domain analysis. These included *building design and layout* (score 63, up from 4), *marketing* (score 39, up from 9), *service level* (score 35, up from nil), *flat organization* (score 64, up from nil) and *information technology* (score 28, up from nil). These concepts were apparently perceived as secondary or underpinning influences on productivity. Concepts which received a lower score in central analysis than in domain analysis included *budgeting/cost centres* (not scored) and *control* (score 14, down from 74) and *forecasting* (score 6, down from 44). *Standards* (score 25, down from 60) could be interpreted as meaning 'standards' as a fundamental aspect rather than a secondary influence.

A number of other concepts appeared in the central analysis that were not present in the domain analysis. These included the *role of the personnel and training manager* (score 17), *guest satisfaction* (score 14), *weather* (score 15), *recession* (score 13), *systems and procedures* (score 10) and *atmosphere* (score 6). An interesting dimension of hotel managers' perceptions of productivity was the response: *don't understand the term productivity.* This was presumably related to the issue of defining productivity within the hospitality industry. Negative influences upon productivity included *BS5750* (score 15), *staff* (score 15) and *head office* (score 10).

PATH ANALYSIS RESULTS

Productivity

Managers' overall understanding, or *Weltanschauung,* of productivity was explored by a closer examination of the terminology and symbolism they used. For example, the cognitive map of the manager of a five-star, 300-bedroom hotel showed the complex understanding of the subject illustrated in Figure 7.1. This manager defined productivity as 'achieving best value through the balance of good service and wage costs', and the figure correspondingly shows the output of achieving productivity linked to quality.

This map also shows links between *manning levels, service levels, structure* and *the role of the manager.* Secondary concepts are examined in Figure 7.2, which shows a still greater depth of comprehension.

By contrast, the perceptions of a manager from a four-star, 250-bedroom hotel represented in Figure 7.3 are that productivity is related to *training, motivation, the role of the manager, fear of getting it wrong, don't understand, measurement* and *knowledge of output.*

The manager of a branded roadside hotel related productivity to *design of the building, correct equipment, part-time staff* and the *role of the manager.* This manager defined productivity as 'making the most of what you have got', and viewed productive performance as 'achieving 100 per cent occupancy'. This perception of productivity represents the low–low quadrant in Lovelock's (1991) customization and

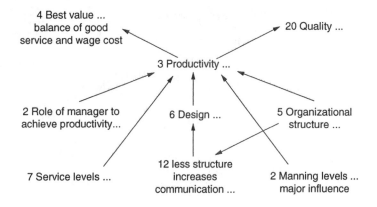

4 Best value ...
balance of good
service and wage cost

20 Quality ...

3 Productivity ...

2 Role of manager to
achieve productivity...

6 Design ...

5 Organizational
structure ...

7 Service levels ...

12 less structure
increases
communication ...

2 Manning levels ...
major influence

Figure 7.1. Domain analysis: productivity: Five Star, 300 bedrooms

judgement model of service delivery. A similar perception of productivity was expressed by the manager of a three-star, 200 bedroom, branded airport hotel. Productivity was linked with the concepts *role of the manager, training* and *measurement,* which this individual defined as 'value for money for the client within the framework of predetermined costs and standards'. *Measurement* and *benchmarking* were seen as the keys to achieving productivity, defined as the 'measure of efficiency within determined costs and guest satisfaction levels'. Managers of smaller hotels exhibited a more general business approach to productivity. The manager of a 20-bedroom coastal hotel emphasized *cash flow* as a factor, and defined productivity as 'giving the customer what he wants at a price'. Concepts that influenced productivity included *location, recession, organizational structure, repeat business* and the *manage-ment of staff.* The manager of a larger (80-bedroom), independent seaside hotel could not define productivity, saying that 'it just seemed to happen'. This manager perceived productivity to be influenced by *building design* (positive), some *unreliable staff* (negative), *training* and the *role of the manager.* The manager of a similar, three-star, 40-bedroom hotel claimed no understanding of the term 'productivity', but was nevertheless able to identify *culture of a small company, location/access* (negative), *personality of staff, the role of the manager* and *weather/seasonal factors* as influences upon productivity. Measurement of success within the hotel was achieved by a series of gross profit ratios. Productivity depended upon a pool of multi-skilled core staff and training was seen as essential. The manager of another three-star, 25-bedroom hotel commented of productivity: 'the hotel has no policy, it [productivity] just happens'. Thus, perceived influences upon productivity differed according to the size of the hotel and the complexity of the operation.

Training

According to domain and central analysis, most of the managers perceived *training* to have a major influence upon productivity. The map displayed in Figure 7.4 represents

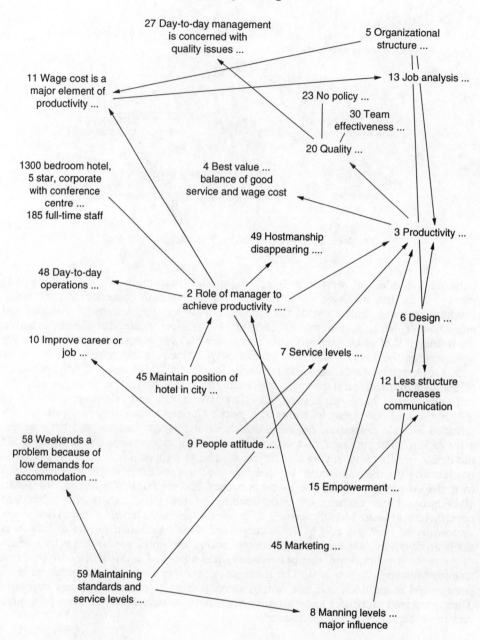

Figure 7.2. Central analysis: productivity: Five Star, 300 bedrooms

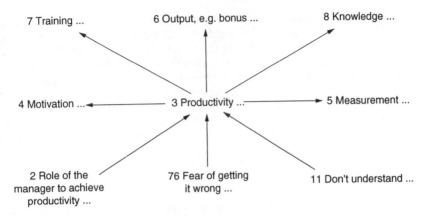

Figure 7.3. Productivity: Four Star, 250 bedrooms

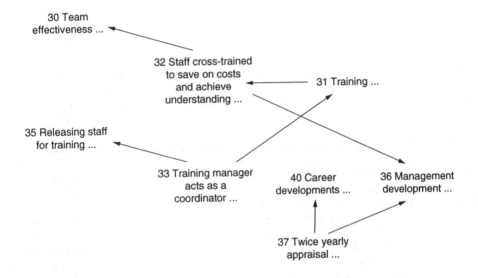

Figure 7.4. Training: Five Star, 300 bedrooms

the perceptions of a training manager in a five-star, 300-bedroom hotel and was one of the most complex models obtained.

This individual felt that training enabled staff to save on costs and gave them a better understanding of team effectiveness. The manager of a four-star, 250-bedroom hotel linked the concept of *training* to those of *training needs* and *legal aspects*. This hotel used an NVQ structure to provide workplace training that was believed to increase the productivity of staff. The manager of a branded airport hotel dedicated 5 per cent of his payroll costs to training, as he perceived it to be directly linked with productivity. This hotel also operated a pilot NVQ scheme in an effort to improve the skill and qualification levels of its staff. An independent, 60-bedroom hotel delivered its training (mostly legislation and food handling) by buying in the services of a local college. The manager of a branded roadside hotel felt that training was a central aspect of productivity improvement, which made staff better qualified, fulfilled legal requirements and improved staff retention. However, for training to be effective, it had to be seen by trainees to be practically oriented. This hotel also operated its own comprehensive training programmes, using a range of on-site, self-learning multimedia software packages for food hygiene and standards training. The manager considered NVQs to be of little value because of the expense they involved. The managers of six small hotels, of under 30 bedrooms, viewed training virtually as unnecessary, expressing the view that operatives were 'born with skills'.

The role of the manager

The 28 hotel managers interviewed rated the *role of the manager* as having the biggest influence on productivity. All the respondents, even those who had experienced problems defining productivity, stated that their role was concerned with improving productivity within the hotel. Managers in larger, branded, company-owned hotels had a clearer perception of their role, which was generally defined by the company. For example, the manager of a 200-bedroom airport hotel stated that his job was concerned with quality, productivity, qualifications, cost management, man management, marketing/sales and organization. His role as a manager therefore required qualities of leadership, common sense, facilitation and communication. By contrast, the manager of a branded roadside hotel saw his role as one of delivering standards, probably because decisions concerning the product/service mix had already been taken at head office level. This manager was concerned exclusively with service delivery and the customer interface. By contrast, the manager in a 56-bedroom, seasonal holiday hotel was concerned mainly with day-to-day activities such as accounts, acting the host and marketing. He felt that he was not directly concerned with productivity *per se*, which 'just seemed to happen'. Another 20-bedroom hotel was so small that the manager's approach was largely 'hands on' and he viewed his role as 'everything'. This hotel also had a high element of family involvement and staff were multi-skilled with little functional demarcation. The manager of a five-star, 300-bedroom hotel saw his role as ensuring that the company's brand image was upheld within the context of day-to-day operations. He perceived 'a lack of hostmanship' to be a negative influence on his role, as much of his time was spent on tactical decisions. Similarly, the manager of a 1000-bedroom, city-centre hotel was concerned with 'strategic management' and 'resource productivity' as his main priorities. The hotel industry is clearly very diverse and the manager's role may vary considerably between strategic and operational poles.

The quality dimension

The manager of a 300-bedroom, five-star hotel understood the complexity and dimensions of quality in similar terms to those of Jones and Lockwood (1989). At the

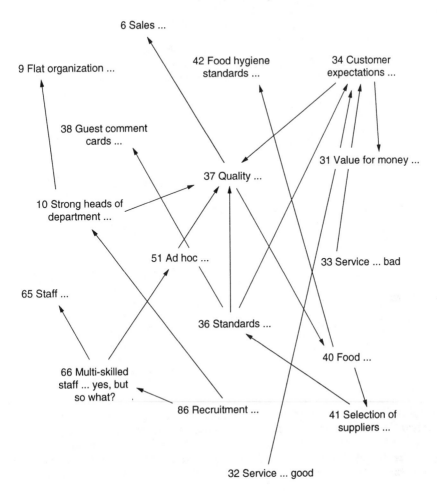

6 Sales ...

9 Flat organization ...

42 Food hygiene
standards ...

34 Customer
expectations ...

38 Guest comment
cards ...

31 Value for money ...

37 Quality ...

10 Strong heads of
department ...

51 Ad hoc ...

33 Service ... bad

65 Staff ...

36 Standards ...

40 Food ...

66 Multi-skilled
staff ... yes, but
so what?

86 Recruitment ...

41 Selection of
suppliers ...

32 Service ... good

Figure 7.5. Quality: Three Star, 56 bedrooms

domain level, *quality* was related positively to *productivity* and *intangibility*, and seen as the '*key to success*'. It was related negatively to *BS5750*. Quality outcomes were perceived as related to *team effectiveness* and *day-to-day management*. The negative influence of *BS5750* was perceived as being because of the systems and procedures involved, which were seen as too demanding upon managers' time. Problems of implementation were also perceived. The manager of a branded roadside hotel viewed quality as a fundamental aspect of the productivity equation. Quality was located at the core of the cognitive map, linking to all departments, to *consistency, delivery of standards, central reservation systems* and *part-time staff*. The delivered standards of a branded operation were seen as the quality threshold. Hotel managers all had their own understanding of quality, but all linked it directly with productivity. The manager of a 56-bedroom seasonal hotel related quality to standards and customer expectations, which were measured using guest comment cards. A central analysis view of this hotel manager's perceptions of quality is shown in Figure 7.5.

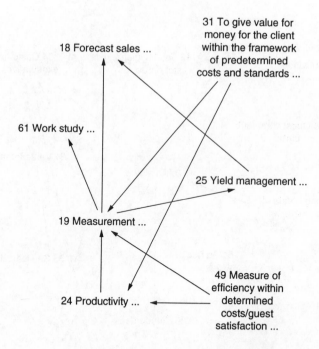

Figure 7.6. Measurement: Airport Hotel, 200 bedrooms

This map includes the dimensions *service, selection of suppliers, value for money, recruitment, multi-skilling* and *staff*. This central analysis view demonstrates how quality crosses a wide spectrum of concepts, so that a holistic view must be taken to comprehend it. Managers of small hotels also understood these dimensions of quality although they seldom operated systematic quality management procedures.

Productivity measurement

Domain and central analysis indicated a perceived overall need for productivity measurement. Concepts linked with *measurement* and *productivity* are shown in a cognitive map of the manager of a 200-bedroom airport hotel (Figure 7.6).

This manager viewed the link between productivity and measurement as 'the measure of efficiency within determined costs/guest satisfaction'. Productivity management techniques at this hotel included sales forecasting, work study and yield management. The manager of a four-star, 200-bedroom hotel viewed measurement in terms of yield management, plus a combination of different techniques. As productivity is such a complex area, no single measure could be used in isolation. The cognitive map also highlighted other problems of measurement, such as the different environments in which hotels operated and the intangibility of the hospitality 'product'. Managers of smaller hotels tended to view measurement as a matter of management accounting, e.g. simple gross profit statements on wages, food and liquor. Measurement seemed to be very much *ad hoc* in hotels of this kind, relying upon traditional management accounting controls, with little further development. Exceptions to this were housekeeping departments, which often used rule of thumb measures in smaller hotels. Managers might, for example, use a ratio of one room attendant to ten rooms as a working basis, but when asked why, replied: 'We have always used those standards.'

Motivation

Hotel managers perceived a clear link between *productivity* and *motivation*, a concept which they also related to *reward* and *effort*. This would seem to imply a perception that productivity improvement is linked to *reward systems*, but the latter concept received only a moderate score. Thus there appeared to be no universal perception of this link in the hotel industry, where reward systems were the exception rather than the rule. The manager of an 80-bedroom seaside hotel linked the concepts of *motivation*, *staff retention* and *the entrepreneur*. That of a similarly located, four-star, 200-bedroom hotel saw *motivation* as related to *personal objectives*, *personality traits* and *productivity*. Problems were perceived in connection with linking *motivation* to *reward* and *productivity*. These included the design of effective reward systems based upon individual, team or hotel-based productivity. This hotel manager had previously experienced problems with reward schemes, as some staff became jealous and team effectiveness was marred by conflict.

Building layout and design

Building design scored low in domain analysis but much higher in central analysis. Thus managers perceived little relationship between the design of premises and their day-to-day roles, but they did recognize the concept as influencing productivity in a more general sense. Figure 7.7 shows the cognitive map of *building layout and design* for the manager of a purpose-built, branded, roadside hotel. For this individual, the concept was linked to *correct equipment*, *ergonomics*, *productivity* and *wage cost percentage*.

Budgeting

Verbs relating to *budgeting* scored highly against productivity in domain analysis, but received very low scores in central analysis. This difference probably reflected the influence that managers felt they had over both productivity and budgeting. They were closely concerned with maintaining income, costs and therefore productivity at unit

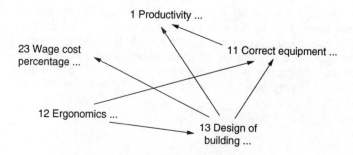

Figure 7.7. Building design: Branded Roadside Hotel

level. However, budget setting, and hence the design of productivity, tended to be a matter for head office, with which they were not concerned.

Staff

The concept of *staff* was strongly related to that of *productivity*, as well as to a number of other concepts. The cognitive map of a manager of a 20-bedroom, central London hotel showed *staff* as a key concept, with links to *lazy*, *mix of staff*, *selection* (a very important perceived link), *training* and *efficiency*. The output of the staff concept was related to good productivity. In effect, this manager believed that if the concepts influencing productivity were right, the staff would achieve good productivity. The manager of a three-star, 80-bedroom hotel expressed a similar view. Concepts that influenced staff were motivation, training and seasonality. The manager of a three-star, 100-bedroom hotel saw the staff resource as a cost centre, so that direction and resource productivity were the focus of management. Achievement of resource productivity was linked with the concepts of *training*, *multi-skilling*, *motivation*, *leadership*, *heads of department*, *flat organization*, *recruitment* and *measurement*. Central analysis revealed the importance of 'softer' issues of management, such as *motivation* and *reward*, in many of the cognitive maps. Domain analysis showed the predominant input into staff to be *training*, seen as influencing staff to achieve productivity.

A HIERARCHICAL MODEL OF HOTEL PRODUCTIVITY

A model of the factors perceived to influence productivity is shown in Figure 7.8. It uses the principles of Hitchins's (1992) unified systems hypothesis (UHS) and presents a four-level systems hierarchy in which the focus is the hotel managers' perception of productivity.

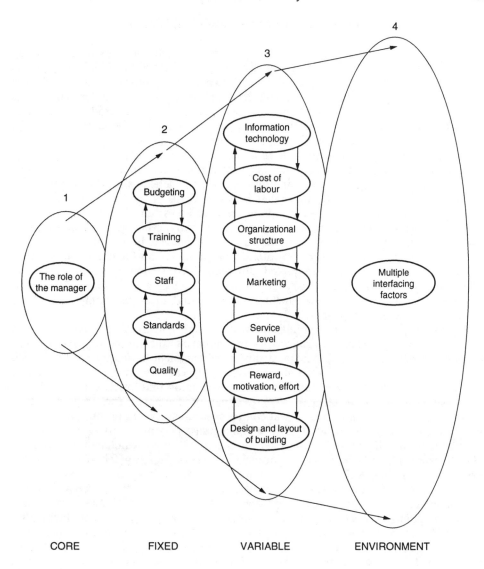

Figure 7.8. Model of hotel productivity hierarchy

THE CENTRAL CONCEPT OF PRODUCTIVITY

Central to the hierarchical model is the role of the hotel manager, viewed as a shaper, whose tasks and understanding are crucial to the achievement of productivity. This recalls the model proposed by Kast and Rosenzweig (1985), in which the manager and management task are central to the organization. It is also compatible with Jones and Lockwood's (1989) concept of productivity as an interface between employee performance and asset protection.

FIXED CONCEPTS OF PRODUCTIVITY

Budgeting, training, staff, standards and *quality* are the 'fixed' concepts which make up the next level of the hierarchical productivity model. One of the USH principles is concerned with 'interacting systems design', where the output from one system becomes the input into another. Outputs from the core concept thus become inputs into fixed concepts within the hierarchical model. Concepts at the 'fixed' level are also inputs into subsequent levels and therefore cannot be viewed in isolation.

Training is perceived as having a strong influence upon productivity, perhaps because hotel managers understand it as an easily managed element. Training can be delivered in the workplace through a systematic procedure, such as the use of NVQs. However, many managers seemed indifferent towards these qualifications, preferring an *ad hoc* approach, especially in smaller hotels. Perhaps NVQs need re-examination to make their image more appealing, or to improve access and availability.

All the cognitive maps related *quality* to productivity. Managers' commitment to quality varied, with 26 hotels from the sample pursuing a bottom-up approach to quality/productivity, while a very few attempted the more satisfactory top-down type of approach. 'Quality' was interpreted differently in different types of operation. Hotels with low–low service delivery (according to Lovelock's (1988) model) tended to emphasize the importance of productivity and quality, often using the delivery of standards as a quality benchmark.

Hotel managers also perceived links between *standards, measurement, budgeting* and productivity. In smaller units productivity measurement was viewed as part of wider business measurement, and specific productivity measurement techniques were not used. These hotels did not see productivity as a separate entity worthy of measurement, concurring with Lee-Ross and Ingold's (1994) observation that 'owners of small hotels may have more important business objectives than productivity'. The strong perceived links between cost centres, budgets and control measurement and productivity were in line with the findings of Brown (1994), and suggested that productivity measurement must be seen as tangible to be effective. Managers of affiliated hotels recognized the limitations of a purely budgetary approach. For example, they felt that budgetary control systems might stifle initiative by removing opportunity or motivation.

High scores in both domain and central analysis showed the perceived overall importance of *staff* to productivity but opinion about this varied between managers. Smaller, unaffiliated hotels tended to emphasize partial factor productivity (Pickworth, 1994) and costs over which they had direct control. Larger, affiliated hotels tended to view staff as an input into the productivity equation and measured output against staff numbers or hours. For example, they would measure service times for room cleaning, or the ratio of restaurant staff to covers. This approach to staffing has been encouraged by the economic recession, which has placed a greater premium on wage costs (Wood, 1994). However, this approach to productivity was used by only two hotels in the sample. The alternative possibility of a behaviourist approach, involving a top-down strategy of productivity improvement, was not found.

Variable concepts of productivity

Variable concepts of productivity represent the third level in the hierarchical model. They include *information technology, cost of labour, marketing, service level, organizational structure, design of building* and *reward/motivation/effort.* The manager's influence over these elements varied widely. For example, the manager of a roadside branded hotel was directly concerned only with the delivery of standards, and had to make no choices with regard to service design. *Organizational structure* also has a variable influence on productivity. For example, Heap (1992), Watson and D'Annunzio-Green (1994) and Pickworth (1994) all note that improved lines of communication and reduced levels of 'flattened' organizational structure enhance productivity

The *design and layout* of hotels cannot be dismissed as an ingredient of productivity. According to Brown (1995), 80 per cent of hotels are not purpose built and this was evidently perceived as a productivity issue by the hotel managers interviewed, who linked it with a number of operational problems. *Information technology* is also seen as facilitating productivity, by improving decision-making and communication within hotels. Jones and Ferroni (1994) note that computer-based information systems allow the development of competitive advantage and better management decisions. Computer-based systems are also perceived as important because of their function as distribution channels (e.g. through central reservation systems).

RECOMMENDATIONS

On the basis of the research described above, the authors make a number of observations about the management of productivity in UK hotels:

1. Hotel managers appear to identify a strong relationship between productivity and quality. They also view themselves as central to the achievement of both of these targets. Perhaps they should therefore adopt quality management practices shown to be successful in the manufacturing sector (e.g. Ingold and Worthington, 1994; Johns and Chesterton, 1994). The authors do not recommend BS5750 or similar schemes, as these seem to be too procedure-dominated for the hospitality industry. The 'continuous quality improvement' or TQM approach is probably more appropriate.
2. A successful implementation strategy for productivity improvement requires a user-friendly system of training. It would seem that NVQs are here to stay, but there is a distinct need to communicate the benefits of NVQs to hotel managers.
3. Productivity must be continuously measured, and managers should be aware of the different types of productivity measurement. Productivity is a complex concept, and no one single measure can be used. A multi-dimensional approach is required, suitable for benchmarking successful management.
4. Successful productivity improvement should be based on a relationship between recognition, reward, effort and outcomes. Hotel managers seem able to see the connection between these factors, but have generally failed to introduce recognition or reward systems.
5. The role of management should be concerned with defined competencies to achieve productivity improvement rather than with technical skills.
6. Productivity management, measurement, quality improvements, recognition/ reward and training all require a 'top-down' approach in which management takes the lead.

7. Operational productivity should be built into the design and refurbishment of hotels, involving closer liaison between the operator and the design team.
8. Service quality must never be sacrificed for the sake of apparent improved productivity. Customers go elsewhere if quality is inadequate, and the productivity gain becomes irrelevant.

The authors wish to acknowledge the contributions of Sally Reynolds, Birmingham College of Food, and Mark Sasse, HCTC, for their assistance with the interviews and Jim Forsyth of Napier University for his help with the diagrams.

REFERENCES

Ackermann, F., Eden, C. and Cropper, S. (1994) 'Getting started with cognitive mapping'. Paper presented at the Young Operations Society Bi-Annual Conference, March, University of York.

Arnaldo, M.J. (1981) 'Hotel general managers: a profile'. *Cornell Hotel and Restaurant Quarterly*, November, 53–6.

Arnold, J., Robertson, I. and Cooper, C. (1991) *Work Psychology*. London: Pitman.

Atkinson, J. (1985) *Flexibility, Uncertainty and Manpower Management*. Brighton: Institute of Manpower Studies.

Bagguley, P. (1990) 'Gender and labour flexibility in hotels'. *Service Industries Journal*, **10**, October.

Ball, S. (1994) 'Improving labour productivity'. In P. Jones and P. Merricks (eds), *The Management of Food service Operations*, pp. 188–203. London: Cassell.

Barker, D. (1989) *Hotel Management Systems – Training Techniques*. Geneva: International Labour Organisation.

Baum, T. (1989) 'Competencies for hotel managers: industry expectations of education'. *International Journal Of Contemporary Hospitality Management*, **2**(4), 13–16.

Beer, I.R. (1987) 'Efficiency plus productivity equals profit'. *Restaurant Business*, November, 147–60.

Boyatzis, R. (1982) *Competent Manager*. Chichester: Wiley.

British Standards Institute (1983) *BSI 4778: BSI Handbook*. London: BSI.

Brown, J. (1994) 'Behavioural implications of management control systems in hotel companies'. Paper presented to the CHME Third Annual Research Conference. April, Napier University, Edinburgh.

Brown, J. (1995) 'Energy policy in the hotel industry'. Unpublished Master of Philosophy thesis, De Montfort University, Leicester.

Checkland, P. (1981) *Systems Thinking, Systems Practice*. Chichester: Wiley.

Connell, J. (1992) *Forte Hotels Rebranding Exercise 1991*. Bedford: European Case Clearing House, Cranfield Ltd.

Eden, C. and Ackermann, F. (1992) 'The analysis of causal maps'. *Journal of Management Studies*, **29**(3), 309–24.

Eden, C., Jones, S. and Sims D. (1983) *Messing about in Problems*. Oxford: Pergamon.

Glover, W.G. (1987) 'The cult of effectiveness'. In D.G. Rutherford (ed.) *Hotel Management and Operations*. London: Van Nostrand Reinhold, pp. 29–33.

Guerrier, Y. and Pye, G. (1994) 'Managing human resources in restaurant and catering outlets'. In B. Davies and A. Lockwood (eds), *Food and Beverage Management*. Oxford: Butterworth-Heinemann.

Heap, J. (1992) *Productivity Management: a Fresh Approach*. London: Cassell.

Heizer, J.H. and Render B. (1993) *Production and Operations Management: Strategies and Tactics*. Boston: Allyn and Bacon.

Hitchins, D. (1992) *Unified Systems Hypothesis*. Chichester: Wiley.

Hutchins, D. (1982) *Quality Circles Handbook*. New York: Nicholls.

Ingold, A. and Worthington, T. (1994) 'Extraordinary customer satisfaction: the road to success'. In R. Teare *et al.* (eds), *Achieving Quality Performance*. London: Cassell.

Jewell, B. (1993) *An Integrated Approach to Business Studies*. London: Pitman.

Johns, N. (1993) 'Productivity management through design and operation: a case study'. *International Journal of Contemporary Hospitality Management*, **5**(2), 20–4.

Johns, N. (1994) 'Food service layout and design'. In P. Jones and P. Merricks *et al.* (eds), *The Management of Food Service Operations*. London: Cassell.

Johns, N. and Chesterton, J. (1994) 'ICL: snapshot of a changing culture'. In R. Teare *et al.* (eds), *Achieving Quality Performance, Lessons from British Industry*. London: Cassell.

Jones, P.L. and Ferroni, L. (1994) 'Management of information systems for food and beverage operations'. In B. Davies and A. Lockwood (eds), *Food and Beverage Management*. Oxford: Butterworth-Heinemann.

Jones, P.L. and Lockwood, A. (1989) *The Management of Hotel Operations*. London: Cassell.

Kast, F.E. and Rosenzweig, J.A. (1985) *Organization and Management: a Systems and Contingency Approach*. New York: McGraw-Hill.

Kirk, D. (1994) 'Design and layout'. In B. Davies and A. Lockwood (eds), *Food and Beverage Management*. Oxford: Butterworth-Heinemann.

Lee-Ross, D. (1993) 'Two styles of hotel manager, two styles of worker'. *International Journal of Contemporary Management*, **5**(4), 20–4.

Lee-Ross, D. and Ingold, A. (1994) 'Increasing productivity in small hotels: are academic proposals realistic'. *International Journal of Management and Tourism*, **8**(3–4), 135–43.

Lovelock, C.H. (1991) *Services Marketing*. London: Prentice Hall.

McKenna, E.F. (1987) *Psychology in Business*. London: Erlbaum.

McLaughlin, C. and Coffey, S. (1990) 'Measuring productivity in services'. *Services Industries Journal*, **1**(1).

Mahoney, T.A. (1988) 'Productivity defined'. In R.J. Campbell and J.P. Campbell (eds), *Productivity in Organizations: New Perspectives from Industrial and Organizational Psychology*. New York: Jossey-Bass.

Maslow, A.H. (1943) 'The theory of human motivation'. *Psychological Review*, **50**(4), July, 370–96.

Medlik, S. (1988) *Tourism and Productivity*. London: BTA/ETB Research Services.

Mills, R.C. (1989) *Managing Productivity in the Hospitality Industry*. New York: Van Nostrand Rheinhold.

Mintzberg, H. (1973) *The Nature of Managerial Work*. London: Harper & Row.

Moriarty, K. and Jones, M. (1992) *Graphics Cope*. Glasgow: Strategic Decision Support Research Unit, Department of Management Science, University of Strathclyde.

National Economic Development Council (NEDC) (1992) *Working Party, Competitiveness in Tourism and Leisure, Sub-Group Report. Costs and Manpower Productivity in United Kingdom Hotels*. London: NEDC.

National Institute Economic Review (1986) *Productivity in Services*, February, 44–7.

National Institute of Economic and Social Research (1989) 'Productivity and vocational skills in Britain and Germany: hotels'. *National Institute Economic Review*, November.

Peters, T. J. and Waterman, R.H. Jr. (1982) *In Search of Excellence: Lessons from America's Best Run Companies*. New York: Harper & Row.

Pickworth, J. (1994) 'Productivity improvement'. In B. Davies and A. Lockwood (eds), *Food and Beverage Management*. Oxford: Butterworth-Heinemann.

Prokopenko, J. (1987) *Productivity Management: a Practical Handbook*. Paris: International Labour Office.

Ranfti, R.M. (1984) 'Training managers for high productivity: the Hughes approach'. *National Productivity Review*, Spring, 24–31.

Reynolds, S. and Ingold, A. (1994) 'Evaluation of total quality management tools and techniques in the United Kingdom hotel industry'. Paper presented at the Young Operations Research Conference, March, University of York.

Russell, B. (1991) 'Teamwork pays off'. *Hotels*, p. 25.

Sasser, W.E., Olsen, R.P. and Wyckoff D.D. (1992) *The Management of Service Operations*. New York: Allyn and Bacon.

Schroder, H.H. (1989) *Managerial Competence: the Key to Excellence. A New Strategy for Management Development in the Information Age*. Iowa: Kendall and Hunt Publications.

Schroeder, R.G. (1985) *Operations Management: Decision Making in the Operations Function*. New York: McGraw-Hill.

Secor, P.F. and Backman, C.W. (1969) *Social Psychology*. New York: McGraw-Hill.

Slattery, P. (1991) 'Hotel branding in the 1990s'. *Economic Intelligence Unitt Travel and Tourism Analyst*, **1**, 23–35.

Slattery, P. (1992) 'Unaffiliated hotels in the UK'. *Economic Intelligence Unit Travel and Tourism Analyst*, **1**, 99–102.

Sornchai, W. (1986) 'How to build the attitudes of hotel staff'. Report of Asian Seminar, November.

Stewart, R. (1982) *Choices for the Manager: a Guide to Managerial Work and Behavior*. New York: McGraw-Hill.

Swan, J.A. and Newell S. (1994) 'Managers beliefs about factors affecting the adoption of technological innovation. A study using cognitive maps'. *Journal of Managerial Psychology*, **9**(2), 3–11.

Van der Hoeven, W.H.M. and Thurik, A.R. (1984) 'Labour productivity in the hotel business'. *Services Industries Journal*, **2**(2), 161–73.

Watson, S. and D'Annunzio-Green, N. (1994) 'The influence of organizational structure on personnel management: a move towards human resource management'. Paper presented at the CHME Third Annual Research Conference, April, Napier University.

Witt, C.A. and Clark, B.R. (1990) 'Tourism: the use of production management techniques'. *Services Industry Journal*, **10**(2), 306–19.

Witt, C.A. and Witt S.F. (1989) 'Why productivity in the hotel sector is low'. *International Journal of Contemporary Hospitality Management*, **1**(2), 28–33.

Wood, R.C. (1994) *Organizational Behaviour for Hospitality Management*. Oxford: Butterworth-Heinemann.

EIGHT

Influencing hotel productivity

Mark Sasse and Stephen Harwood-Richardson

INTRODUCTION

It has for some time been widely accepted that productivity measurement and improvement should not be limited to manufacturing sectors (National Institute Economic Review, 1986). There is scope for productivity measurement and improvement in the services sectors where products are less tangible. The hotel sector of the catering and hospitality industry is no exception and productivity in this sector has received growing attention in recent years.

Over the past 20 years many writers have significantly advanced our understanding of productivity issues in hotels and the sheer complexity of isolating factors that impact on productivity. It is all too easy to criticize their findings, because no one has solved the basic problem of isolating factors that impact on productivity. Such criticism needs to be viewed constructively and it is anticipated that this work will be equally susceptible to criticism. This chapter reviews much of the previous work that has been carried out to develop global measurements of productivity for hotels. This work was intended to enable some assessment of overall productivity in hotels, permit comparisons of productivity between hotels (and between countries) and enable some means of assessing changes in total hotel productivity over time. It is apparent that the variety of hotels, of different sizes and standards, serving different markets with different products makes such global measurements and comparisons quite impractical. The greatest strides in productivity improvement are therefore most likely to come from the development and application of practical guidance for hotel managers on how to monitor and influence productivity in their establishments. This is a key aim of the work of the Hotel and Catering Training Company (HCTC) examined in this chapter.

While many writers have acknowledged the complexity of productivity measurement in hotels and the need to take account of a wide range of factors that influence productivity, few, if any have attempted to take account of all these factors in a practical application. Past studies have typically resolved these difficulties by limiting the scope of their study to particular operations or business of the hotel (e.g.

accommodation (Prais *et al.*, 1989), or restaurant productivity (Ball *et al.*, 1986)) and by using a limited range of measures: for example, relating some element of output (such as guest nights or covers), to labour input (numbers of full-time employee equivalent). Previous studies have also tended to look at larger hotels and frequently those of hotel chains, where arguably knowledge of productivity and action to improve it is more widespread, while issues in smaller hotels, which form a larger part of the industry, are overlooked (Lee-Ross and Ingold, 1994).

The HCTC have begun an exploration of the scope for measurement of productivity in hotels of all sizes. The ultimate aim is to develop a productivity model that could be applied in individual hotels, of all sizes, enabling them to identify productivity improvement from adjustments in working practices and in particular from training. It is not anticipated that this will enable direct comparison between hotels, although it is hoped that it will enable causes of productivity improvement to be isolated in particular hotels and cases of best practice to be shared with others.

To achieve this it is necessary to identify for hotels:

- the range of productivity measures that can be used;
- the ability of managers to undertake practical measures;
- the factors that impact on productivity;
- the relative impact of different factors on productivity.

The HCTC, in collaboration with researchers based at Birmingham College of Food, Tourism and Creative Studies (BCFTS), is part way through its study of productivity in hotels. To date a literature review to identify previous work in this area has been completed, along with considerable exploratory work leading to a survey of managers of hotels. Analysis of the findings from the survey has begun and brief preliminary findings are presented in this chapter. The broad aim of the survey was to assess the scope for common measures of productivity and to identify the relative impact of different factors on productivity.

BACKGROUND

Productivity in general has long been a major concern of national economists. Increased productivity is generally seen as beneficial to the national well-being, bringing improvements in standards of living and having a favourable impact on the balance of payments. It means that better use is made of resources and wastage is reduced. In recent years there has been growing concern about productivity growth rates in the UK and the USA: these have been relatively low in comparison with those in other industrialized countries. In the UK, there have been major changes in the structure of the economy and the way the workforce is employed. In the mid nineteenth century, roughly a third of the workforce was employed in agriculture, a third in manufacturing and a third in the service sector (Milward, 1990). Since then, the proportion employed in agriculture has fallen to less than 2 per cent, with the introduction of more efficient practices. In more recent years, the proportion employed in the manufacturing sector has also declined somewhat, owing to new technology and overseas competition: about 25 per cent of the workforce are now working in this sector. The service sector is now the largest employer, accounting for two-thirds of the workforce, and contributing about 70 per cent of the country's gross national product (GNP).

Ray (1986), writing in the National Institute Economic Review, examined the changes in the services sector between the mid-1970s and the mid-1980s, during which time the output of services rose considerably while that of manufacturing fell. During this time, 1.3 million new jobs were created in the services sector. The average annual growth rate of output was 2.4 per cent for the sector as a whole. This sector consists of many divisions, of which some, most notably banking, finance, business services and air transport, showed very high growth, while others, like wholesale distribution, sea transport and railways, actually showed negative growth. The hotels and catering division performed poorly, with output growth of just 1 per cent per annum. However, in this division the average output per full-time (or equivalent) employee was actually found to decrease by 1 per cent per annum during this time, which may be taken as a drop in productivity. It is widely accepted that increasing productivity in the service sector generally is important. Poor productivity in the service sector is often attributed to the nature of the work involved. Witt and Witt (1989) mention various problems, in that the work is typically labour-intensive, frequently individually processed, often an intellectual task performed by professionals and often difficult to mechanize or automate.

In the early 1980s pressure for increased productivity in the service sector arose from an increase in inflation, increasing demand for services and increasing competition, which resulted in companies changing their objectives and styles of management. During the 1990s, there will be even greater pressure for productivity improvements owing to environmental factors such as demographic changes, new employment practices, new legislation, changing economic and political boundaries and changing consumer trends.

CONCEPT, DEFINITION AND MEASUREMENT OF PRODUCTIVITY

The productivity ratio

Productivity measurements are always in the form of ratios of one factor (output) to another factor (input). Productivity is generally recognized as the relationship between input and output in a system (Schroeder, 1985), or as a measure of the results achieved (output) using given resources (input). As Ball *et al.* (1986) state, writing about their work, 'Productivity ratios can be identified for any feature of hotel operation once the inputs and outputs have been identified.' There are three main categories of measurements:

- financial, calculated using financial factors for both input and output;
- physical, calculated using physical factors for both input and output;
- combination, calculated using a physical and a financial factor.

Financial measurements of productivity include such factors as sales revenue, operating costs, value added and profit. Labour costs are often of particular interest, as these tend to account for a large percentage of the total operating costs. Examples of productivity ratios that are commonly calculated are profit against sales revenue and sales revenue against labour costs.

The most common physical measurements of productivity are for room occupancy, covers served per chef or per waiter and ratios of guests to staff. Other measurements that may be made include floor space per guest, numbers of complaints, electricity consumption per guest and materials utilization or wastage (for example, in the kitchen, kilograms of chips prepared as a percentage of kilograms of potatoes used). Rates of working, such as rooms cleaned per hour, are useful physical measures, time being an essential resource. There is also an extensive range of combination measurements, using a physical output and a financial input, or vice versa. Examples of physical outputs used are numbers of rooms sold, numbers of covers served and numbers of bar customers. The most commonly used financial output is sales revenue. Typical physical inputs might include staffing levels, man-hours worked or rooms available. Examples of financial inputs are labour costs, material costs (e.g. for kitchen and bar) and capital expenditure.

Many hotels might be expected to have this kind of basic information, which would enable them to calculate productivity ratios, but not all of them make use of it in monitoring their productivity. Two aims of the HCTC research were to measure the extent to which hotel managers could provide this type of information (not just claim that they collected it!) and whether or not they actually used it to measure productivity.

Prokopenko (1987) points out that quality as well as quantity should be taken into account when considering the inputs and outputs: 'Although productivity may mean different things to different people, the basic concept is always the relationship between the quantity and quality of services produced and quantity and quality of resources used to produce them.' Quality is a key issue when we are examining productivity in hotels, where the product is highly differentiated or customized. Unfortunately, 'quality' means different things to different people and although the 'quality' of hotels is arbitrarily recognized through a number of national and international rating schemes, it is extremely difficult to measure. Bain (1986) says in the first part of his book *The Productivity Prescription* that the concept of productivity tends to be associated with manufacturing, but can be applied to other situations where there is not a tangible physical output. He gives a car's miles per gallon rating as a simple example: the fuel is the input, and the distance travelled is the intangible output. If intangible but measurable inputs and outputs are used, the concept of productivity can be applied to education, government, the professions and the service sector generally. It is the problem of measuring quality in hotels that remains one of the major stumbling blocks to the effective comparison of productivity between hotels. Even for hotels in the same group operating with identical products and services, quality can be perceived to be different; for example, because of the efficiency of staff, or even the location of the hotel.

Labour is a very important resource and so is often taken as an input in the productivity equation. However, it is only one input and comparing the value of output only to the value of labour ignores the relative efficiency with which all the other resources within the operation are used. In fact, criticism is frequently levelled at partial productivity ratios, in that they tend to consider only one input and output at a time. In recent years there has been growing promotion of the use of broader-based productivity measurements to include such elements as capital, materials and energy as well as labour. The single index of total factor productivity attempts to view the efficiency of the transformation of all inputs in combination into outputs. A total productivity measure (TPM) attempts to include all inputs and all outputs in a system (Thorpe and Horsburgh, 1991). As Chew (1986) comments, 'A multi-factor view of productivity is important . . . but it is difficult for one index to encompass all inputs. Using several different single-factor measures can yield a multi-factor perspective.' The use of several productivity measures over time would help a manager to pinpoint the causes of changes observed.

Value-added productivity measures

The Hotel and Catering Tourism Committee (1989) of the International Labour Organisation recommends measuring the output in the form of value added. Value added is sales revenue minus the variable costs directly attributable to those sales, and it can be taken as an output in the productivity equation. The Committee describes it as 'the only measure that can be used with reasonable effectiveness and reliability to compare one enterprise with another'. This is supported by Medlik (1989), who defines output as value added at factor cost (constant prices) and output per head as value added per full-time equivalent person employed. He states: 'Value added has a common application at the level of an individual firm and establishment, and economy level.' The advantage of using a value-added output measure is that it enables account to be taken of the costs of resources (through contribution to profit), rather than just sales revenue. But, while it is argued that such value-added measures permit comparison between establishments, they do so only at the financial level, and ignore the issues of quality and customer satisfaction with the service or product supplied.

In practice, various different measurements have been used to investigate productivity in the working environment and this has led to disagreement and confusion over the concept of productivity (Mahoney, 1988). Some measurements relate to efficiency of performance (for example, return on investment, cost per unit, output per employee); other measurements relate to outcomes (for example, sales, customer satisfaction, profits). Efficiency measures can show whether an organization is doing things in the right way, but do not indicate whether the organization is doing the right things (Thorpe and Horsburgh, 1991). It is outcomes rather than efficiency that lead to the ultimate success or otherwise of the organization. The types of measure that are most appropriate depend on the purpose for which they are to be used.

It can be seen that productivity measurement is often a complex matter, but it is important as it allows monitoring of operations and performance, and helps in planning corrective action. Teague and Eilon (1973) give the following reasons why an organization should measure its productivity:

- strategic purposes, to allow the organization to compare its overall performance with competitors or similar firms;
- tactical purposes, to allow management to control the overall performance of the organization via the individual sectors;
- planning purposes, to compare the relative benefits yielded by different inputs and different ways of operating;
- internal management purposes, such as assessing individual performance.

MEASUREMENTS TAKEN IN PREVIOUS PROJECTS

Traditionally, productivity is a concept associated with the manufacturing sector, but much work has been done on improving productivity in various service sector industries, and a number of researchers have already carried out some important projects examining productivity in the hotel industry. Van der Hoeven and Thurik (1984) investigated labour productivity in a number of German and Dutch hotels. They found that, in general, labour requirements consisted of two components: a fixed threshold level and a sliding level, which varied in proportion to the volume of business. The fixed threshold level depended largely on the size and rating of the hotel. The rate at which the sliding level varied depended on various factors, including the size and rating of the hotel, but also the rates of staff pay and the average length of guests' stay.

Ball *et al.* (1986) carried out a study in a sample of nine hotels, all four-star and in urban areas, offering similar facilities and services, and operated by the same company. They concentrated on the food and beverage departments because these had the most variation in levels of customer use, and therefore, it was believed, had most potential for performance improvement. They stated that a hotel could increase its profitability by increasing its volume of business or by reducing its operating costs, but that ideally both issues should be addressed together. They recommended determining and measuring various inputs and outputs of a hotel, calculating productivity ratios from these and evaluating their significance; and they suggested a wide range of measurements that could be used. These covered such areas as labour productivity (e.g. the ratio of number of meals cooked to number of kitchen staff and the ratios of sales revenue to payroll for different departments of the hotel), the use of raw materials (e.g. mass of chips produced against mass of potatoes and the number of bar customers against the cost of liquor used) and capital measures (e.g. total hotel customers per square foot of hotel). Following a pilot study, where they experimented with a variety of measurements connected with labour productivity, they decided to concentrate on two measurements: revenue against numbers of full-time equivalent employees (FTEEs) and numbers of covers served against FTEEs. These were monitored on a month by month basis for the restaurant/coffee shop, for room service and for kitchen and stewards, over a period of two years from May 1983 to April 1985 for each of the nine hotels. Further analysis was proposed to investigate the causes of periods of good and poor performance. Similarly, hotel departments that seemed to have higher productivity could be compared with those with lower productivity, in an attempt to identify the reasons for this.

Labour productivity in hotels was investigated further when the National Institute of Economics and Social Research (NIESR) undertook a comparison of British and German hotels (Prais *et al.*, 1989). The study investigated a small but carefully matched sample of 14 medium-sized hotels in the UK and 24 in West Germany, and looked at the utilization of human and physical resources and at training. It was found that German hotels seemed to have higher levels of training and lower staffing requirements; German hotels also seemed to make more use of labour-saving equipment and ergonomically designed rooms. The NIESR made many qualitative comparisons between UK and German hotels, but in quantifying differences in levels of productivity, it concentrated mainly on staffing levels, particularly the ratio of guest nights to FTEE. It is, however, difficult to pinpoint the causes of lower levels of staff productivity if other factors are ignored. Critically, the NIESR ignored the financial contribution of staff, which ultimately determines the viability of a hotel. Concentrating on staff productivity, the NIESR researchers also drew conclusions about training issues, but ignored the possible impact of other factors like marketing. If a hotel is poorly marketed and is half empty as a result, no amount of staff training will increase productivity.

It has generally been claimed that British hotel managers have lower levels of training, and do not make sufficient use of appropriate management techniques. Witt and Clarke (1990) sent questionnaires to 167 hotels, to investigate how widespread was the use of various techniques. Of these hotels, 43 responded and out of 26 techniques listed in the questionnaire, the only ones that over 40 per cent of respondents claimed to use occasionally or frequently were activity sampling, classification and coding, critical path analysis and time study. It is possible, however, that these techniques were used but under different names.

In 1992, the National Economic Development Committee (NEDC) published a comprehensive report, which attempted to build on the earlier work of the NIESR. The NEDC project compared productivity levels in matched samples of 20 UK, French and German hotels, using a wider variety of measurements: physical, financial and combinations of these. The main measurements used were: (physical) FTEE to available rooms, (financial) ratio of profit to sales; and (combination) sales revenue per room, costs per room, value added per FTEE, sales revenue per FTEE and costs per FTEE. Averages of each measurement for all hotels in each country were calculated and then used to compare productivity between the three countries. The NEDC also concluded that productivity in UK hotels seemed to compare poorly with that of French and German hotels. The NEDC study, however, only looked at hotels in each of the three countries that were on the Horwath Consulting Client database, which were unlikely to be representative of the population of hotels in the UK, France or Germany. The NEDC also carried out a survey of 144 UK hotels to ascertain opinions and productivity practices, which revealed an apparent lack of knowledge and use of operations management techniques. The authors drew the conclusion that there was insufficient short-term forecasting of workload, and corresponding matching of workforce rostering to match the workload, in the UK and recommended that a major project be undertaken to determine best practices and to demonstrate the benefits that these can yield.

AIMS AND METHODOLOGY OF THE HCTC PROJECT

It was the published findings of the NIESR and NEDC that prompted the HCTC to commence a study of productivity in hotels. The wide press coverage resulting from these studies and the NIESR study in particular put the UK hotel industry in a poor light and placed heavy emphasis on training as the primary cause of the UK hotel industry's poor productivity performance. Through the HCTC, industry representatives questioned the conclusions of the reports, but were also anxious to address the productivity issue through training. The overall objective of the HCTC project is to investigate the impact of training on productivity and ultimately to demonstrate how productivity improvements can be achieved. In order to do this it has been necessary to identify appropriate measures of productivity and develop a productivity model identifying key factors that impact on productivity. This will then enable managers to isolate and assess factors influencing productivity in their operations. A further aim of the project is to identify cases of best practice in productivity improvement. The key stages of the project are shown in Figure 8.1.

Productivity Management

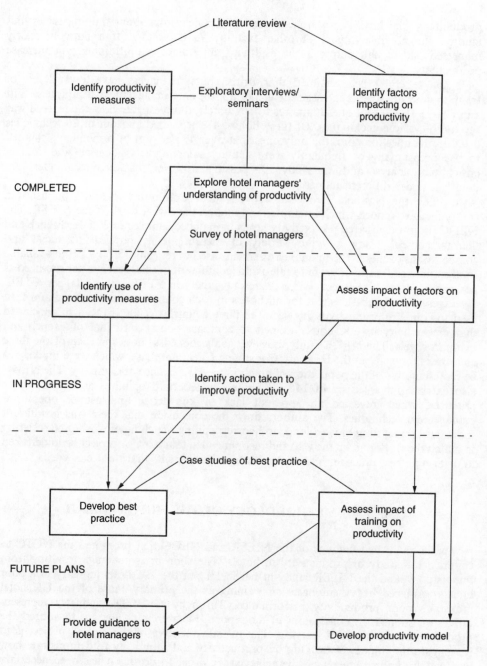

Literature review

Identify productivity measures

Exploratory interviews/ seminars

Identify factors impacting on productivity

Explore hotel managers' understanding of productivity

COMPLETED

Survey of hotel managers

Identify use of productivity measures

Assess impact of factors on productivity

Identify action taken to improve productivity

IN PROGRESS

Case studies of best practice

Develop best practice

Assess impact of training on productivity

FUTURE PLANS

Provide guidance to hotel managers

Develop productivity model

Figure 8.1. Key stages in HCTC Productivity in Hotels Study

Literature review

Initially a literature review was undertaken of the previous work on the subject of productivity measurement and particularly on productivity in hotels and the service sector in general. This identified the sheer complexity of measuring and monitoring productivity in hotels, but enabled the HCTC to avoid duplicating the valuable work already undertaken.

Exploratory work

In order to put the HCTC work into context it was necessary not only to review previous work in the field, but also to explore hotel managers' understanding and appreciation of the issues. During the autumn of 1993, a number of interviews were carried out with the managers of about 30 different hotels, of various sizes and standards, located in London, Birmingham, Edinburgh, Bournemouth, Norfolk and South Wales. The purpose of these was to find out how these establishments were run, to probe managers' perceptions of productivity, to identify what factors and action they saw as influencing it and to reveal any measurements they took of performance. In order to explore current industry understanding and definitions of productivity further, two seminars were held in November 1993 in collaboration with Birmingham College of Food, Tourism and Creative Studies. These seminars, attended by many leading industrialists and academics, also provided an opportunity to discuss the factors that might influence productivity.

Survey of hotel managers

Following this preparatory work, questionnaires were developed and piloted for a survey of hotel managers. The main survey of UK hotels was carried out over a period of about five months up to December 1994. Hotels of all sizes, gradings and types of management and ownership were invited to participate in the study, Previous studies have concentrated on large hotels, particularly those that are members of a chain, but it is the smaller hotels that represent the majority of the industry, where productivity improvement is likely to have the greatest impact. Managers of 208 hotels participated in the survey (representing a response rate of 56 per cent from the initial sample). They were asked about the type of hotel they operated, the kinds of market they served and what facilities they provided. Information was collected about productivity, measurements made by hotel managers, their perceptions of the impact of various factors on productivity and any special action they had taken to improve their productivity. In 95 per cent of cases, the managers took part in detailed telephone interviews lasting 40 minutes on average; the remaining 5 per cent of respondents chose to complete postal questionnaires.

Analysis of survey findings

The full analysis of completed questionnaires will yield information on what measurements, if any, are taken by hotel managers, the relative perceived importance of the various factors that can affect productivity and how these vary for different kinds of hotel. The responses will also identify what kind of action has been taken in connection with these factors, enabling further exploration of cases of best practice that might be shared with other hoteliers. This chapter includes only a brief analysis of preliminary findings from the survey. The full analysis has yet to be completed.

PERCEPTIONS WITHIN THE INDUSTRY

During the initial HCTC exploratory interviews it was established that some of the managers had little or no formal training in hotel management, while others were highly qualified. When managers were asked about their understanding of productivity, the following definitions were given:

- making the best use of what you have;
- getting the most out of what you have got;
- a ratio of output to input;
- how much you measure and can get out of a given unit;
- the amount of input and the level of production from that;
- proportion of resources used, against a given benchmark;
- what is produced against the energy input;
- relationship between work produced and time (a rate of working);
- how we can use the facilities of the hotel and skills of the staff;
- in terms of kitchen and food and beverages, it has to do with efficiency and attitude of staff;
- product you have to sell and how efficiently you sell it (the product here is the service);
- to give value for money to the customers, within the framework of a predefined cost system;
- value for money, for guests and for holding company;
- producing the best service at the lowest price and getting the maximum profit.

All the definitions provided were valid interpretations of productivity (i.e. a ratio of output to input), although the variety of definitions provided for different fields of activity was perhaps unexpected. Respondents had, however, shown a general understanding of productivity, which enabled a full survey of hotel managers to explore productivity issues without the need to define it explicitly.

THE HCTC SURVEY OF HOTEL MANAGERS

For each hotel, information on physical and financial resources (inputs and outputs) was sought. While it was anticipated that many managers would have a general

Table 8.1. Proportion of hotel managers who provided input and output figures for the previous year

Inputs/outputs	Proportion recording (%)
Room occupancy for last year	82
Bed occupancy for last year	4
Guest nights for last year	1
Total sales revenue last year	46
Operating profit last year	18
Total assets last year	14
Total payroll last year	28
Property overheads last year	12

understanding of productivity, it was important to gather data that would indicate what input and output measures were taken, as well as those which were actively converted into productivity ratios. Respondents were asked to supply actual input and output figures, rather than simply being asked whether such data was recorded. The physical resources investigated were the human resources, in terms of staffing levels, by department where appropriate, the facilities for diners and the accommodation for overnight guests. Physical outputs elicited were the occupancy figures (or total guest nights) for accommodation and the numbers of covers served for food and beverage operations. The financial resources investigated were the value of the assets and labour costs, while sales revenue and profits were recorded as financial outputs.

As expected, almost without exception, respondents were able to supply information concerning the physical inputs mentioned above (available staff, rooms, beds and covers for restaurants, etc.). However, few managers were able to supply output figures (numbers of guests, covers served, etc.), though many indicated that such information was accessible to them. In terms of occupancy (Table 8.1), room occupancy rates were most likely to be recorded but, because many of the hotels charged per room rather than on any other basis, bed and guest occupancy was rarely recorded. Many managers, however, indicated that such information could be fairly easily obtained. In almost all cases, when examining accommodation, it would therefore be possible for each hotel to calculate the productivity ratios in the form of guests to staff, rooms to staff and guest nights to staff. In addition, the ratio of occupied rooms to available rooms was nearly always calculated by the hotel. For the productivity of the food and beverage operations of the business, the ratios of covers served to chefs/cooks and to waiters/waitresses could generally be calculated. It was also possible to estimate the utilization of restaurant capacity. It is perhaps not surprising, therefore, that many earlier studies have concentrated on these measures of productivity to the exclusion of many others.

It was apparent in many cases that financial information was not readily available to hotel managers, although in some cases respondents were unwilling to supply financial data. Clearly, for accounting purposes they would be required to collect some financial information for the establishment as a whole (e.g. sales and profits per member of staff), although they might generally be unable to calculate ratios for separate departments, such as accommodation, and food and beverages. In addition to all these combination measures, some financial productivity measurements, namely the ratios of profits to sales, profits to assets and sales to assets, could be calculated.

It was generally apparent, therefore, that although many managers could access a variety of information on inputs and outputs few did so and few were able to provide any indication of recent trends to indicate that regular monitoring was taking place.

Table 8.2. Proportion of hotel managers taking productivity measures by size of hotel

	Number of bedrooms				
	1–19	20–49	50–99	100+	Total
Sample	76	83	24	17	200
Measurements taken (%)	16	23	46	82	28
Measurements not taken (%)	84	77	54	18	72

Table 8.3. Hotel managers' stated measures of productivity

Physical	Financial or combination
Occupancy	*Sales revenue*
Room occupancy	Takings per hour, by department
Bed occupancy	Takings per FTEE
Guest nights	Takings per guest (average spend)
	Takings per room or guest night (room rates)
Staff	
Staffing levels	*Costs*
Staff to guest ratios	General costs per room let
Staff to guest nights ratios	Labour costs per room let
Staff to rooms ratios	Laundry costs per guest night
Staff turnover	Energy or fuel costs (inc. water) per guest night
Staff absenteeism	Labour costs, as percentage of revenue or expenditure
Staff availability for ancillary work	Costs per cover
	Materials costs
Use of resources	Food and beverage costs
Energy or fuel per guest night	
Materials/consumables per room	*Profits*
	Per guest night
Staff performance	Per room let
Chambermaids (rooms/h)	Per FTEE
Waiters (covers/h)	Margin (per cent) on food and beverages
Cooks/chefs (covers/h)	
Reception/booking	
Performance management/administration	
Performance	Note: /h stands for 'per head'.

PRODUCTIVITY MEASUREMENTS USED BY RESPONDENTS

Only 28 per cent of respondents indicated that they specifically measured productivity. It was the larger hotels that were more likely to take such measures (Table 8.2). Hotels aimed primarily at the business market and the higher quality hotels were those most likely, but not exclusively, to record productivity measurements. However, there is a need for caution in interpreting these findings; there was evidence of differing ideas of what constituted a measure of productivity. A few respondents made measurements that strictly speaking were not productivity measurements. Rather, they were measures of inputs or outputs, which in isolation could not be used as a measure of productivity. Conversely, other managers were in fact taking productivity measurements, without necessarily recognizing them as such.

Those respondents who had replied positively were asked to give the measurements that they took (Table 8.3). The 'productivity' measures given have been divided into seven categories, of which four categories are physical and three financial or combination. In a few cases, hotel managers were able to list a number of measures that they took, but felt unable to give an exhaustive list because of the very wide range of measures taken by the hotel. This was, however, exceptional.

In the majority of cases hotel managers did not directly measure or monitor productivity over time. Those hotel managers who did measure productivity provided a wide range of different measures, indicating little consistency in how and what was measured. Only a few hotels, typically those belonging to groups with a thorough approach to productivity control, were likely to calculate values for a number of these measurements. Further analysis will reveal the most frequently adopted measures in different types of hotels.

FACTORS INFLUENCING PRODUCTIVITY

The HCTC study of productivity in hotels is ultimately intended to provide a means of assessing the particular impact of training on productivity. Clearly, however, with a complex issue like productivity the effect of training, or any other single factor, on productivity cannot be observed in isolation. At any one time a whole host of factors are impacting on the productivity of a hotel; moreover, the individual impact is in a continual state of flux. It stands to reason, however, that any manager observing a change in productivity, however measured, will seek to identify the nature of the factors causing the change. The degree to which a factor will then be considered and tackled will depend upon its perceived importance as a factor influencing productivity. The HCTC study therefore sought to establish the key factors influencing productivity and how the relative impact of these factors varied between hotels in different circumstances.

In the exploratory interviews, hotel managers had been asked what factors they saw as influencing productivity, whether positively or negatively, and all the factors mentioned were collated. Many of these factors were related to staff, either directly or indirectly: they included such factors as staff training and qualifications, staff motivation and attitude, recruitment, turnover, rates of pay, rewards and incentives. At the two seminars held by the HCTC in conjunction with staff of Birmingham College of Food in November 1993, attending academics and industrialists were asked to consider factors influencing productivity through a number of practical workshops where their ideas were recorded. The material examined during the literature review also revealed a number of key factors thought to influence productivity and chiefly covered such factors as training of staff and management, staff morale and motivation, quality, physical facilities and new technology, especially computers. Having drawn up a comprehensive list of over 40 suggested factors, from these different sources, we noted that a few of them (e.g. occupancy) were really measurements of productivity rather than factors affecting it, so these were excluded from the list. It was also apparent that a number of the factors could be grouped together (e.g. rates of pay, rewards and incentives). Eventually a condensed list of 16 factors was drawn up. It may be possible to identify infinite things impacting on productivity, but in practice it is necessary to eliminate factors with minimal impact. This list is not therefore intended to be exhaustive, but rather representative of the key influences identified with productivity in hotels.

The 16 factors were as follows:

- staff recruitment and selection;
- staff morale and satisfaction;
- staff training and qualifications;
- staff pay, bonuses and incentives;
- management training;
- customer perceptions and satisfaction;
- quality of service and product;
- advertising and promotion;
- forecasting;
- hotel facilities;
- new technology;
- weather;
- economic climate;
- competition;
- local events;
- property overheads.

To establish the impact of these factors on productivity in different types of hotels, hotel managers were asked, for each factor in turn, to say whether it had a major influence on productivity in their establishment, a moderate one, a minor one or no influence at all. For each of the factors, respondents were then invited to describe any special action that they were taking in connection with this factor, or to make any comments that they considered relevant. Respondents were also given an opportunity to add any other factors to the list as appropriate. In only a few cases (less than 3 per cent) did the respondent choose to add any additional factors to the list. Additional factors mentioned in the main survey were:

- security (the threat of terrorism had affected London tourism);
- parking facilities (cheap and secure parking is important, but is scarce in many cities);
- local environment (local government should try to improve amenities);
- political framework (the government has a poor attitude towards tourism).

The responses given by hotel managers as to the influence of each of the 16 factors on productivity in their establishment were coded as follows:

Response	Coding
None	0
Minor	1
Moderate	2
Major	3

This enabled average (mean) ratings to be calculated for the responding hotel managers (Table 8.4). For each factor, the number of valid responses is also shown.

Customer perceptions and satisfaction were the factors thought to have the greatest overall influence on hotel productivity by managers. In all the subsequent analyses these remain the most important factors overall. Many hotels indicated that they go to

Table 8.4. Average influences of factors on hotel productivity according to managers

Factor	Average rating	Valid response
Quality of service and product	2.91	203
Customer perceptions and satisfaction	2.91	201
Staff morale and satisfaction	2.71	176
Hotel facilities	2.62	201
Economic climate	2.51	202
Property overheads	2.36	199
Staff training and qualifications	2.29	174
Advertising and promotion	2.21	201
Staff recruitment and selection	2.17	151
Staff pay, bonuses and incentives	2.12	174
Management training	2.11	174
Competition	2.00	202
Forecasting	1.92	197
Local events	1.83	201
New technology	1.57	202
Weather	1.50	202

considerable lengths to obtain customer feedback and to act upon it: customer feedback questionnaires were frequently mentioned, as was the importance of open communications between guests and staff. Other strategies used to gauge customer opinion were asking old customers to come back as 'mystery guests', and asking staff to spend a night as a guest in their own hotel. Quality of service and product was also seen to have a major influence on productivity and is undoubtedly a key issue in an attempt to compare productivity between hotels. Confirming Prokopenko's (1987) assertions that it is the quality as well as the quantity that is the key to productivity, Prais *et al.* (1989) and the NEDC (1992) used matched samples of hotels in comparing productivity between hotels in different countries in order to try to compare like with like. All hotels, however, pitch themselves at a different level of the market and provide quite different products and services in terms of quality. In the HCTC survey, hotel managers identified that customers have certain expectations of their hotel and that there was a need to try to exceed those expectations. Few researchers identify the impact of customer satisfaction or the quality of service on productivity. They are some of the hardest factors to measure and take account of, which undoubtedly explains their absence from previous research. They are not, incidentally, factors that have been widely explored in the HCTC study to date!

The next most important factor was staff morale and satisfaction, where managers recognized the importance of a well motivated workforce in generating higher levels of productivity. Also highly rated were hotel facilities and the economic climate. The first of these factors is something in connection with which the hotel can adopt a proactive strategy, making improvements where possible. The second is an external factor over which the hotel manager has little control or influence. It seems likely that the recent recession has put this factor into a sharper context for many hotels. It is easy to see how diminishing occupany rates can lower productivity in hotels, since there are a number of fixed costs that have to be met by the hotel regardless of whether or not guests are present. This may explain why property overheads are regarded as having a relatively high influence on productivity. Staff training and qualifications were also placed in the top half of influencing factors.

Relatively low on the list was forecasting, identified by the NEDC as a key means

Productivity Management

Table 8.5. Average influences of factors by market type

| Factor | Market | | |
	Over 50% business	Over 50% tourism	Other
Quality of service and product	2.88	2.91	2.94
Customer perceptions and satisfaction	2.82	2.92	2.94
Staff morale and satisfaction	2.68	2.72	2.80
Hotel facilities	2.56	2.63	2.63
Economic climate	2.59	2.59	2.60
Property overheads	2.18	2.33	2.34
Staff training and qualifications	2.56	2.11	2.37
Advertising and promotion	1.91	2.29	2.43
Staff recruitment and selection	2.16	2.20	2.19
Staff pay, bonuses and incentives	2.12	2.02	2.40
Management training	2.34	1.93	2.40
Competition	2.24	1.82	2.11
Forecasting	2.12	1.70	2.26
Local events	2.06	1.77	1.83
New technology	2.03	1.32	1.71
Weather	0.76	1.78	1.60

of improving productivity. This appears to support the NEDC findings that hotel managers do not regard forecasting as a factor that can influence hotel productivity. Surprisingly, new technology was also very low on the list of influences, despite generally being recognized in most industries as a key to productivity improvements. It may be that appropriate software is not yet available to improve productivity significantly, particularly for the small operator. Weather was regarded as the least influential factor on hotel productivity, though subsequent analysis shows that weather, like some other factors, can be very important to some sectors of the hotel industry.

Analysis of the sample by market type

The sample was split into three groups: those that were mainly business hotels, those that were mainly tourist hotels and a smaller number that did not fall directly into either category, which provided permanent residence for some guests or catered through food and beverage facilities for local residents. When we compare these groups with each other, there is little overall variation in the perceived influence of the various factors for the sample as a whole, but a few significant points were noted (Table 8.5).

The weather had little or no influence on productivity in business hotels, but could be a moderate factor in some tourist hotels, a few even classing it as a major factor for them. New technology was a more important factor in business hotels than in tourist hotels, although even here it was often seen more in terms of providing facilities for the business customer to use rather than as a means of directly providing a more efficient service to the customer. Business hotels generally rated advertising and promotion a little lower than tourist hotels, partly because they relied more on repeat

Table 8.6. Average influences of factors by hotel rating

Factor	Rate		
	4/5 stars, 5 crowns	2/3 stars, 3/4 crowns	Fewer than 2 stars/ 3 crowns
Quality of service and product	2.93	2.89	2.92
Customer perceptions and satisfaction	2.87	2.84	2.96
Staff morale and satisfaction	2.80	2.72	2.68
Hotel facilities	2.80	2.51	2.67
Economic climate	2.53	2.52	2.50
Property overheads	1.93	2.16	2.58
Staff training and qualifications	2.67	2.29	2.21
Advertising and promotion	2.14	2.16	2.27
Staff recruitment and selection	2.43	2.13	2.16
Staff pay, bonuses and incentives	2.40	2.10	2.09
Management training	2.50	2.25	1.90
Competition	2.20	2.00	1.98
Forecasting	2.33	2.08	1.74
Local events	2.33	1.82	1.76
New technology	2.27	1.77	1.31
Weather	0.93	1.40	1.66

business and partly because they belonged to groups or chains and could leave promotion more to their head offices. It was also noted that business hotels rated the influence of training and qualifications for both staff and management more highly, mentioning various kinds of ongoing training for their staff. Business hotels also recognized both forecasting and competition to be more important than did the tourist hotels. A number of differences in perception between business and tourist hotels were therefore observed which need to be explored further, first to ensure they result from the nature of their clientele, and not some other factor (e.g. business hotels being larger) and second to review more thoroughly why these factors are given a different emphasis by these hotels.

Analysis of the sample by rating of the hotel

The sample was also split into three groups according to quality ratings: the high group was for hotels with four stars (five crowns) or more, the middle group was for hotels with two or three stars (three or four crowns) and the low group was for other hotels with fewer than two stars (three crowns). There were only 16 hotels in the high group, though this was considered sufficient for the findings to be fairly representative; the middle and low groups had 83 and 109 hotels, respectively (Table 8.6).

In all groups, customer perceptions and satisfaction and quality of service and product remained the most highly rated factors, with staff morale and satisfaction coming closely behind. Weather generally seems to be about the least important factor in terms of ranking, though it is noteworthy that the hotels in the low group seem to consider it to be more important than the middle group and a lot more important than the high group.

When we compared the groups with each other, it was noted that hotels in the low group seemed to rank property overheads more highly than those in the middle group, and much more highly than those in the high group. Perhaps hotels of a more modest standard generally have older buildings, and so maintenance and improvements require more attention. If more resources (inputs) are required for this, this may rightly be perceived as a major influence on overall productivity. The more luxurious hotels regarded training and qualifications of relatively high influence for both staff and management. New technology was rated more highly in these hotels, as was forecasting.

Analysis of the sample by size

For the purposes of analysis the sample was divided into four size groups, according to the number of bedrooms:

Group	Number of bedrooms	Number in group
1	1–19	79
2	20–49	84
3	50–99	24
4	100+	17

Customer perceptions and satisfaction, quality of service and product, and staff morale and satisfaction were generally rated as major influences on productivity by hotels of all sizes. Hotel facilities were also thought to have an important impact on productivity, particularly in the largest hotels (Table 8.7).

As would be expected, the larger hotels generally appeared to have a more structured approach to management. It was noted that forecasting was seen to be more significant for the larger hotels; these would have the most resources (physical and human) at their disposal, and so it was most important for them to match resources to demand accurately, in order to avoid wastage or loss of business. All hotels seemed to rate staff morale and satisfaction very highly, but it is significant that the larger hotels considered staff recruitment and selection to have a bigger influence on productivity than did the smaller hotels. The larger hotels also indicated that training and qualifications for both staff and management had a significant impact on productivity. Staff pay, bonuses and incentives were not thought to have much influence by the smallest hotels.

The larger hotels rated the influence of new technology more highly than smaller hotels. The term 'new technology' was deliberately left fairly open, but managers tended to mention information technology and computing equipment as being most important in this area. A few mentioned the benefits of fax machines to help communication, but only a few discussed improvements to their equipment in the kitchen or in the bars.

It is also noteworthy that the smallest hotels (those with fewer than 20 bedrooms) in the sample rated property overheads rather more highly than hotels in the other groups. It may be that these kind of hotels have older buildings which require considerable maintenance and upkeep; and rising customer expectations may have

Table 8.7. Average influence of factors by hotel size

		Size of hotel by number of bedrooms			
Factor		1–19 rooms	20–49 rooms	50–99 rooms	100+ rooms
1	Quality of service and product	2.88	2.93	3.00	2.88
2	Customer perceptions and satisfaction	2.95	2.88	3.00	2.71
3	Staff morale and satisfaction	2.70	2.73	2.78	2.59
4	Hotel facilities	2.68	2.58	2.43	2.76
5	Economic climate	2.51	2.51	2.65	2.53
6	Property overheads	2.64	2.19	2.17	2.24
7	Staff training and qualifications	2.10	2.28	2.48	2.53
8	Advertising and promotion	2.17	2.28	2.04	2.24
9	Staff recruitment and selection	2.04	2.10	2.41	2.56
10	Staff pay, bonuses and incentives	198	2.23	2.13	2.12
11	Management training	1.87	2.17	2.41	2.19
12	Competition	1.90	2.09	2.17	1.94
13	Forecasting	1.73	1.96	2.13	2.35
14	Local events	1.80	1.81	1.96	1.94
15	New technology	1.29	1.67	1.91	2.00
16	Weather	1.64	1.48	1.39	1.12

necessitated costly improvements in recent years. Further analysis by the age and style of the building (information which was collected) will confirm whether or not this is the case.

Analysis of the sample by changes in occupancy

When asked whether they had experienced a change in occupancy over the previous year, 90 of the respondents said it had gone up, 37 said it had gone down and 61 said there had been no significant change. (The others did not know, or omitted this question.) Having divided the respondents into these three groups, and examined the data for significant trends, we found that the hotels which had experienced an increase in occupancy tended to rate such factors as staff recruitment and selection, staff morale and satisfaction, and also training for both staff and management as quite influential on productivity. Those which had experienced a drop in occupancy seemed to attach greater importance, or perhaps to blame it upon, such external factors as economic climate, the weather and competition.

When asked about occupancy for the coming year, 90 of the respondents expected a further increase, 62 expected no change and only eight expected a decrease.

Analysis of the sample by perceived changes in staff productivity

When the respondents were asked whether they considered staff productivity to have changed in the previous year, 91 said that it had increased, 63 said it had stayed the same and ten said it had fallen (the remainder did not know, or omitted this question). After dividing the respondents into these three groups, it was found that those hotels which reported a rise in productivity seemed to rate staff training and qualifications as having a greater influence on productivity than the other hotels. Those which reported a fall in productivity seemed again to place greater emphasis on the influence of the weather and the economic climate on productivity than the other hotels.

When respondents were asked about their expectations concerning staff productivity for the coming year, only one expected a drop. However, 57 expected an increase and 93 expected it to stay about the same. Comparing these two groups, it appears that those expecting an increase rated staff issues generally as a little more influential, together with management training, forecasting and local events.

Analysis of the sample by group membership

About a third of the respondents belonged to group companies. Preliminary analysis suggests that group hotels rated both staff training and qualifications and management training as more influential than other hotels. They also rated forecasting and new technology to be significantly more important.

Analysis of the sample by whether or not they take productivity measurements

About a quarter of the respondents said that they took measurements of productivity. Such hotels tended to be those run by more professional and highly trained management. As might be expected, when compared with the other hotels, these placed significantly more importance on management training, as well as on forecasting and new technology.

CONCLUSIONS

The concept of productivity is often overlooked in the management of many hotels, particularly the smaller ones, where managers have typically had little training in professional management. It was apparent that some simple productivity measurements, like occupancy, are taken in some establishments, but are not recognized as being such (i.e. nearly all of the managers in the HCTC survey recorded occupancy, but only about a quarter of respondents claimed to take productivity measures). Virtually all hotels, however, have sufficient physical and financial data to enable the calculation of a variety of productivity measurements. Basic physical data, such as the number of bedrooms, the numbers of guests, the numbers of covers served and details of the staff employed, together with fairly basic financial information from the accounts on sales revenue, costs and profits, would allow the calculation of a range of productivity measurements for the hotel. This information is not therefore being put to good use to monitor performance. Yet surprisingly, while productivity in hotels has been quite widely investigated and numerous academic journals and books provide advice on the subject to modern students of hospitality management, little has been done to emphasize the value of productivity measurement and monitoring to the industry generally. There is therefore scope for the production and wide dissemination of a user-friendly guide to measuring and monitoring productivity.

From the HCTC survey of hotel managers, it was apparent that most hotels could take measurements of room nights per FTEE, sales per FTEE and profits per FTEE. It was also apparent that many previous studies had concentrated on these measures in examining productivity in hotels. It became clear, however, that these measures alone would not permit comparisons between hotels unless the hotels were very similar in terms of size, standard and market. Within a particular hotel, these productivity measurements could be useful for monitoring performance over a period of time, although more sophisticated measures, such as value-added measures, or combinations of measures are likely to provide a better indication of productivity change over time and a better indication of causes of changes in productivity.

Although, as mentioned above, it was only a minority of hotels that said they took measurements of productivity, when asked whether there had been a change in staff productivity over the previous 12 months, only 10 per cent of the respondents said they did not know, or omitted to reply. About 5 per cent of managers said that productivity had fallen, usually giving the cause as falling levels of business. About half said it had risen, and a third said it had stayed the same. When an increase was reported, the reason most often given seemed to be an increase in the overall level of business. From this, it would appear that some, but by no means all, managers perceive productivity as being more or less the same thing as the level of business: in other words, rather than perceiving it as a ratio of outputs to inputs, they tend to regard only the outputs. This finding was supported by some of the managers who said they measured productivity, but then gave only details of outputs that they recorded.

To a large extent expectations of how occupancy and covers in restaurants would change over the next year also reflected expectations on future staff productivity. However, whereas only one hotel manager expected staff productivity to fall, more managers expected business levels to fall, suggesting that a few managers generally understood productivity changes and planned either to reduce staffing levels or to take other measures to maintain or improve staff productivity. If, however, as appears to be the case from preliminary findings, most managers generally only consider the influence of demand on productivity, it will require a significant change in perception on the part of managers to see the potential benefits of training, forecasting and new technology, for example, in terms of productivity improvement.

Productivity is influenced by a number of factors, all of which are important and many of which are interrelated. The HCTC study has attempted to identify the factors that might have most impact on productivity. While the perceptions of hotel managers provide only a limited assessment of the influence of factors on productivity, it is likely that they will provide a better assessment than could be generated by an external researcher observing hotel performance.

The two factors that were most important to all establishments in the HCTC survey were customer perceptions and satisfaction, and the quality of the service and product. Other factors concerning staff, particularly their morale, job satisfaction and training, were also regarded as important influences on productivity. Yet few studies, including the HCTC study as yet, have attempted to take account of the impact of these factors on productivity. With so many factors potentially impacting on productivity, the real problem is isolating the impact of change in any one of the factors. It will be extremely difficult to vary any of these factors in practice and then measure their impact on productivity, although training may offer greater opportunities for such investigation. Training may not be strictly quantified but, the provision of training can be relatively well controlled and its impact assessed perhaps more readily than the impact of improved quality, or changing customer perceptions.

In relation to each of the factors, various comments made by the respondents were collected and collated, to gather opinion from the industry and to identify cases of good practice for productivity improvement. A number of hotels in the survey have been identified as being of particular interest because of their impressive strategies in connection with one or more of these factors. It is planned to study these in more detail, with the aim of identifying best practice for the industry as a whole. These strategies could then be tested in hotels through demonstration projects (as proposed by the NEDC, 1992), in order to demonstrate their effectiveness in bringing about improvements in performance.

In time, it is hoped to broaden the scale of investigations to include hotels in continental Europe. The recently announced 'benchmarking project', an initiative of the Department of National Heritage (1995), alongside a similar initiative of the CBI, may yet see the fulfilment of many of these long-term objectives. But any such study needs to address the issues for hotels of all sizes, and in particular smaller hotels, if it is to be of significant value to the UK hotel industry.

The authors wish to acknowledge the contribution made to the HCTC project by Dr Tony Ingold, Sarah Peters and Sally Reynolds of the Birmingham College of Food, with both the literature review and exploratory work; Ian Yeoman of Napier University with exploratory work; and former HCTC staff member Penny Lane with the initial literature review.

REFERENCES

Bain, D. (1986) *The Productivity Prescription*. New York: McGraw-Hill.

Ball, S.D., Johnson, K. and Slattery, P. (1986) 'Labour productivity in hotels: an empirical analysis'. *International Journal of Contemporary Hospitality Management*, **5**(4), 265–9.

Chew, B.W. (1986) 'No-nonsense guide to measuring productivity'. *Harvard Business Review*, Jan/Feb.

Department of National Heritage (1995) *Tourism: Competing with the Best*. London: HMSO.

Hotel and Catering Tourism Committee (1989) *Productivity and Training in the Hotel, Catering and Tourism Sector*. International Labour Organisation Report 3, First Session, Sectorial Activities Programme. Geneva: ILO.

Lee-Ross, D. and Ingold, T. (1994) 'Increasing productivity in small hotels: are academic proposals realistic?' *International Journal of Hospitality Management*, **13**(3), 201–7.

Mahoney, T.A. (1988) *Productivity in Organizations: New Presentation from Industrial and Organizational Psychology*. San Francisco: Jossey-Bass.

Medlik, R. (1989) 'The main features and underlying causes of the shift to services'. *Tourism*, **61**, January/February, 13–18.

Millward, R. (1990) 'Productivity in the UK services sector: historical trends 1886–1985 and comparisons with the USA'. *Oxford Bulletin of Economics and Statistics*, **25**(4), 423–36.

NEDC (1992) *Costs and Manpower Productivity in UK Hotels Sub Group Report*. London: National Economic Development Office.

Prais, S.J., Jarvis, V. and Wagner, K. (1989) 'Productivity and vocational skills in services in Britain and Germany: hotels'. *National Institute Economic Review*, November, 52–74.

Prokopenko, J. (1987) *Productivity Management: A Practical Handbook*. Geneva: International Labour Office.

Ray, G.F., (1986) 'Productivity in services'. *National Institute Economic Review*, February, 44–7.

Schroeder, R.G. (1985) *Operations Management Decision Making in the Operations Function*. New York: McGraw-Hill.

Teague, J. and Eilon, S. (1973) *Productivity Measurement: a Brief Survey*. London: Chapman and Hall.

Thorpe, R. and Horsburgh, S. (1991) *The Management Services Handbook*, 2nd edn. London: Pitman.

Witt, C.A. and Witt, S.F. (1989) 'Why productivity in the hotel sector is low'. *International Journal of Contemporary Hospitality Management*, **1**(2), 28–33.

PART 3
THE PRODUCTIVITY OF OPERATIONS

NINE

Perceptions and interpretations of productivity within fast-food chains: a case study of Wimpy International

Stephen Ball

INTRODUCTION

Improving productivity is important to the fast-food industry. It is thought that labour productivity in the hospitality industry has traditionally been very low compared to that in many other industries. Recent evidence supports these thought (Medlik, 1988; Mill, 1989). Similar findings have been reported for service industries more generally. Elfing (1989), for instance, identified a service lag when comparing productivity of services with that of manufacturing on an international basis. Other international comparative studies have highlighted differences between hotel productivity in different countries and in particular show levels in UK hotels (Prais *et al.*, 1989; Worldwide Hospitality Industry, 1991).

Advances in national and industrial productivity are determined primarily by decisions, actions and productivity performance within individual firms and unit (Adam *et al.*, 1981; Gold, 1981; Prokopenko, 1987). Prokopenko considers the enterprise or the company as 'the place where productivity growth is actually created'. In a competitive environment firms are confronted with the need to improve continuously the productivity of their operations to achieve profitability and growth. Additionally, it is they who have the best opportunity for direct and rapid productivity improvement and it is they and their managers who are increasingly being urged to give greater emphasis to productivity and productivity management programmes. The need for higher productivity levels within individual fast-food organizations, and hospitality organizations more generally, would therefore seem clear.

However, the various perspectives in the literature often imply inconsistent definitions and interpretations of the basic productivity concept. Behavioural scientists, economists, accountants, trade unionists, politicians, managers and other groups all appear to differ on an operational definition of productivity. These inconsistencies and diversities can only serve to confuse and retard productivity endeavours within an organization.

This chapter is concerned with the productivity perspectives of different people groupings associated with the operations function of fast-food chain restaurants. Essentially it is divided into two parts. The first part aims to analyse the literature in order to develop a sound conceptual foundation of productivity in the context of fast-food chain restaurants. This will be achieved by examining the basic definition of productivity and the multiple viewpoints of different people groups involved with operational activities in fast-food chain restaurants. The aim of the second part is to report some findings from recent empirical research undertaken by the author (Ball, 1993) on productivity perceptions and interpretations in one fast-food restaurant chain, namely Wimpy International. Throughout, implications of the differing notions of productivity for the improvement and management of productivity within fast-food chain restaurants are discussed.

THE BASIC PRODUCTIVITY CONCEPT

A number of authors, including Mali (1978), Kazarian (1989) and Sink (1985), have claimed that productivity and productivity management have been restricted in organizations. According to them this has been owing in part to a limited, or lack of, understanding of the basic concept.

In a broad sense, productivity is regarded as the utilization of resources in creating goods or services from an entity. If this entity is taken as an organization then it can be simply viewed as a microeconomic system. According to this system's model, organizations are in constant interaction with their environment and as such can be referred to as open systems. Resources are taken from the environment and used as inputs to the organization. Inputs then interact with each other and are transformed to produce outputs that return to the environment.

Productivity is generally defined in systems terms and is usually stated as the relationship between the amount of output of goods and/or services obtained from a system and one or more of the input(s) employed in yielding this output. Thus:

$$\text{productivity} = \frac{\text{output obtained}}{\text{input(s) employed}}$$

For fast-food chain restaurants, as other organizations, the concept can be basically expressed in either a partial or a total form. Total productivity is the ratio of total outputs to the sum of all contributing and associated resource inputs. In partial form the ratio relates outputs to one class of resource input.

Two assumptions are made in the traditional productivity concept. These are that inputs and outputs are perfectly defined and measurable and that the utility of outputs is in no doubt. These assumptions will now be shown to be imperfect when applied to the realities of fast-food chain restaurants.

THE DEFINITION OF INPUTS

Inputs are simply the resources needed to operate an entity and can be categorized into such broad types as labour, capital, raw materials, energy and information resources. In fast-food restaurants customers can also be considered as inputs, as they may be actively involved in helping to create the service product – either by serving themselves to, for example, salads or meal accompaniments such as cruet sachets, serviettes and straws, or by interacting with service staff (even if this is usually brief and controlled) over the order, payment and collection. When customers do serve themselves this is in effect substituting their labour for that of service staff. The self clearing of tables is another example where the labour input is replaced by customer 'labour'.

The service sector and the hospitality industry more specifically have concentrated particularly upon the partial measure which links output to the labour input, i.e. labour productivity (see, for example, Pedderson *et al.*, 1973; Pavesic, 1983; Pine and Ball, 1987; Jones and Lockwood, 1989; Mill, 1989). Ball *et al.* (1986) argue that labour is a legitimate focal point for hotel managers managing productivity, because labour is present in almost all output-generating endeavours and represents a significant proportion of hotel costs. Similar arguments could be presented for fast-food restaurant managers. Fast-food chain restaurants are labour hungry (Ball, 1992), have a significant proportion of total operating costs devoted to labour (although at approximately 20 per cent of total costs this is less than those identified as typical of hotels) and have a variable cost over which management can, and does (Transnationals Information Centre, 1987, p. 9), exert some control. A further reason for focusing upon the labour input is productivity in fast-food restaurants is that labour measurements (e.g. hours worked) are normally readily available through electronic point of sales systems, rotas and clock-in clock-out machines.

Critics argue that there are shortcomings in only considering the labour input and that it obscures the relevance of other resource types. Blois (1984), for instance, regards it as unsatisfactory as output production is normally the consequence of a combination of input factors. In the same vein, Hall (1973) criticizes the use of labour inputs in productivity measures as it 'implies, quite incorrectly, that all productivity gains are the result of labour's efforts'. The use of labour hours or labour costs as indicators of the labour input might also be regarded as too narrow, because they fail to pay regard to the heterogeneity of employees working in the same positions. Workers have different skills, abilities, attitudes, levels of motivation, degrees of job satisfaction and loyalty. These, it could be argued, mean that different labour makes different contributions to output. Certainly any conception of productivity that omits consideration of different employees and their different attributes and quality of input is short-sighted. Better application of social skills with customers may stimulate sales and thus have a positive impact upon productivity. However, the problems of incorporating these factors into input measures are far from clear and rarely mentioned, let alone resolved, in the literature. Doutt (1976) notes that such 'other characteristics can only be noted in the most casual way'.

Other counter arguments exist to the above criticisms of focusing only on labour and on traditional quantitative measures of labour. These include the reality that there are considerable difficulties in measuring and accumulating different types of resources and also that calculating labour by hours worked or employee costs in fast-food restaurants is relatively easy, particularly where the technologies previously mentioned are in use. These plus the fact that in many cases units of labour input can be used, according to Bernolak (1980), as an alternative to the more complex multi-input factor productivity concept mean that, rightly or wrongly, the labour factor and traditional labour measures will continue to be considered or used in productivity calculations in fast-food restaurants for the foreseeable future.

THE DEFINITION OF OUTPUTS

The composition of output in the productivity ratio of fast-food restaurants poses some difficulties. In contrast with primary and secondary sectors of the economy, which produce physical units or goods, fast-food restaurants, and service industries in general, supply customers with a mix of physical products, facilities and services. This mix makes the quantification and summation of all the ingredients in physical terms impossible because of their diversity. Financial measures, such as sales and added value, have been advocated as ways of overcoming this. The expression of output in monetary values is also advantageous where common ground is desired between output and input. However, such measures of output may be affected by inflation, which would give false interpretations of output changes. Physical measures are inflation proof but given the earlier point could at best be applied to part of the product–service mix of fast-food restaurants, namely the physical product ingredient.

According to Adam *et al.* (1981), outputs are easiest to measure when physical units of limited type are produced and can be used. Output measurement should therefore be easy in manufacturing settings. In food service the closest analogy to manufactured physical goods might be numbers of meals provided, yet these cannot be stored, making their counting more time restricted. Fast-food restaurants do, however, normally produce menu items of a limited type and, when part of a branded and franchised chain, strive to produce and serve standardized and comparable items. Here the use, and measurement, of served menu items as an output does have some logic even if they are only part of the total provision.

Within fast-food restaurants an array of outputs is identifiable and can be utilized for different purposes. For instance, fast-food chains normally include pavement flows of pedestrians when they select high street sites for restaurants. Likewise, drive-through sites are heavily determined by vehicle flows. Operations management would therefore be interested in the proportion of customers served who are 'peeled off' from passing pedestrians or drivers. Another output of interest might be the number of children's birthday parties provided by a restaurant. Fast-food chains have regarded the under-16s as a major target market and have become involved in party provision as one way of tapping it. The number of items produced by a particular piece of equipment in a given time would be an output to focus upon, especially as some fast-food chains have been aware of the leverage that technology can give them and of the subsequent savings in costs.

All outputs of fast-food restaurant operations can be conceived as secondary or primary outputs. Secondly outputs result from the conversion of inputs prior to selling or delivery to the customer. The production of food in a restaurant's production area would be an example. Primary outputs on the other hand, have a 'sales' element such as gross margin, customer served, pieces (menu items) sold or seating utilization. The choice of output and productivity ratio is dependent upon the use to which they are put. A catalogue of ratios can be compiled by fitting outputs to associated inputs.

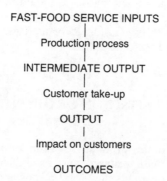

FAST-FOOD SERVICE INPUTS
|
Production process
|
INTERMEDIATE OUTPUT
|
Customer take-up
|
OUTPUT
|
Impact on customers
|
OUTCOMES

Figure 9.1. Model of fast-food service delivery

Each ratio relates to different aspects of operating performance and to different organizational activities. Ball (1994) gives examples of the range of food service productivity ratios.

From Figure 9.1 it can be seen that productivity can relate either to the relationship between inputs and intermediate (secondary) outputs or to that between inputs and (primary) outputs. Each of these ratios is different and has different measurement and improvement implications. It is important that the differences between these ratios are recognized to enable inputs and outputs to be more easily standardized, to achieve a constancy in the relationship between inputs and outputs and to facilitate more accurate measurement of inputs and outputs (Jones and Lockwood, 1989). The outcome factor in Figure 9.1 is significant as the effectiveness of transforming outputs into desirable customer outcomes is a matter of quality. This again shows how productivity interrelates with quality.

PRODUCTIVITY AND THE QUALITY FACTOR

Productivity can be and has been regarded in quantitative terms. Maximizing the efficiency with which inputs are converted to outputs has traditionally formed the basis of productivity improvements within firms. Efficiency perspectives have underpinned the productivity practices of the McDonald's and Burger King fast-food chains, where industrial engineers have shaped technological efficiency strategies related to plant, equipment and processes to increase productivity (Levitt, 1972; Filley, 1983; Transnational Information Centre, 1987). However, the sustained and exclusive reliance by any management upon the efficiency and quantitative criteria of productivity to the exclusion of other dimensions, such as effectiveness, dynamism and quality, has been questioned (Crandall and Wooton, 1978; Thorpe, 1986; Pickworth, 1987). The difficulty with many measures of output is that they fail to take any account of changes in quality. If quality of a product or service is increased without additional costs and result should be an improvement in customer satisfaction. There are approaches to overcome the pitfalls associated with quality changes to outputs. These are referred to by Ball and Johnson (1994). They include the adjustment of output to the number of usable, saleable or acceptable outputs, which in the case of services could mean using the number of satisfied customers served rather than just the number of customers served. Quality control techniques, such as the use of standard packages, service audits and direct customer feedback mechanisms, could minimize quality change adjustments to outputs. They have the key intention of maintaining quality of output as a constant level.

The failure of a fast-food chain to incorporate quality within its concept of productivity would be particularly short-sighted given the presence of customers on site in fast-food restaurants, (unless they are customers of a home delivery fast-food operation) and their involvement in the service process. For example, it might be possible to product more menu items or serve more customers with no increase in resources, but this may lead to errors in the production and assembly of those items and inadequate interaction between front-of-house workers and customers. Furthermore, as Cowell (1984) claims, marketing in the service exchange process has a distinctive role. Rathmell (1974) sums this up.

> Goods are produced, sold and consumed. Services are sold and then performed and consumed simultaneously. . . . In place of the one interface between buyer and seller of goods – marketing – there are two interactions between the buyer and the seller of services – marketing and production.

Hence, any attempts to increase productivity in quantitative terms through efficiency-oriented productivity measures would be very likely to impinge upon the customer's perception of the service offered and might, if excessive, result in customers' expectations not being met and thus in customer dissatisfaction. In other words, a 'trade-off' between the quantity and quality of outputs in fast-food restaurants may result in an adverse effect upon productivity. So fast-food providers taking productivity actions should have a sensitivity to the customer and should take both quality and quantity into account. They need to focus upon the outcomes of their endeavours by concentrating on how well customers are served as well as how many are served, by enquiring whether services are required rather than merely providing them and by examining how well complaints are dealt with as opposed to merely logging them. Such a sensitivity can be achieved by the establishment of a relationship between the provider and the customer. Such a relationship can improve productivity.

The output of fast-food restaurants, although to a lesser extent than some service organizations, is entwined with the provider's efforts/input. Thus an important concern for fast-food restaurants is the quality of the workforce, management and working conditions. Similarly, the quality of other inputs will have an effect upon the output of fast-food restaurants. Production equipment that regularly breaks down through inadequate maintenance will reduce the potential quantity of output and may have adverse consequences upon quality. The purchase or receipt of sub-standard commodities may result in increased waste or an inferior end product. The presence of these additional qualitative factors in both inputs and outputs in food service situations is recognized by Freshwater and Bragg (1975). They contend that traditional productivity computations have been unrealistic as they failed to take account of the quality of resources, training and motivation.

Thus productivity is linked with quality of output, input and, indeed, the process itself, and quality has to be married to quantity. As Mill (1989) says, hospitality 'Management will also have to make customer satisfaction, service and quality part of the productivity equation.' Quality judgements and expectations in fast-food restaurants are influenced by external or environmental factors. Fast-food management needs to recognize this.

Productivity in the fast-food restaurant context lies beyond this scope of a simple quantitative input–output relationship. Qualitative dimensions are also significant with regard to both inputs and outputs. Hence the basic definition of productivity needs to be expanded so that specific reference is made to both the qualitative and quantitative dimensions. Such a definition would be that productivity is the relationship between the quantity and quality of goods or services produced and the quantity and quality of resources used to produce them. This can be alternatively expressed as:

$$\text{partial fast-food restaurant productivity} = \frac{f(\text{quality of outputs, quantity of outputs})}{\text{quality and quantity of a single class of resource, e.g. labour}}$$

$$\text{total fast-food restaurant productivity} = \frac{\text{total } f(\text{quality of outputs, quantity of outputs})}{\text{quality and quantity of labour} + \text{capital} + \text{energy} + \text{raw materials, etc.}}$$

An understanding of this by fast-food managers is required if they are to realize the full benefits of productivity interventions.

THE PRODUCTIVITY PERSPECTIVES OF DIFFERENT PEOPLE

While few would disagree with the basic meaning of productivity cited in the previous section it has been postulated by Mohanty and Rastogi (1985), Sink (1985), Thorpe (1986), Prokopenko (1987), Pickworth (1994) and others that in reality different people have different definitions and perceptions of productivity. Such claims are logical given that people have varying backgrounds, positions of responsibility, goals, etc. Thorpe (1986) even argues that often these perceptions conflict. He contends that it would be desirable for each organization to recognize this and avoid any conflict by bringing together a range of people within the organization to discuss productivity and the organization's priorities. Lane (1976), for example, in contrasting several viewpoints of productivity, says that 'Confusion over just what productivity is has frequently hampered the search (for ways to secure greater employee productivity) and clouded the discussion.'

Of the above authors only Sink (1985) provides any empirical data to support his claims, and these are limited. It is often implied or stated, and again usually with no evidence, that people's awareness of productivity is low and that people perceive the significance of productivity as low. This is a situation that Riggs and Felix (1983) regard as undesirable. They consider it important to make people in organizations aware of productivity and its significance. Ball and Johnson (1994) state that the many contemporary connotations of productivity are dependent upon the discipline and reference point of the definer. Mohanty and Rastogi (1985) go further than this and examine the different views people have of productivity under a variety of headings: expectational incongruencies, definitional incongruencies (based particularly upon the discipline of the definer), temporal incongruencies, valuational incongruencies and spatial incongruencies. The influence of peoples' expectations upon their interpretations of productivity and the time at which they are defining productivity and implementing productivity actions (the temporal factor) are especially relevant to an analysis of productivity perspectives associated with fast-food chain restaurants and are therefore examined below. The temporal factor is analysed in dynamic and strategic terms.

PEOPLE'S EXPECTATIONS OF PRODUCTIVITY

A fast-food chain restaurant can be considered as an exchange system comprising varied expectations and satisfactions of the persons involved, sometimes referred to as stakeholders. These stakeholders – franchiser, franchisees, managers, operatives, customers, etc – make varied contributions to the restaurant's operation and expect something back in return. Some of these expectations may be conflicting while others are complementary.

Franchisers normally expect to collect an initial franchise fee and continuing royalties from the franchisee. Franchisers normally seek to maximize control and expect standardization of operations. Franchisees, on the other hand, expect some independence, even if it is restricted. Such independence may be acceptable to the franchiser but if abused could result in franchiser–franchisee conflict, particularly if standards are being compromised. An example of this related to Wimpy International is vividly detailed by Pollard and Voss (1985). Lane (1976), Mohanty and Rastogi (1985) and Thorpe (1986) identify generalized productivity expectations of other stakeholders and groups. It is suggested, for example, that managers, in return for their labour, attempt to maximize production and profitability through coordination of resources and labour control. Workers, on the other hand, aim to maximize net earnings, improve the quality of work life and enjoy more leisure time. Customers look for quality of service at lowest possible price. Stakeholders' expectations, then, may not be entirely economic and may be socially orientated. Stakeholders provide different forms of input and have certain expectations of the nature of the output that should be produced.

Hence a person's expectations will influence his or her understanding and interpretation of productivity. This view is supported by Mohanty and Rastogi (1985), who claim that the diversity of perceptions about productivity is partially explained by the expectational incongruencies of different behavioural groups.

Just as Zeithaml *et al.* (1990) suggest that various factors might shape customer expectations of quality, so, it is proposed, do several factors influence peoples' expectations of productivity. Customers' expectations of productivity in fast-food chain restaurants might be determined by communications with other customers, past experiences, personal needs and external communications from providers of fast food (e.g. radio and television commercials and promotional advertisements). Operatives' expectations might be shaped by communications with other operatives, past experiences, personal needs, education and communications from management about company attitudes and policy towards productivity. An appreciation by fast-food chain restaurant managements of the determinant factors of these expectations would provide them with opportunities to shape peoples' (e.g. operatives' and customers') perceptions of productivity and therefore reduce any potentially damaging perceptual diversity.

STRATEGIC AND DYNAMIC INFLUENCES UPON PERSPECTIVES OF PRODUCTIVITY

Measures of productivity may need to change to something more appropriate as priorities alter. There is a danger that if measures are not reviewed, and if necessary changed, the productivity focus bears no relationship to currently important issues and patterns of behaviour becomes rigid. Rather than just counting the number of customers served in a restaurant, it may become important (for instance, because of complaints from customers about the shortage of facilities) to focus upon the number of people entering a restaurant in order to monitor lost customers and the utilization of facilities, such as toilets, by the general public. Thus it follows that productivity in fast-food restaurants, as in any organization, contains a dynamic element. This is a factor recognized by both Mohanty and Rastogi (1985) and Thorpe (1986). Thorpe states that a dynamic element is important in productivity to ensure that patterns of behaviour change according to currently important issues.

Mohanty and Rastogi and Thorpe also consider that productivity can be perceived in strategic terms. Essentially they re-emphasize and develop a contention made by Crandall and Wooton (1978), and supported here, that productivity interpretations, strategies and actions relate to the development of an organization.

Strategies for improving productivity have been classified as either contractive or expansive (Johns and Wheeler, 1990). However, if one considers that productivity can be improved by changing the output to input ratio in one of five ways (these are indicated in Figure 9.2), then it is apparent that productivity strategies could alternatively be divided into five. Furthermore, each of these strategies can be related to the different stages of development that an organization like a fast-food chain or each of its restaurants undergoes. In each stage of development the problems and priorities change, the specific activities undertaken change and the input–output relationships change. Numerous models of company and organizational development have been proposed. Figure 9.2 is another. It draws upon Ross (1981), Sandler (1982) and Jones and Lockwood (1989) in order to illustrate in simple terms how for one cycle of development the strategic factors and approaches relevant to the management of productivity in a fast-food chain will be dependent upon the stage that has been reached. It also shows what these strategic approaches mean in terms of input and output changes. From this discussion it is argued that productivity has strategic dimensions and that different people may have different perspectives of productivity according to the phase of development they believe the chain, or an individual restaurant, is in.

Thus far, the existence of a diversity in productivity perceptions among people associated with fast-food chain restaurants has been explored and the possible reasons

PRODUCTIVITY STRATEGY	WORKING EFFECTIVELY	WORKING SMARTER	MANAGING GROWTH	COST REDUCTION	PARING DOWN
Input/output change for greater productivity	Increase output, decrease input	Increase output, maintain input	Increase output > increased input	Decrease input, maintain output	Decrease output < decreased input
STAGE OF THE SERVICE LIFE-CYCLE	INNOVATION	DEVELOPMENT	GROWTH	MATURITY	DECLINE
Main features of firm at each stage	Slow growth, one or two prototype operations	Growth by opening new outlets	Very rapid geographic growth	Saturation of sites	Close down less profitable units
Main features of operation at each stage	Trying out new ideas by trial and error	Adopt model, trial elsewhere	Adapt slightly in new locations	Adapt greatly to meet competetive threats	Revamp completely

Figure 9.2. Organizational life cycle and productivity strategies

for this identified, the point being that if diversity does exist and remains unrecognized then it could be damaging. Thorpe (1986) provides an example of the conflicting effects of different groups improving productivity based upon their own definitions.

> In their efforts to secure employee compliance and co-operation, supervisors very often agree to work schedules which suit the employees but which waste materials or machine-running time. Top management in pursuing their aim of expanding to secure a greater market share could well invest in technology which, perhaps temporarily, increased costs and made the investor's return on capital less attractive, at the same time as increasing costs and adversely affecting inflation, albeit in a small way.

The inference from this is that the management of productivity within the context of fast-food restaurants requires an awareness by managers of their workers' and customers' perceptions of productivity and of any differences in perception. Furthermore, a knowledge and understanding of the factors that determine people's perspectives would be invaluable. Without these the successful management of productivity (and consequently success of the business) may take longer to achieve or at worst may not be achieved.

DIMENSIONS OF PRODUCTIVITY

A number of dimensions of productivity have emerged in this chapter which represent peoples' explanations of productivity. These are: that productivity refers to the output from one class of input, usually labour in catering organizations; that productivity relates to the total output produced from all the inputs utilized; that productivity is concerned with quality as well as quantity; and that productivity has a temporal or dynamic interpretation. It is hypothesized that these dimensions, along with a number of others drawn from Katzell (1975), Riggs and Felix (1983), Sumanth (1984), Sink (1985 and Pickworth (1987), represent a good cross-section of the explanations that managers, workers and customers of a fast-food chain restaurant would have of productivity. These dimensions are not necessarily independent of one another. For instance, absenteeism and employee turnover may be connected to an employee's loyalty, morale and job satisfaction. Similarly, the quality of output is likely to impinge upon customer satisfaction. Any overlap of dimensions is considered to be partial rather than total and is not such that any of the following dimensions should be excluded.

D1 Productivity refers to the relationship between what a country or industry produces and what it uses in doing this.
D2 Productivity means the output each employee hour.
D3 Productivity means the quality of an employee's output as well as the quantity.
D4 Productivity includes loyalty, morale and job satisfaction.
D5 Productivity includes absenteeism and employee turnover.
D6 Productivity includes stoppages, vandalism and other disruptions.
D7 Productivity includes customer satisfaction.
D8 Productivity means different things to an individual at different times.
D9 Productivity means different things to different groups associated with a fast-food restaurant at any one time.
D10 Productivity means the overall efficiency and effectiveness of a fast-food organization.

Successful management is integrated and holistic. In a fast-food chain this means that senior management must aim to integrate the views of others within their perspective of productivity to enable synchronized productivity performance to be achieved. Senior management would therefore be likely to embrace the broadest range of productivity dimensions. On the other hand, while restaurant management and operatives should be aware of the way in which senior management interprets productivity, it is likely that because of their limited discretion over operational activities they would focus on fewer dimensions of productivity than senior management.

Key functions of senior managers of fast-food chains, independent of time or place, must be to make their restaurants and employees productive and to focus upon meeting customers needs. These functions, as previously discussed, are inseparable. Customer service and productivity have been crucial to the success of McDonald's and other service organizations (Albrecht and Zemke, 1985). To meet customer needs fast-food chains and their restaurants must be productive. From this the customer benefits and so should management, operatives and other stakeholders. Given this argument, senior management's explanation of productivity should reflect that of customers as it is through the customer that senior management succeeds. Therefore one would expect both groups to explain productivity in very similar terms or, to put it another way, one would expect both groups to include to the same extent the same dimensions in their general interpretations of productivity. Losing sight of customers' explanation of productivity could lead to the fast-food chain experiencing problems.

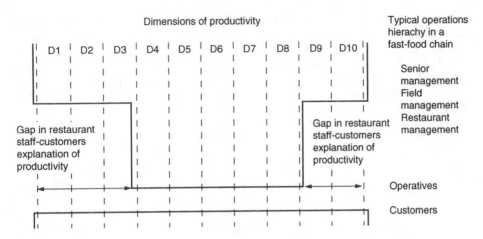

Figure 9.3. Hypothetical model comparing the explanations of productivity held by different people associated with a fast-food chain restaurant

Note: The dimensions included between continuous lines represent each group's explanation of productivity.

If senior management and customers explained productivity through a similar yet greater range of dimensions than operatives, then at the operative–customer interface a gap would exist that might prove damaging to both customers and managers. Customers' expectations of productivity, based upon their particular explanations, may not be being met. Senior management's task in such circumstances should be to increase operatives' awareness of their interpretation of productivity. This would be necessary even when operatives have limited discretion. The ideas in this section are central to this chapter and are illustrated in Figure 9.3.

PRODUCTIVITY PERCEPTIONS IN THE WIMPY INTERNATIONAL FAST-FOOD CHAIN

In the United Kingdom the fast-food sector generates significant revenues for its providers and is a valuable contributor to government revenues, economic growth, the balance of payments and employment. Since the mid-1970s the chain operators have revolutionized fast food in the UK and have been largely responsible for the dramatic growth of the sector. As the chains push to expand their share of the market, which in 1993 was estimated to be 40–45 per cent of the total £5.2 billion fast-food market, competition among them is expected to intensify. In such a competitive environment fast-food chains have a compelling need to be productive in their restaurants to ensure increased profitability and growth.

In the remainder of this chapter certain key findings from an empirical study of productivity and productivity management in Wimpy International's fast-food restaurant operations (Ball, 1993) are reported and discussed. The empirical research was designed and undertaken to determine actual productivity perspectives of distinctive groups within the company and then to compare and contrast them. These perspectives embraced productivity awareness, perceptions and practices. They related to corporate executives based at head office, field management who were not based at head office and had responsibility for a number of restaurants, restaurant management, operative staff and customers in both the company-managed and franchised divisions of the company. The findings presented here represent only part of the research carried out.

When the data were collected during 1988–9 the name Wimpy was synonymous with the fast-food scene in the UK. Wimpy International was a division of UB Restaurants, part of United Biscuits (UK). Wimpy was selected for study because of its size and longevity of operation in the UK. It was assumed that productivity management would be more advanced in a well established chain than in one of the newer chains.

The research adopted a case study approach and included in-depth interviews with eight head office executives/managers and field managers and the use of questionnaires in 12 Wimpy fast-food counter service restaurants (both company-owned and franchised), with 33 restaurant managers, 45 restaurant operatives and 106 customers. The restaurants and respondents chosen were intended to be representative of defined populations.

EXECUTIVES' AND FIELD MANAGERS' VIEWS OF THE PRODUCTIVITY CONCEPT

Top managers in fast-food companies are responsible for steering their companies through highly competitive circumstances and for the long-term viability of their companies. While productivity can be taken as a short-term concept, it is argued that it also has a longer-term orientation and must be regarded as interdependent with strategy. Strategy is a head office concern in most large organizations and thus the need for Wimpy's top management, given the size of the organization, to adopt a strategic emphasis on productivity in the 1990s would seem to be strong. Jones (1990) and Johns and Edwards (1994) uphold identical beliefs for hospitality managers in general.

When asked, all the head office executives in Wimpy regarded productivity in Wimpy and Wimpy restaurants in strategic terms (see Table 9.1). The finance director epitomized this consensus.

In the seventies there were a lot of inefficiencies you could eradicate without damaging the short term, i.e. there was overmanning. We were not moving technologically quickly in terms of industry. Those were all things we have benefited from. They are not things that affect the long term. But you have the 'Hanson' approach where you cut back on R and D and you can reach short-term rewards and promoting, advertising and developing a strong brand, and I think it is that side of productivity – squeezing the cash cow dry – that's wrong. It's a question of balancing the short and long term. (Finance Director, Wimpy International, 1988)

Table 9.1. Head office executives' understanding of productivity in Wimpy and Wimpy Restaurants

	Those in agreement	Those in partial agreement	Those in disagreement	No indication of agreement or disagreement
Productivity in restaurants relates sales to labour usage	All	–	–	–
Productivity in restaurants relates sales/outputs to other resources	All	–	–	–
Productivity in restaurants includes quality and customer satisfaction	All	–	–	–
Productivity in restaurants includes job satisfaction, absenteeism, loyalty	FD, MDM	MD, OD	OD	–
Productivity in restaurants means different things to different people in Wimpy	MDM, MD	OD FD	–	–
Productivity in restaurants means different things at different times	FD, MD OD	–	–	MDM
Productivity in restaurants is/should be a strategic issue	All	–	–	–
Concept of productivity is the same in Wimpy as in:				
(a) Manufacturing	–	–	FO, OD, MD	MDM
(b) Other catering operations	MD	–	OD	MDM, FD
Productivity is a goal of Wimpy	All	–	–	–
Productivity is not the major goal of Wimpy	MDM, FD	–	MD, OD	–

Note: FD, finance director; OD, operations director; MD, managing director; MDM, management development manager.

This response highlights the adverse and sacrificial consequences of adopting a short-term perspective and supports the notion that productivity factors and strategic considerations must be seen as interdependent. The converse is also possible: concentrating upon long-term ambitions rather than short-term success. Wendy's, the major US-owned burger chain, is a good example. It had long-term aspirations and strategies when entering the UK but was unsuccessful and withdrew from the market because of losses, poor productivity and a failure to reach a critical mass. This was in spite of it opening 18 units. Wimpy's finance director commented upon this converse situation:

> Maybe it is a question of balancing the short and long term. Everyone says you have to take 100 per cent long term; don't worry about this year, in five years time we'll earn a lot. In businesses that say that . . . It's always jam tomorrow and never today. It is actually wrong as we have to earn the crusts today.

Management of productivity begins from knowing what it is and how important it is. The conventional catering view that operational productivity in restaurants relates sales to labour usage was unanimously held by all the head office executives and management. The finance director typified their beliefs.

Productivity in restaurants; there I would look at generating sales, and you generate sales by two things – people walking in through the door, and increasing the spend per head of those people, and obviously relating that to the variable cost of running the restaurant, which is basically labour and food.

However, the inclusion of all variable costs in the denominator of the productivity equation defines productivity more as the 'total productivity concept'. It includes capital and fixed costs. Wimpy executives all agreed that comparison of the value of outputs to resources additional to labour was part of their understanding of productivity in Wimpy (see Table 9.1). This is sensible as exclusive concentration upon labour productivity within any company obscures the relative efficiency with which the other factors of production are used. In fast-food operations these other factors, especially raw materials, are significant.

The use of innovative delivery systems in modern fast-food restaurants has implications for the efficient management of a variety of resources and processes and thus the adoption of a definition of productivity which embraces all inputs is valid (Jones, 1990). The widest perception of productivity was held by the managing director, who said that he took the core meaning of productivity as

volume by volume the sheer weight of physical sterling sales that we generate through our restaurants, and without that I haven't got a company. I'm not allying productivity to output/man or whatever for the minute. My crude definition is: those are the number of restaurants – that's the volume of sales I expect.

This interpretation of productivity reflects the joint impact of all the inputs into restaurants in producing sales and therefore equates to the 'total productivity concept'.

Sasser *et al.* (1978) position fast-food and take-away meals towards the goods end of their goods–service continuum owing to their manufactured orientation. However, any similarities of the productivity concept in Wimpy and manufacturing was discounted by the executives. Three out of four executives perceived productivity to be different.

The importance of linking quality to productivity in fast-food chains has been emphasized. All the Wimpy executives, when asked, regarded productivity as including quality and customer satisfaction. In different ways they thought that the production of the Wimpy product and its delivery must be effective, efficient and dependable for it to be acceptable and to have value to their customers. The philosophy that service must be predictable and consistent and offer customer dependability in appearance, delivery time and cost is upheld by other fast-food chains (Albrecht and Zemke, 1985).

Wimpy executives also agreed, but to varying degrees, that factors such as job satisfaction, employee loyalty and the negative factor of absenteeism were included in their conceptions of productivity. Absenteeism could be used as a surrogate measure of productivity where output is not physically measurable. In the case of fast-food operations this would not be required, as the output is measurable in quantitative terms and, with some effort, in qualitative terms. According to the operations director, job satisfaction and worker loyalty were needed 'if you are going to achieve good productivity'.

Productivity also has a dynamic element according to the executives, with productivity being shaped differently at different times. To a fast-food chain dynamism is significant despite the limited individual discretion and flexibility that usually characterizes standardized and highly branded and often franchised operations. Wimpy was continually seeking ways to improve its service and product quality. Productivity measures also changed to reflect the priorities of different service attributes. According to the operations director, productivity 'has changed, it has evolved, not abruptly, through necessity. Will it change in the future? Of course it will as customers' needs change.'

Support for the contention that productivity means different things to different people groups (e.g. executives, restaurant managers and operatives) in Wimpy was provided by the responses from the executives. However, among the executives the overall conclusion is that there was very little difference of opinion about the nature of productivity. They all believed that productivity related output to resources and all perceived it to embrace quality and customer satisfaction. Virtual unanimity also existed over the necessity to consider the strategic and dynamic dimensions of productivity. Thus the empirical findings of the perceptions of the executives greatly support the general theoretical arguments presented earlier. Despite the above findings, 'productivity' was not a word used at executive level. Sales growth, labour percentage and urgency were the words used, according to the operations director. He stated that one of the reasons for this was that 'productivity' was previously used widely and by everyone in Huckleberry's (taken over by Wimpy in 1985). However, here it was interpreted as cutting back on staff. This, he said, resulted in lost customers and revenue, which he did not want in Wimpy. He felt that the opposite was often necessary: employing more staff would increase customer numbers. He also wanted 'to see customers being served properly, a good environment, staff that are happy and efficiently doing a good job, and a sense of urgency'.

It would be expected that field managers, like others, perceive productivity from their own circumstances. This in their case would be mainly in operational terms, i.e. related to the achievement of sales, standards and margins. Their distance from head office decision-making, particularly in the case of the operations executives, and their specific roles would suggest that strategic aspects would not be particularly pronounced ingredients of their productivity conceptions.

The empirical findings substantiate this hypothesis. All four field managers interviewed first and foremost viewed productivity as the relationship between output and some measure of labour utilization. Labour cost percentages were mentioned by all of them. One of the regional managers exemplified this labour productivity orientation.

> As far as I am concerned productivity is getting the best out of a person, or people, employed to do a job. It is important to make sure they are productive all the time and that you get value for money as an employer, and hopefully that they are getting value from the job, by not being allowed to get bored.

The view that productivity in Wimpy includes employee factors such as morale and job satisfaction was not accepted by all field managers. Only one agreed that it should be included. The inclusion of other inputs in the productivity equation was not immediately forthcoming, as with the head office executives. But when asked three out of four said that they did include other costs, such as food and operating expenses. Only one thought capital was important. 'We are constantly looking at the total restaurant operation and obviously it is important for us to utilize every facility and every piece of equipment the best we can'.

Regional managers and operations executives, commonly termed field managers as they operate 'out there in the field' as opposed to inside a specific restaurant, have the role of maintaining standards of quality in Wimpy restaurants, whether franchised or not, and are responsible for ensuring consistency between restaurants. Such tasks are key to a business wishing to be an effective branded operation. Quality and customer satisfaction were regarded by all the field managers as part of productivity. As one manager said,

> They are paramount to productivity within Wimpy because if the customers are not satisfied with the product quality at the end of the day they will go and they won't come back. So no matter what we do with equipment or anything we do to change the system we should look at the end customer, at speed and product quality'.

All the field managers considered productivity to be seen differently by different people groups in Wimpy. One manager argued that to operations it meant serving more people and getting more money; to marketing it was involved with 'bundling the product up properly for sale'; to training it was their ability to help operations achieve targets. Although these are different, they do all have an operations orientation and if accurate suggest that the crux of productivity lies with operations. One field manager remarked that 'operations is very much the be all and end all' and that operations was 'the dog and everybody else the tail'. Another recommended that a common operations-centred understanding of productivity throughout the company could be achieved by arranging for all people from non-operations departments to spend time working in restaurants. Two operations executives reiterated what had been said at head office about the non-use of the word productivity in induction, training and day-to-day operations. 'We talk around it', said one, while another said 'We use more terms like efficiency and the quickest way to do something.' Two reasons were suggested for its non-use. One was that staff would not like the word because it means job losses and other undesirable things. This was similar to a view of one of the head office respondents. The other reason suggested was that it was a word associated with manufacturing and was unsuitable for fast-food restaurants.

COMPARISONS OF THE VIEWS OF RESTAURANT MANAGEMENT, RESTAURANT OPERATIVES AND RESTAURANT CUSTOMERS

Figure 9.4 shows the percentage agreement with the statements explaining basic productivity in Wimpy. It is important to note that percentage agreement varied with statements explaining productivity. In other words, it could be said that different aspects of productivity had different levels of importance attached to them by

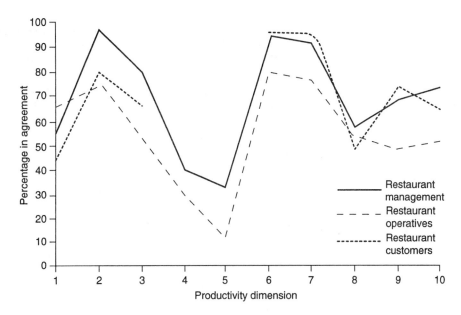

Figure 9.4. Percentage of Wimpy restaurant management, operatives and customers in all restaurants who agree with different dimensions of productivity

restaurant management, restaurant operatives and restaurant customers. Percentage agreement was greatest in general for interpretations of productivity that were clearly customer-oriented, i.e. the interpretations that included customer satisfaction and quality (dimensions 2 and 6), and for dimension 7, which could be considered to contain a customer element, though less overt. The complete productivity statements to which the dimension numbers (1 to 10) refer are shown in Table 9.3. It is interesting to note that while all three groups interviewed were very likely to relate productivity to that of Wimpy in general (dimension 7), customers and managers were far less likely than operatives to consider productivity in terms of the individual (dimension 1). Figure 9.4 shows, at a glance, that there were differences between perceptions of the basic concepts of productivity (dimensions 1 to 10) on the part of management, operatives and customers in Wimpy restaurants.

For all the dimensions of productivity (except dimension 1), the extent of restaurant management agreement was closer to that of customers than it was to that of operatives. In fact, as Table 9.2 shows, the average difference between the perceptions of management and operatives was almost twice that of management and customers. This implies that restaurant management's and customers' understandings of productivity were generally more alike than those of management and operatives. Comparisons of the perceptions of customers and management and of customers and operatives show that the average difference was greater for the latter pair than for management and customers (see Table 9.2).

Around 20 per cent, or greater, difference in agreement existed between management and operatives, related to the views that productivity included loyalty and job satisfaction (dimension 3), productivity means different things to different groups

Table 9.2. Perceptual differences of various dimensions of productivity between restaurant management, restaurant operatives and restaurant customers

Dimension	Percentage difference in agreement about dimension										Maximum difference	Average difference
	2	6	7	3	10	9	1	8	4	5		
Management: Operatives	21.5	11.7	13.1	25.5	22.5	23.8	9.9	7.0	8.3	19.2	25.5	16.3
Management: Customers	19.8	6.2	4.1	12.8	9.8	1.8	12.1	1.5	NK	NK	19.8	8.5
Operatives: Customers	1.7	5.5	9.0	12.7	12.7	25.6	22.0	5.5	NK	NK	25.6	11.8

Note: NK – not known as customers, therefore not questioned about these dimensions.

Table 9.3. The significance of the difference of restaurant managers' and operatives' opinions about various statements of productivity

	Calc. χ^2	Tab χ^2 for d.f. = 2 $\alpha = 0.05$	Opinions of groups are/ are not significantly different
Productivity means the output of Wimpy staff each hour (dimension 1)	1.141	5.99	Not significantly different
Productivity means the quality of output of Wimpy staff as well as the quantity (dimension 2)	7.389[a]	5.99	Significantly different
Productivity includes loyalty, morale and job satisfaction (dimension 3)	5.361	5.99	Not significantly different
Productivity includes absenteeism and employee turnover (dimension 4)	2.838	5.99	Not significantly different
Productivity includes stoppages, vandalism and other disruptions (dimension 5)	4.722	5.99	Not significantly different
Productivity includes customer satisfaction (dimension 6)	6.162[a]	5.99	Significantly different
Productivity means the overall efficiency and effectiveness of Wimpy International (dimension 7)	2.551[a]	5.99	Not significantly different
Productivity means different things at different times (dimension 8)	4.819	5.99	Not significantly different
Productivity means different things to different groups in Wimpy at any one time (dimension 9)	7.672	5.99	Significantly different
Productivity refers to the relationship between what a country or industry produces and what it uses in doing this (dimension 10)	4.544[a]	5.99	Not significantly different

Note: a Between one and four cells with expected counts < 5.

(dimension 9), productivity refers to the relationship between what a country or industry produces and what it uses in doing this (dimension 10), productivity means the quality of output as well as quantity (dimension 2) and productivity includes stoppages, vandalism and other disruptions (dimension 5). Restaurant management was more inclined to include all of these dimensions than operatives. Only dimension 2, which included a quality and a quantity element in productivity, exhibited the same order of difference when the perceptions of management and customers were compared. Interestingly, it was managers who were more inclined to include this dimension than customers.

Comparisons of the perceptions of customers and operatives show greater than 20 per cent differences only for dimension 9 (productivity means different things to different groups) and dimension 1 (productivity means employee output per hour). More operatives than customers agreed that the latter dimension should be included in their definition of productivity, while the reverse was true for dimension 9. The size of the differences between the pairs of groups for the other dimensions is noticeably smaller.

The χ^2 statistical significance test was used to determine whether there was any significance in the perceptual differences of various dimensions of productivity between the respondent groups. Table 9.3 shows that the difference between restaurant managers' opinions and those of operatives was only significant when they were asked

Table 9.4. The significance of the difference of restaurant operatives' and customers' opinions about various statements of productivity

	Calc. χ^2	Tab χ^2 for d.f. = 2 $\alpha = 0.05$	Opinions of groups are/ are not significantly different
Productivity means the output of Wimpy staff each hour	7.575	5.99	Significantly different
Productivity means the quality of output of Wimpy staff as well as the quantity	4.078[a]	5.99	Not significantly different
Productivity includes loyalty, morale and job satisfaction	6.175[a]	5.99	Significantly different
Productivity includes customer satisfaction	1.207[a]	5.99	Not significantly different
Productivity means the overall efficiency and effectiveness of Wimpy International	2.060[a]	5.99	Not significantly different
Productivity means different things to you at different times	25.429	5.99	Significantly different
Productivity means different things to different groups in Wimpy at any one time	16.768[a]	5.99	Significantly different
Productivity refers to the relationship between what a country or industry produces and what it uses in doing this	9.257[a]	5.99	Significantly different

Note: [a]Either one or two cells with expected counts < 5.

about their agreement with the statements: that productivity means the quality of output of Wimpy staff as well as the quantity (dimension 2); that productivity includes customer satisfaction (dimension 6); and that productivity means different things to different groups in Wimpy at one time (dimension 9). When the χ^2 test was performed the difference between restaurant managers' opinions and those of customers was only significant when they were asked about their agreement with the statements: that productivity means the quality of output of Wimpy staff as well as the quantity (dimension 2); and that productivity means different things at different times (dimension 8).

Table 9.4 shows that there were more statements where the difference between operatives' and customers' opinions was significant than where it was not. The difference was significant when they were asked about their agreement with the statements: that productivity means the output of Wimpy staff each hour (dimension 1); that productivity includes loyalty, morale and job satisfaction (dimension 3); that productivity means different things at different times (dimension 8); that productivity means different things to different groups in Wimpy at one time (dimension 9); and that productivity refers to the relationship between what a country produces and what it uses in doing this (dimension 10).

From these tests it can be concluded that the gap, as defined earlier in this chapter, explaining and understanding productivity is greatest between operatives and customers. This is because there are more statements where the difference between operatives and customers is significantly different than where the difference between either restaurant managers and operatives, or between restaurant managers and customers, is significantly different. On the same basis the gap between managers and customers was less than that between managers and operatives. This confirms what

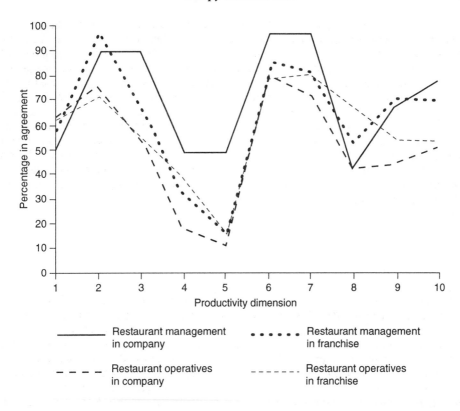

Figure 9.5. Percentage of Wimpy restaurant managers and operatives in company and franchise outlets who agree with different dimensions of productivity

was implied earlier in this section from the comparison of percentages of agreement: that managers' and customers' understandings of productivity were more alike than those of managers and operatives.

COMPARISONS BETWEEN MANAGERS AND OPERATIVES IN COMPANY RESTAURANTS AND MANAGERS AND OPERATIVES IN FRANCHISED RESTAURANTS

It was possible, given the sample frame, to analyse all the questions according to the franchise and company categories. Figure 9.5 shows that restaurant management in a company were more inclined than those in franchise to include all dimensions of productivity within their definition of productivity, except for dimensions 1, 2, 8 and 9. For each of these the difference in the response rates was less than 10 per cent. This was also the case for dimension 10. Thus the greatest differences occurred over the inclusion of such factors as employee loyalty, morale, job satisfaction (dimension 3) and customer satisfaction (dimension 6); over the inclusion of the so-called productivity surrogates of absenteeism and employee turnover (dimension 4); over the inclusion of the negative intangibles of stoppages, vandalism and other disruptions (dimension 5); and over the view that productivity means the overall efficiency and effectiveness of Wimpy (dimension 7). The higher proportion of company managers including the last in their definitions would be expected given that managers in franchised restaurants have responsibilities and loyalties to their franchise companies. For dimensions 4 and 5 more than 30 per cent more managers in franchises than in companies actually disagreed with their inclusion in their definition of productivity. As far as operatives were concerned, the only occasions when the differences in the response rates between those in franchises and those in companies were greater than 10 per cent occurred with respect to dimensions 4, 8 and 9. When the χ^2 test was performed upon the data collected, related to the opinions of franchise and company staff about their explanations of productivity, no significant differences were found.

CONCLUSION

Productivity is usually, and basically, regarded as the quantitative relationship between output and resource inputs. This chapter contends that this conception of productivity in fast-food restaurants should be broadened. Productivity in such contexts is inextricably linked with the quality of outputs, inputs and, indeed, the process itself. While quality of workers, managers and working practices and conditions are all of key importance, it is quality of service and customer satisfaction (usually considered a measure of service quality) that are particularly important given the nature of the fast-food service package and service delivery system. Hence productivity must be considered in both qualitative and quantitative terms. Because of the complex inter-action between the quality and quantity dimensions of productivity it would be understandable if they were, as some advocate, managed separately. The view here is that a fast-food chain's quantitative and qualitative results must be put alongside one another and evaluated in an integrated manner. Any decisions and actions taken as a consequence must also be integrated.

The identification, and subsequent measurement, on inputs and outputs in fast-food restaurants might be viewed as a conundrum, especially if the quality factor is included. Certainly these tasks are challenging. Some insights and approaches have been considered in this chapter.

The output to input definition of productivity is very likely to conceal varying perspectives and dimensions of productivity. These taken collectively represent people's explanations of productivity and are influential factors upon productivity performance. It is argued that these explanations must be recognized by management, through the use of market research, before any attempt to change productivity. Fast-food chains need to manage productivity by incorporating an organizational consensus about productivity. Without this, managers and staff may follow a common interpretation of productivity that conflicts with or does not match customer expectations of productivity based upon their particular explanations. The importance of satisfying customers means that the explanations of all fast-food staff must reflect the expectations their customers have of restaurant productivity. Alternatively managers and staff may pursue their own definitions and possibly work at cross purposes. Both alternatives would be detrimental to the business.

Dimensions of productivity

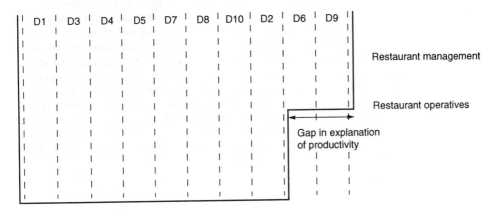

Figure 9.6. Comparison of the explanations of productivity held by restaurant management and operatives in Wimpy International

Management can actually shape the productivity perceptions and perspectives of its employees, through, for example, internal marketing, induction and training processes. Marketing approaches also offer an opportunity for management to influence customers' understanding of, and expectations from, productivity in fast-food restaurants.

A number of conclusions may be drawn from the empirical data presented relating to Wimpy International. An encouraging finding, from Wimpy's perspective, was that head office executives and management had a wide interpretation of productivity. This included quantitative, qualitative, strategic, dynamic and surrogate dimensions. It can therefore be concluded that these executives and managers did have an adequate understanding of the productivity concept. It was also found that certain conceptual elements, especially the core quantitative and qualitative dimensions, were regularly contained in the other respondent groups' explanations of productivity.

It is a conclusion from this research that the basic concept of productivity is perceived differently by restaurant management, operatives and customers associated with Wimpy fast-food restaurants. Thus evidence has been provided to substantiate the unsupported claims of Mohanty and Rastogi (1985), Thorpe (1985) and others that each group within an organization (in this case in a chain of fast-food restaurants) has its own understanding of productivity and that these differ. Some of these differences were shown using statistical instruments to be significant, while others were not. Where a significant difference occurred between two respondent groups about particular dimensions of productivity a gap in productivity explanation occurred. These gaps are identified in Figures 9.6 to 9.8.

From Figures 9.6 to 9.8 it can be concluded that customers' expectations of productivity, based upon their particular explanations, would probably be met by restaurant management (see Figure 9.7) but would probably not be completely met by operatives (see Figure 9.8). This was because restaurant managers, in contrast to operatives, included all the dimensions of productivity in their explanations of the concept which customers included in theirs. The managers' task is therefore to improve

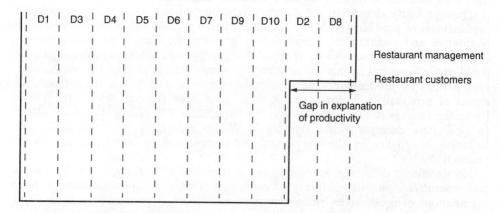

Figure 9.7. Comparison of the explanations of productivity held by restaurant management and customers in Wimpy International

Dimensions of productivity

```
| D3 ! D9 !D10!! D2 ! D4 ! D5 ! D6 ! D7 ! D1 ! D8 !
Gap in explanation
of productivity                                   Restaurant management
                                                  Restaurant customers
                                    Gap in explanation
                                    of productivity
```

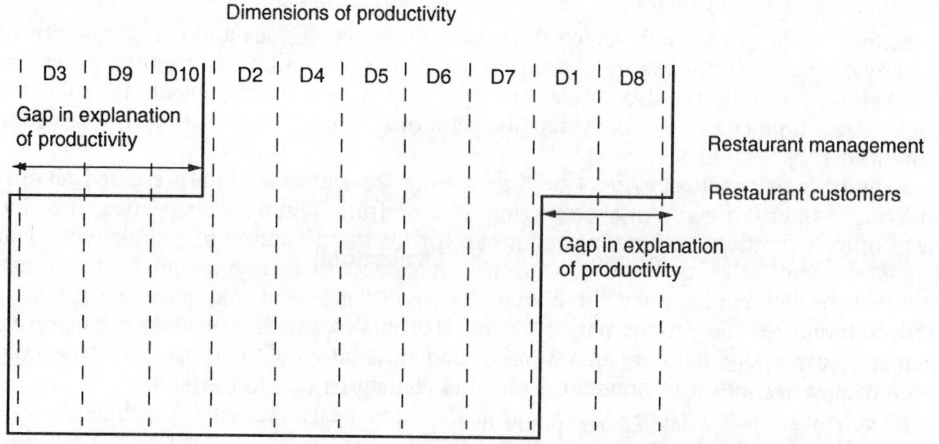

Figure 9.8. Comparison of the explanations of productivity held by restaurant operatives and customers in Wimpy International

operatives' understanding of productivity if they wish operatives to meet customer expectations and avoid experiencing any problems. In particular, operatives need to be made aware of and include dimensions 3, 9 and 10 in their interpretations of productivity. Emphasis needs to be placed especially on dimension 9, as this is not included significantly in operatives' explanations when compared to both managers' and customers' explanations of productivity (see Figures 9.6 and 9.8).

Wimpy restaurant managers explained productivity through a greater range of dimensions than operatives. This means that there was inconsistency in the interpretation of productivity among staff within Wimpy restaurants. This inconsistency needs to be removed in order to avoid the possibility of any conflicting effects or adverse consequences as a result of the different groups improving productivity based upon their own definitions, rather than on a definition understood and accepted by all.

The qualitative dimension did commonly feature among the Wimpy respondents' explanations of productivity. Many respondents recognized a relationship between the qualitative and quantitative dimensions of productivity. This is promising for the improvement of productivity in Wimpy and, if replicated in other fast-food chains, could prove beneficial to them. For Wimpy it shows that, at least in the respondents' explanations of productivity, the relationship between quality and the quantitative aspect of productivity is not overlooked, as is so often the case (Pickworth, 1987). From the findings it also appeared that the importance that Wimpy customers attach to qualitative elements of the outputs of Wimpy employees was matched by the inclusion of quality in the operatives', managers' and executives' definitions of productivity.

No significant difference was found in the responses of restaurant staff (managers and operatives) in the company division of Wimpy to questions about their explanations of productivity when compared with those of restaurant managers and operatives in franchised outlets. This suggests that ownership type does not have an influence upon the perceptions of restaurant staff about the basic meaning of productivity, and thus if there are any differences in productivity performance between franchised and company restaurants they are because of other factors associated with the management and operation of company and franchised outlets.

REFERENCES

Adam, E. Jr, Hershauer, J. and Ruch, W. (1981) *Productivity and Quality – Measurement as a Basis for Improvement.* Englewood Cliffs, NJ: Prentice Hall.

Albrecht, K. and Zemke, R. (1985) *Service America.* Homewood, IL: Dow Jones–Irwin.

Ball, S. (1992) *Fast Food Operations and Their Management.* Cheltenham: Stanley Thornes.

Ball, S. (1993) 'Productivity and productivity management within fast-food chains – a case study of Wimpy International'. MPhil dissertation, University of Huddersfield.

Ball, S. (1994) 'Improving labour productivity', In P. Jones and P. Merricks (eds), *The Management of Foodservice Operations.* London: Cassell.

Ball, S.D. and Johnson, K. (1994) 'Productivity measurement – hotels'. In S.F. Witt and L. Moutinho (eds), *Tourism Marketing and Management Handbook*, 2nd ed. Englewood Cliffs, NJ: Prentice Hall.

Ball, S.D., Johnson, K. and Slattery, P. (1986) 'Labour productivity in hotels: an empirical analysis'. *International Journal of Hospitality Management*, 5(3), 141–7.

Bernolak, I. (1980) 'The measurement of outputs and capital inputs'. In D. Bailey and T. Hubert (eds), *Productivity Measurement: an International Review of Concepts, Techniques, Programmes and Current Issues.* Farnborough: Gower, pp. 148–66.

Blois, K. (1984) 'Productivity and effectiveness in service firms', *Service Industries Journal*, 4(3), 49–60.

Cowell, D. (1984) *The Marketing of Services.* London: Heinemann.

Crandall, F.N. and Wooton, L.M. (1978) 'Developmental strategies of organizational productivity'. *California Management Review*, 21, 37–47.

Doutt, J.T. (1976) 'Productivity in fast-food retailing'. PhD thesis, University of California, Berkeley.

Elfing, T. (1989). 'The main features and underlying causes of the shift to services'. *Service Industries Journal*, 9(3), 337–56.

Filley, R.D. (1983) 'IEs make good use of people-orientated skills in helping their organizations provide service productivity'. *Industrial Engineering*, January, 36–47.

Freshwater, J.E. and Bragg, E.R. (1975) 'Improving food service productivity'. *Cornell Hotel and Restaurant Administration Quarterly*, 15(4), 12–18.

Gold, B. (1981) 'Improving industrial productivity and technological capabilities: needs, problems and suggested policies'. In A. Dogramaci (ed.), *Productivity Analysis, a Range of Perspectives*. London: Nijhoff.

Hall, C. (1973) 'Foreword'. In T.B. Pedderson *et al.*, *Increasing Productivity in Food Service*. Chicago: Cahners.

Johns, N. and Edwards, J.S. (1994) *Operations Management: a Resource Based Approach for the Hospitality Industry*. London: Cassell.

Johns, N. and Wheeler, K. (1989) 'Productivity and performance measurement and monitoring'. In R. Teare and A. Boare (eds), *Strategic Hospitality Management*. London: Cassell, pp. 45–69.

Jones, P. (1990) 'Managing foodservice productivity in the long term: strategy, structure and performance'. *International Journal of Hospitality Management*, 9(2), 143–54.

Jones, P. and Lockwood, A. (1989) *The Management of Hotel Operations*. London: Cassell.

Katzell, M.E. (1975) *Productivity: the Measure and the Myth*. New York: AMACOM.

Kazarian, E.A. (1989) *Foodservice Facilities Planning*, 3rd edn. New York: Van Nostrand Reinhold.

Lane, H.E. (1976) 'The Scanlon plan: a key to productivity and payroll costs'. *Cornell Hotel Restaurant and Administration Quarterly*, 17(1), 76–80.

Levitt, T. (1972) 'Production line approach to service'. *Harvard Business Review*, September/October, 41–52.

Mali, P. (1978) *Improving Total Productivity*. New York: John Wiley & Sons.

Medlik, S. (1988) *Tourism and Productivity*. London: BTA/ETB Research Services.

Merricks, P. and Jones, P. (1986) *The Management of Catering Operations*. London: Cassell.

Mill, R.C. (1989) *Managing for Productivity in the Hospitality Industry*. New York: Van Nostrand Reinhold.

Mohanty, R.P. and Rastogi, S.C. (1985) 'An action research approach to productivity measurement'. *International Journal of Operations and Production Management*, 6, 47–61.

Pavesic, D. (1983) 'The myth of labour-cost percentages'. *Cornell Hotel Restaurant and Administration Quarterly*, 24(3), 27–30.

Pedderson, T.B. *et al.* (1973) *Increasing Productivity in Food Service*. Chicago: Cahners.

Pickworth, J. (1987) 'Minding the P's and Q's: linking quality and productivity'. *Cornell Hotel Restaurant and Administration Quarterly*, 28(1), 40–7.

Pickworth, J. (1994) 'Productivity improvement'. In B. Davis and A. Lockwood (eds), *Food and Beverage Management: a Selection of Reading*. Oxford: Butterworth-Heinemann.

Pine, R. and Ball, S. (1987) 'Productivity and technology in catering operations'. *Food Science and Technology Today*, 1(3), 174–6.

Pollard, C. and Voss, C.A. (1985) 'Case study: Wimpy International (A) and (B)'. In C.A. Voss *et al.* (eds), *Operations Management in Service Industries and the Public Sector*. Chichester: Wiley.

Prais, S.J., Jarvis, V. and Wagner, K. (1989) 'Productivity and vocational skills in services in Britain and Germany: Hotels'. *National Economic Institute Review*, November, 52–74.

Prokopenko, J. (1987) *Productivity Management: a Practical Handbook*. Geneva: International Labour Office.

Rathmell, J.M. (1974) *Marketing in the Service Sector*. Cambridge: Winthrop.

Riggs, J.L. and Felix, G.H. (1983) *Productivity in Objectives*. Englewood Cliffs, NJ: Prentice Hall.

Ross, J.E. (1981) *Productivity, People and Profits*. Reston, VA: Reston.

Sandler (1982) 'Productivity measurement and improvement in the hospitality industry'. In A. Pizam, R.C. Lewis and P. Manning (eds), *The Practice of Hospitality Management*. AVI, pp. 153–63.

Sasser, W.E., Olsen, P.R. and Wyckoff, D.D. (1978) *Management of Service Operations*. Boston: Allyn and Bacon.

Sink, D.S. (1985) *Productivity Management Planning: Measurement and Evaluation, Control and Improvement*. New York: Wiley.

Sumanth, D. (1984) *Productivity Engineering and Management*. New York: McGraw-Hill.

Thorpe, R. (1986) 'Productivity measurement'. In A.M. Bowey and R. Thorpe (eds), *Payment Systems and Productivity*. London: Macmillan.

Transnationals Information Centre (1987) *Working for Big Mac*. London: TIC.

Zeithaml, V.A., Parasuraman, A. and Berry, L. (1990) *Delivering Quality Service*. New York: Free Press.

TEN

Productivity measurement in food service systems

Mike Rimmington and John Clark

INTRODUCTION

Measuring productivity in the food service industry presents a number of challenges. When seeking guidance in the literature, the researcher is immediately confronted with divergent views regarding the fundamental issue of what is meant by productivity. Although Fletcher and Grice (1985) identify the requirement to define precisely the output of a given industry, many different and sometimes conflicting views of how to approach this prerequisite have been proposed. Witt and Witt (1989) add that even if this obstacle is surmounted, there remains the question of whether like is being compared with like. They argue that, while organizations can be involved in the same area of service provision, differences in ways of operating can result in productivity variation owing to inherent operational features, rather than deviation from comparable performance targets. How these and other issues impinge upon the task of measuring catering productivity is explored in more detail in the following pages. There is undoubtedly potential tension between what is desirable and what is feasible. However, a literature review and analysis of the issues raised reveal that research in the area to date has sometimes been constrained more by conceptual limitations than practical difficulties.

APPROACHES TO PRODUCTIVITY MEASUREMENT

As Jones (1990) remarks, definitions of productivity all involve some variation around comparing inputs (the resources used in making products and providing services) with outputs (the product or service itself). The root of the productivity concept lies in economic theory and one dictionary definition is '*the arithmetical ratio between the*

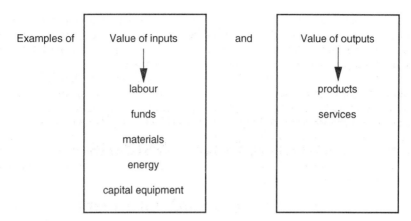

Figure 10.1. Productivity measured quantitatively

Source: Adapted from Heap (1992).

amount produced and the amount of resources used in the course of production' (*Oxford English Dictionary*). As implied by this definition, productivity was originally associated primarily with the manufacturing of products and with an emphasis on quantity. These origins explain some of the limitations experienced when applying the concept within service industries.

In considering productivity measurement within the hospitality industry, some writers have based their recommended approach on this original concept. For example, Dilworth (1989) defines productivity as the ratio of all outputs over all inputs, while Rose (1980) refers to the measurement of resources needed to produce an identified output. However, as Jones (1990) has commented, such definitions can be simple to state, but complex to apply, particularly in a food service context.

Quantitative approach

Complexity in application to an extent depends upon the perspective taken. For example, Heap (1992) demonstrates that inputs and outputs can be specifically identified and measured financially to provide a quantitative perspective. He illustrates this with the examples shown in Figure 10.1. Such measurement is straightforward because only readily available, objective criteria are considered. By the same token, the basis of measurement is very limited, since only financially measurable, tangible inputs and outputs are taken into consideration.

Financially measured inputs and outputs can be compared at a broad aggregate level by measuring the value added, i.e. the difference between the value of outputs and the value of inputs. The higher the value added, the higher the productivity, i.e.

$$\text{value added} = \text{value of outputs} - \text{value of inputs}$$

Value added measures are particularly useful in macro measurement for comparing productivity among different food service organizations, or even across industries. As well as broad measures such as this, inputs and outputs can be compared in a variety of meaningful ways that provide more specific measurements.

Ball *et al.* (1986) note that once the boundary of measurement has been determined it is a fairly straightforward task to identify appropriate financial and other relevant quantitative measures. Their approach involved categorizing measures into physical, combined physical/financial and financial, after which they constructed boundaries around different input classifications identified as labour, energy, capital and raw material. The measures selected for the labour input classification under each category, which apply to measurement of labour productivity within the different departments of an hotel, are as follows the physical measure is:

$$\frac{\text{meals produced}}{\text{number of kitchen staff}}$$

The combined physical/financial measure is:

$$\frac{\text{restaurant revenue}}{\text{restaurant hours}}$$

The financial measure is:

$$\frac{\text{banqueting revenue}}{\text{banqueting labour cost}}$$

Jones (1990) makes a valuable contribution in proposing that productivity boundaries should be considered, while taking into account the particular characteristics of the food service system being considered and the need to sustain productivity advances in the long term, not just the short term. To ensure that productivity is given a high profile throughout the organization, he recommends three focuses that consider different aggregates of employees within the organization. Jones's approach considers productivity measurement boundaries from individual, group and organization-wide orientations. For example, Figure 10.2 illustrates how labour cost measures can be related to revenue at different levels within the organization. Such measurement (even down to specific time periods) has become feasible as many organizations now utilize electronic point-of-sale (EPOS) technology, linked to computer-based management information systems (MIS).

Jones's recommended approach provides an effective framework for specific tangible measures. However, it can also accommodate some of the broader based alternative approaches described below, and Jones himself argues a need to derive the approach from the standpoint of the actual food production system being considered.

Thus far, only tangible inputs and outputs, which can be quanitified and measured financially, have been considered. Many literature contributions in fact go beyond this. However, the introduction of intangible and indirect factors necessarily makes the measurement much more problematic and complex. On the other hand, this is necessary if total factor approaches, measuring all aspects of productivity, are to be developed.

Measure	Overall organization	Restaurant department	Individual food service worker
Labour cost % revenue			
Labour cost per labout hour			

Figure 10.2. Intra-organization productivity measurement perspectives

Source: Adapted from Jones (1990).

Total factor approaches

One area of complexity is introduced in frequent recommendations (see, for example, Brown and Hoover, 1990) that a 'total factor' productivity model which relates total organizational output to all input resources be adopted. They note that 'a measurement technique that considers only one or a few of the resources used to produce goods and services may result in limitations and potentially inaccurate productivity measurement'. In an effort to provide such comprehensive measures, some authors (Jones, 1990; Heap, 1992) have argued that, because of their importance in the hospitality industry, intangible as well as tangible inputs and outputs should be included when productivity is measured. Intangible factors are those that, while difficult to specify in physical terms, are nevertheless an intrinsic part of the meal experience. Such intangibles as atmosphere, management style, staff flair and expertise are important inputs. If a long-term view is taken, the intangible customer satisfaction is perhaps the most important food service output. Such intangibles are undoubtedly very important elements in both inputs and outputs. However, their very nature provides problems of definition for those attempting to determine the boundaries and substance of productivity measurement.

While some authors are interpreting a total factor approach as one that involves consideration of intangible as well as tangible inputs and outputs, others use the term within the context of the financial/quantitative approach. For example Ball *et al.*'s (1986) interpretation of a total factor approach involves the generation of broad aggregate measures that intrinsically encapsulate all individual aspects of productivity. (Individual aspects are classified as labour, energy, capital or raw material.) Interestingly, the proposed example of a total factor physical measure for a hotel proposed by Ball *et al.*, is

$$\frac{\text{number of satisfied customers}}{\text{total number of hotel customers}}$$

Although described as a physical measure, the notion of 'satisfied customers' implicitly incorporates an intangible aspect of the ouput. The 'hardness' of the number depends upon how effectively these satisfied customers can in fact be identified and counted.

While customer satisfaction can be, and is, measured in practice, it is a concept that clearly goes beyond what would normally be considered as physical. In so doing it necessitates the incorporation of qualitative measurement, with all its inherent difficulties. It is also difficult to envisage how the broad measure of 'number of satisfied customers' could be derived as anything other than a composite index of more specific satisfaction measures. This would involve evaluating customer reaction both to aspects of the hospitality environment and to important operational features.

However, it is also possible to argue that truly quantitative aggregate 'broad' measures such as value added in fact implicitly encapsulate intangible qualitative performance. In the long term, only if intangibles are being delivered in a way that customers find acceptable can value added be achieved and sustained at its potential. If this argument is accepted, then broad financial or other quantitative measures in fact represent aggregates of both tangible and intangible productivity performance.

This argument can even be extended to broad aggregate financial measures such as return on capital:

$$\frac{\text{profit achieved}}{\text{capital employed}}$$

Here the 'total factor' measure is purely financial, yet it can be held to represent both tangible and intangible aspects of performance. Only if the intangibles are as they should be will customer levels be sustained and income earned. Only if the tangibles are as they should be will income and costs be controlled in such a way that profit is produced at the required rate in relation to the capital employed.

While we recognize that such broad aggregate measures represent both tangible and intangible dimensions of performance, the relative effect of each dimension cannot be identified. For instance, good profit performance may result from, say, good performance in intangible areas resulting in high revenue generation; on the other hand, this may have been more or less offset (in an unnoticed way) by inadequate control over tangible input resources. To resolve such uncertainties, more precise measures are needed.

Brown and Hoover (1990) recognize that a total factor approach to productivity can also be built up from multiple partial as well as aggregate measures. Use of multiple partial measures of productivity is recommended by them as enabling managers to identify the relationships and trade-offs among all the various resources used. A wide range of partial measures drawn from food service and business literature are reported within the classifications of labour, materials, energy and capital. Examples of these are shown in Table 10.1.

Inspection of a range of multiple partial measures such as those illustrated in Table 10.1 will clearly show any trade-offs that may be occurring. For example, in a technological approach to food service system provision, higher labour productivity may be achieved, as represented by different partial measures of labour productivity. However, this may be at the expense of lower capital productivity, as shown by capital measures. Brown and Hoover also raise as a possibility the interesting prospect of combining partial measures in an aggregated composite index. This could even be weighted to reflect the relative importance of different partial measures.

Table 10.1. Total factor productivity via multiple partial measures

Type of measurement	Examples of measurement
Labour ratios	Total outputs/labour expenses
	Meals produced/labour hours worked
Material ratios	Total outputs/material expenses
	Food cost/number of meals produced
Energy ratios	Total outputs/energy expenses
	Total outputs/British Thermal Units (BTUs) used
Capital ratios	Total outputs/capital expenses

Source: Examples drawn from Brown and Hoover (1990).

Behavioural impact of measurement

An organization that considers such measures to be important should also take account of the fact that measures selected will in themselves be an influencing factor on management behaviour. Innovative thinkers such as Hopwood (1976) and Anthony *et al.* (1992) have drawn attention to the fact that information and control systems are not neutral, but in themselves shape and affect behaviour through the signals that they give to employees. Responsibility centre managers faced with single factor productivity measures, or measures which emphasize few variables, may not impact in the way intended. For example, the previous discussed return on capital is an important measure of productivity. However, a high return on capital can be achieved either by generating high sales and profiits, or by employing a low level of capital relative to a lower level of sales and profits. If only this narrow measure of capital productivity is selected, then conservative managers may be motivated more towards the latter than the former. This may not be what the organization had in mind, and it lends further weight to the argument that a more sophisticated approach to productivity measurement is required. Multiple partial measures that have been carefully selected may be the best to use if management behaviour is to be influenced in a balanced and positive direction. As Drucker (1973) states, it is the specific productivity objectives that are essential to give a business direction and without productivity measurement there is no control.

QUALITY IMPLICATIONS

The consideration of intangible dimensions to productivity, discussed above, links with the assertion made by some authors that issues to do with productivity should always be considered alongside those of quality. Arguments against too much concentration on quantitative measures of productivity have been articulated by Pickworth (1987). He asserts that productivity is inextricably linked with quality and that the two together can form a 'wheel of fortune' where productivity and quality reinforce each other in a potent relationship based on innovation and giving value to customers. The negative side of this positive synergy is of course the downward spiral, where productivity 'gains' based on cost cutting can lead to a fall in quality standards. These in turn result in falling sales, which are responded to by further cost cutting and a further loss of quality, with further loss of customers, until the business eventually ceases trading. Whatever the specific dynamics of the relationship, it seems self-evident that any food service organization that pursues higher short-term productivity only at the expense of quality will inevitably suffer lower productivity in the long term. The logical conclusion is that quality assurance and control should always be considered alongside productivity. Any consideration of productivity must also include quality (and vice versa) if dysfunctional outcomes are to be avoided.

If this argument is accepted then quality measures should be produced alongside those measures which reflect value of output and value of inputs. Johns and Wheeler (1991) propose that a quality dimension should be included in the basic productivity formula. Rather than value, they argue, wealth is in fact a function of both the quantity and quality of what is produced. The basic productivity equation can consequently be re-expressed as follows:

$$\text{productivity} = \frac{\text{volume} \times \text{quality}}{\text{resources used}}$$

While measurement of quality perhaps presents more problems than that of 'harder', more tangible productivity factors, many food service organizations carry out quality measurement as an ongoing control activity. For example, 'mystery diner' control activity is often used to assess a wide range of quality criteria, points being awarded out of 100, perhaps using criteria weighting. Negative customer reaction is also often recorded by logging the quantity and nature of complaints received. Even the strength of customer feeling and attitude towards intangible aspects of quality, such as 'ambience' or the friendliness of food service staff, can be measured by such techniques as semantic differentials. These aspects are important, as confirmed by Olsen and Meyer (1987) in the following statement: 'One of the most important initial elements of productivity measurement is the extent to which the actual service transaction is productive and to what degree does participation of the customer in the process affect productivity.'

Quality control is also carried out to ensure that the service complies with laid down operational standards and procedures. For example, hygiene audits are commonly carried out by food service organizations to ensure that the food safety aspect of quality control is being maintained. Here again a percentage score is often awarded to represent the standard being achieved. Individual units also maintain their own records of temperature checks and other process control measures. While an academic researcher may query the validity of some of these techniques, they at least ensure that quality issues are constantly under consideration, alongside narrower, 'purer' productivity measures, and thus provide some basis for the assessment of achievement.

EFFECTIVENESS

The quality issue also impinges on productivity through its impact on system effectiveness. As Ball *et al.* (1986) maintain, it is important to achieve *simultaneous* efficiency and effectiveness. Too often in the literature it is the efficiency aspect of productivity that is emphasized at the expense of other goals and objectives of the organization. In considerations of the relationship of inputs to outputs, the outputs are taken as given, and emphasis is placed on controlling inputs to achieve higher productivity. Despite protestations that total factor productivity is the way forward, there are many examples in the literature of productivity strategies based on containing cost, particularly labour cost, rather than, for example, on maximizing output (see, for example, Pope, 1971; Rose, 1980). Possibly this is because hotels and catering is a labour-intensive industry and productivity measurement has often been based on manufacturing work study methods.

Even if cost containment is not the explicit strategy, there is the danger that it can become central to the corporate culture, through the incentive effect of measures that influence in a dysfunctional way. This danger may be particularly evident in times of recession when cost control is necessary, but where it is also important that managers possess the incentive to maintain revenue at as high a level as possible. As Watson (1994) points out, over-emphasis on bottom line returns 'often leads to denominator management because executives soon learn that reductions in investment and head count – the denominator – improve the financial actions by which they are measured more easily than growth in the numerator – revenues'. Thus it is easier to control costs than to generate revenue. Managers who are quick to reduce investment and dismiss workers find it takes much longer to regain lost skills and to catch up on investment when the industry turns up again.

Over-concentration on cost control at the expense of effectiveness (whether intended or brought about as a consequence of dysfunctional measures) is clearly detrimental. For those experienced in food service management, the link between effectiveness and achieved productivity is very evident. To achieve productivity targets is much easier during busy operating periods than slack periods.

Some simple examples of this relationship are as follows. A food service attendant can service either one cover or perhaps as many as 30 or more during a period of opening. Labour productivity will vary considerably between these two extremes. However, a minimum brigade of food production and management is required even if a very low customer count is present. Substantial productivity gains are thus possible if customer count can be increased (via enhanced effectiveness). This is because the marginal costs (the value of extra inputs) involved in serving more customers are relatively low when compared to the extra revenue (outputs) that can be generated.

This connection has been recognized by Heap (1992), who explicitly includes quality factors in productivity measurement through incorporation of what he describes as 'top-line factors'. The term is used to describe factors that impinge upon the output side of the productivity equation through their contribution to value as perceived by the customer. This need to identify the criteria that customers use when assessing benefits will be familiar to readers who have read the contributions within hospitality marketing literature of such authors as Lewis (1985).

Heap identifies and measures top-line factors classified into the categories of functionality, reliability and aesthetics. Composite indices for these categories are then combined with an index based upon the normal financial measure of output or throughput to give a new weighted index. In Heap's worked example, the index based on financial output is given a 70 per cent weighting, whereas 30 per cent weighting is given to the top-line factors.

top-line productivity index = financial productivity index (70%) + functionality index (15%) + reliability index (9%) + aesthetics (6%)

While Heap's top-line factors are representative more of a product than a service, it would be possible to generate factors more specifically relevant to food service productivity. However, the end point weighting decision is inescapably subjective even if quantitative measures are able to be devised for individual top-line factors. Heap acknowledges that this is a difficulty with his proposed approach and methodology. A further caveat is provided by Renaghan (1981), who maintains that customers perceive the hotel or restaurant as a whole, rather than as a series of isolated variables. This can lead to problems in measuring productivity as a series of single discrete aspects, even if quality criteria are identified.

In practice, Heap's theoretical approach would probably meet with resistance in the practically oriented and pragmatic hospitality industry. Nevertheless, he has been extremely creative in his attempt to embed quality issues in productivity measurement techniques. His contribution certainly highlights the importance of effectiveness in positively influencing the productivity equation, however measured. Even if Heap's approach is discounted as being too theoretical for widespread practical application, there are many other more straightforward measures that monitor effectiveness rather than efficiency. The aforementioned quality measures are all concerned with effectiveness. Other measures that place emphasis on effectiveness are those concerned primarily with an emphasis on outputs rather than inputs. Revenue- and activity-related output measures both fit this criterion. Examples of these measures are as follows.

Revenue-related:
● total revenue;
● total revenue/number of covers (seats) available;
● total revenue/number of operating hours;
● total revenue/total meals served;
● total revenue/metres squared of trading area.

Activity-related:
● total meals served;
● total meals served/number of covers (seats) available;
● total meals served/number of operating hours;
● total meals served/metres squared of trading area.

All the above measures emphasize effectiveness rather than efficiency, if used appropriately. There is also an argument for maintaining that they all indirectly reflect intangible dimensions to productivity on an aggregate basis. After all, unless the total food service experience is congruent, customers go elsewhere and the above measures quickly reflect the resulting loss of productivity as revenue falls away.

VOLUME FORECASTING

As well as effectiveness *per se*, it is important accurately to forecast the level of business that will actually be achieved. This is particularly true for food service operations with volatile customer counts, which do not operate a reservation system. If an operation consistently over-estimates its volume of customers, then its level of productivity is bound to be adversely affected, since resources will be planned to meet a higher level of output than in fact materializes. Productivity standards such as staffing ratios and food cost percentages (depending on the food service system actually in place) may be affected detrimentally by poor forecasting as well as a lack of ability to perform to operating standards. This can be illustrated by the following example:

Forecast restaurant revenue (sales volume×average spend)	£800
Forecast (and planned for) labour cost	£120
Forecast labour cost as percentage of forecast restaurant revenue	15

However, if the forecast level of business does not materialize, labour productivity falls, since staffing has been arranged to meet a higher level of business.

Actual restaurant revenue	£700
Actual labour cost	£120
Actual labour cost as percentage of actual restaurant revenue	17.1

Here the restaurant has been less productive when measured against the labour productivity measure, not because of any failure to apply operating standards, but through failure to forecast accurately. Given this situation and the short-term pressures, it is easy to understand how managers can resort to sending staff home when 'not needed', even if this results in longer-term problems with staff morale, staff turnover and the intangible aspects of performance.

The effect on productivity would have been experienced in the opposite way if the forecast had been pessimistic rather than optimistic. If staff served more customers than had been planned for in the labour standards, this would have resulted in a positive effect on achieved productivity. However, while productivity for that particular session would have been higher than planned, it may also be that service standards were not achieved, owing to staff overload. In the longer term productivity would therefore be adversely affected. Though we do not want to overemphasize this, (the authors' own experience is that insufficiently busy staff are more of a threat to service standards than over-stretched ones), it is desirable to avoid wide variations from forecast demand in both directions.

Fluctuations in customer volume are inevitable in sectors of the food service industry that admit customers without prior reservation. The objective must be to forecast these as accurately as possible so that planned levels of productivity can be achieved through design rather than by accident. Measurement has a role in this, since the accuracy of forecasting can readily be monitored on an ongoing basis, either as *forecast covers as a percentage of actual covers*, or as *forecast revenue as a percentage of actual revenue*.

Neither the crucially important key role of forecasting in productivity management nor the measurement of forecasting accuracy is reflected in the literature. However, Jones (1990) does identify the importance of variation and variability as important operational characteristics that directly affect productivity levels. Variation is the extent to which demand increases and decreases over a short time cycle. For example, during a typical week some city restaurants may well supply 75 per cent of covers during the peak Friday and Saturday nights. Monday night may be extremely quiet. Variability is the extent to which the same service period experiences fluctuating demand over a longer time frame, according to seasonality, or even within seasons. For instance, restaurants may experience the phenomenon of being busy on a day in one week and inexplicably quiet on the same day in the next. The responce to such variation can be managed through careful use of part-time labour. Variability presents a more difficult management challenge owing to its unpredictable nature.

MEASUREMENT INTERPRETATION

There are many different approaches to the measurement of productivity, but even if one approach is applied consistently there remains the question of interpretation of data produced by the particular measures used. Witt and Witt (1989) have argued that in many instances direct comparison of data is not possible because like is not being compared with like. Within seemingly similar food production and service areas there is indeed often considerable variation in the operating systems employed. Even where the same basic system configuration is being used, physical and design limitations impose operating constraints that can impact considerably on the levels of productivity it is possible to achieve. However, despite these problems it is still generally possible to make some kind of productivity comparison. To do this requires informed analysis and interpretation of the data, in order to look beyond the straightforward ranking of performance. This can include consideration of particular system features that may have contributed towards the level of productivity achieved. Mill (1989), for example, confirms that productivity improvements should be viewed as a totality of the measuring system, not necessarily variables taken in isolation. It is thus necessary to consider the productivity determinants in as wide a system context as possible.

PRODUCTIVITY DETERMINANTS

Up to this point, the issues discussed have centred on the interpretation of productivity as a concept, with associated implications for its direct measurement. However, consideration must also be given to the conditions that bring about the achieved level of productivity. Here the rationale is that if the organization being measured has the clear aim to improve levels of productivity, then it is also pertinent to measure the presence and extent of conditions that it believes are likely to bring this about. The literature contains several examples where productivity (the dependent variable) has been demonstrated to be influenced by identified independent variables.

The most ambitious of these, the seminal study by Ruff and David (1975), investigates 27 factors predicted to affect productivity within hospital food service systems. Factors were selected through literature review. An index system was used to measure the presence and extent of the variables and correlation analysis was used to assess the extent of the relation to three dimensions of productivity: quantity of output, quality of output and extent of employee satisfaction. While one might argue that the last of these is more properly considered as an independent variable, Ruff and David's study was the first comprehensive attempt to research seriously those conditions likely to lead to enhanced levels of productivity within the hospitality industry.

It is possible to argue that the extent to which these independent variables impact

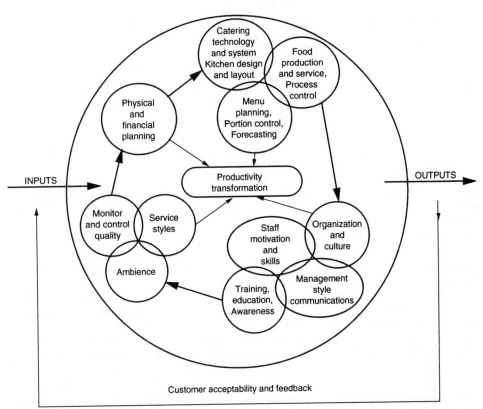

Figure 10.3. Multi-faceted productivity model: factors influencing high productivity transformation of inputs to output in sub-systems and activities

Source: Clark (1994).

upon productivity is as yet unproven and that they should therefore not be considered in this context. However, such a stance overlooks the practical exigencies of food service management. There is a continual need to take operational decisions that affect productivity, and these require empirical information about all the factors perceived as playing a part. Such a perspective accepts the fact that there is still much to be learned regarding conditions which positively impact upon productivity, but that in the interim managers need to take a view on such issues as organizational culture, management style and leadership. While the effect of strategies and policies in these areas may be uncertain, a positive management approach naturally prefers to influence through proactive policies rather than to leave things to chance.

Clark (1994) also identifies conditions affecting productivity via literature review and by analysis of case study situations. He classifies these conditions into broad clusters of factors influencing high productivity transformation of inputs to outputs and displays them graphically in a systems mode (see Figure 10.3). Though Clark did not investigate mathematical correlations between these broad clusters and achieved productivity, it can be predicted that the use of broader boundaries for testing correlations would prevent some of the difficulties that Ruff and David experienced in

Table 10.2. 'Upstream' productivity measurements in 'soft system' areas

Area	Examples of measures
Staff motivation	Absentee/turnover rates
Staff skill and training	Qualifications gained/courses attended
Management style	Leadership styles/personality measures
Organizations and culture	Span of control/hierarchical levels/style appraisal analysis

explaining relationships between such precise measures as length of staff tenure and quantity of meals (expressed as meals per man hour).

Clark (1994) investigated these conditions as a result of research into achieved levels of labour productivity within hospital food production and service systems. Regression analysis was used to compare productivity of systems employing cook–chill and other labour-saving features with those operating conventionally. Although differences in overall productivity between different system types were clearly demonstrated, there was substantial deviation around the performance trend line for each individual system type. Thus factors additional to the technical system being used were clearly influencing productivity in a significant way.

Clark investigated these factors through case studies of units that possessed similar operating systems and equipment configurations, but showed considerable variation in the productivity achieved (measured in terms of meals per chef per day). He identified additional factors that he believed were affecting productivity. Some of these additional factors were 'soft system' factors relating to the management and development of the human resource within the organization and its culture. Such factors are increasingly being recognized as important to the success of organizations. It is perhaps these soft system effects that future productivity research will find most fruitful to investigate. However, the research problems presented by these areas should not be underestimated.

An organization wishing to establish policies in these soft system areas may also wish to measure their effectiveness. Ultimately, the effect of these policies can be expected to impact on actual productivity and could therefore be measured by standard productivity measures. However, it may be that 'upstream' measurement is also desirable, given that some policies may have considerable lead times. Examples of such upstream measures in the soft system area are provided in Table 10.2. Such measurement would fit the idea of productivity strategy being implemented and integrated throughout the organization rather than being limited to a technical approach to food production and service system performance.

CONCLUSION

There are different approaches to productivity measurement. Which approach or combination of approaches is used will to an extent reflect who is undertaking the measurement and for what purpose. External researchers often wish to compare the productivities of different organizations and will not be concerned with the influential effect of ongoing measurement on organizational behaviour. A financial or quantitative approach may well identify suitable comparative data and provide aggregate measures of overall productivity performance in such cases. However, researchers wishing to investigate cause and effect must venture beyond such measures and take account of the intangible objectives of hospitality providers.

If, as demonstrated, effectiveness does impact substantially on achieved productivity, then the argument for including measurement of effectiveness alongside measures of efficiency is very strong. Although measures of effectiveness often concentrate only on one side of the productivity equation, the benefits of achieving enhanced productivity at higher levels of activity rather than lower are self-evident. Certainly higher added value will result even if the ratio of inputs to outputs remains the same. Consequently the argument for including productivity measures that encompass efficiency, effectiveness and quality within any consideration of productivity performance is persuasive.

Those conducting measurement from the management control perspective as part of the ongoing monitoring of an organization's performance need to take a wider range of factors into account when designing and selecting measures. In particular, the effect of measures on management behaviour and the link with quality needs careful consideration. There is also the question of the extent to which measurement should be extended 'upstream' to monitor more immediate results of the wider long-term productivity strategy.

REFERENCES

Anthony, R.N., Dearden, J. and Govindarajan, V. (1992) *Management Control Systems*, 8th edn. Homewood, IL: Irwin.

Ball, S.D., Johnson, K. and Slattery, P. (1986) 'Labour productivity in hotels: an empirical analysis'. *International Journal of Hospitality Management*, 5(3), 141–7.

Brown D.M. and Hoover L.W. (1990) 'Productivity measurement in food service: past accomplishments – a future alternative?' *Journal of the American Dietetic Association*, 90(7), 973.

Clark, J.R. (1994) 'The relationship between productivity and catering technology in the hotel and catering industry'. MPhil thesis, Sheffield Hallam University.

Dilworth, J.B.(1989) *Production and Operation Management*, 4th edn. New York: Random House.

Drucker, P.F. (1973) *Management Tasks, Responsibilities, Practices*. New York: Harper and Row.

Fletcher, J. and Grice, H. (1985) 'The need for output measurements in the service industries: a comment?' *Service Industries Journal*, 5(1), 73–8.

Heap, J. (1992) *Productivity Management: a Fresh Approach*. London: Cassell.

Hopwood, A.G. (1976) *Accounting and Human Behaviour*. Englewood Cliffs, NJ: Prentice Hall.

Johns, N. and Wheeler K. (1991) 'Productivity and performance measurement and monitoring'. In R. Teare and A. Boer (eds), *Strategic Hospitality Management*. London: Cassell.

Jones, P. (1990) 'Managing foodservice productivity in the long term: strategy, structure and performance'. *International Journal Hospitality Management*, 9(2), 144–5.

Lewis R.C. (1985) 'The market position: mapping guests' perceptions of hotel operations'. *Cornell Hotel and Restaurant Administration Quarterly*, 26(2), 86–99.

Mill, R.C. (1989) *Managing for Productivity in the Hospitality Industry*. New York: Van Nostrand Reinhold.

Olsen, M.D. and Meyer, M.K. (1987) 'Current perspectives on productivity in food service and suggestions for the future'. *School Food Service Research Review*, 2, 87–93.

Pickworth, J.R. (1987) 'Minding the Ps and Qs: linking quality and productivity'. *Cornell Hotel and Restaurant Administration Quarterly*, 28(1), 40–7.

Pope, H.H. (1971) 'Establishment of standards can help the food service industry and meet the challenge of the next decade'. *Proceedings of the Society for the Advancement of Food Research*, 20, 15–23.

Renaghan, L. (1981) 'A new marketing mix for the hospitality industry'. *Cornell Hotel and Restaurant Administration Quarterly*, 22(2), 31–6.

Rose J.C. (1980) 'Containing the labour costs of food service'. *Hospitals*, March, 94–8.

Ruff K.L. and David, B.D. (1975) 'How to obtain optimum productivity'. *Hospitals*, December, 77–9.

Watson, T.J. (1994) *In Search of Management – Culture, Chaos and Control in Managerial Work*. London: Routledge.

Witt, C.A. and Witt S. (1989) 'Why productivity in the hotel sector is low'. *Internal Journal of Contemporary Hospitality Management*, 1(2), 29–30.

ELEVEN

Traditional key ratio analysis versus data envelopment analysis: a comparison of various measurements of productivity and efficiency in restaurants

Tommy D. Andersson

When the economy of a nation is analysed, productivity is one of the key factors and partial productivity indices are studied in great detail. Most of these studies deal with the goods-producing sector, despite the growing importance of the service sector, and it is often argued that the service sector is not able to achieve the same growth in productivity as the goods sector (e.g. Griliches, 1992, p. 1). One reason for this may be that these partial productivity measures are not able to capture the total content of a service product. Services are normally made up of tangible as well as intangible parts and to describe 'service output' in terms of one variable may not be possible.

Efficiency and productivity are core concepts in business management too, but the problem of finding reliable and valid measurements remains. In business management, the concept of 'benchmarking', which is based on the notion of comparing different production units, has received a lot of attention lately. The basic idea is to set a standard, a benchmark, that a production unit should strive for. It also introduces an active approach to productivity assessments. Thus, the comparison of various productivity measures is only one part of benchmarking, beside developing and implementing action plans with the aim of closing the 'performance gap' (Camp, 1989; Parsons, 1994).

However, comparisons in terms of productivity measures remain the basis for benchmarking and the question of what to benchmark defines the first step in a benchmarking process (Spendolini, 1992). One objective of this chapter is to discuss 'what to benchmark', i.e. what key ratios or other productivity measures give relevant and reliable information regarding the performance of a production unit. One particular measurement method, data envelopment analysis (DEA), is able to combine several measures into one paramount productivity index (Charnes *et al.*, 1978) and this DEA method receives special emphasis in this chapter.

The restaurant industry is used as a case study of how various measures are able to describe the productivity and efficiency of different units. At the end of the chapter, the ability of these measurements to describe the performance of various restaurants, as well as the information value of various measurements, is discussed.

The objective of this chapter is thus three-fold:

- to discuss various measures of productivity and efficiency;
- to apply these measures to a sample of restaurants;
- to discuss the results in terms of the information value of various measures.

QUANTITATIVE ASSESSMENT OF PERFORMANCE

Performance measures in the form of key ratios are common in most fields of economic activity. Most of these key ratios measure some aspect of productivity and sometimes also efficiency. The distinction between the concepts of productivity and efficiency is not always clear and often the two are used synonymously. In this section, productivity and efficiency will be discussed, and it will also be suggested that they should be kept apart as two different concepts conveying different and complementary information.

The use of key ratios for comparisons between various production units (e.g. restaurants) often gives a feeling of incompleteness. When, in such cases, a comparison is extended by the use of more than one key ratio, the picture may become less incomplete but often more contradictory. This often gives rise to a need to combine two or more key ratios into one measurement based on a multidimensional analysis. In this section, one of these measurement techniques will be discussed.

Productivity

Basic to any performance analysis is the definition of output variables and input variables for a production unit. There is a wide range of variables to choose from. Output variables for a restaurant could include number of guests served, quality ratings by a local newspaper, sales figures, value added, number of drinks served, etc., and input variables could include staff numbers, number of seats, staff skills, advertising budget, salaries, rent, depreciation, etc. Productivity measures are thus based on quantity assessments as well as quality assessments, as discussed by Johns and Wheeler (1991). The concept 'productivity', which was used in the eighteenth century meaning 'faculty to produce' (Sumanth, 1979), is now mostly used as a quantitative performance measure based on output and input variables.

In the middle of this century, productivity became defined as the quotient obtained by dividing output by one of the factors of production (Organization for European Economic Co-operation, 1950). One may thus talk about labour productivity and capital productivity. A similar, but somewhat wider, definition by Siegel (1976) looks at productivity as 'a family of ratios of output to input'. Several other definitions of productivity have also been proposed (e.g. Davis, 1955; Kendrick and Creamer, 1965; Ross 1977; de Ron, 1994) but none as wide as the definition by Siegel. Since too many and too detailed definitions only cause confusion in this important area of scientific enquiry, an even more general definition is suggested. *The concept of productivity will henceforth be defined as an assessment of output in relation to input.*

The advantage of a wide definition is that it leaves room for sub-definitions of partial productivity measures or, in the words of Siegel (1976), 'the family of ratios' may include several family members and the following partial productivity measures may be considered:

- *labour productivity*, where the input variable is a measure of the labour component;
- *capital productivity*, where the input variable is a measure of the capital assets used;
- *total productivity*, where the input and output variables measure all resources used and created in an activity.

Two problems regarding the validity of actual productivity measurements come up most of the time. These are the items that should be measured and the units that should be employed to measure them.

Which items should be covered by output and input variables? Output often comprises more than one 'product'. Service production may include tangible as well as intangible output. A waiter or waitress should not necessarily only serve as many guests as possible, but also make them feel well and welcome. Thus the choice of an output variable may focus on one particular item or try to comprise several items. Similarly, the choice of an input variable should be based on a clear perception about the item to be assessed. Partial labour productivity could, for example, be assessed by the ratio of 'number of guests served' to 'number of full-time equivalent waiters/waitresses'. A general rule is to include in the input variable only such items that can influence the output variable. Overall, the choice of output as well as input variables is only in rare cases able to include all relevant aspects of resources used and created. It is thus important, in analyses of productivity measures, to be aware of the fact that they are incomplete measures. Whether they are relevant or not must be assessed from case to case and always in relation to the purpose of the analysis being carried out.

Which measurement units should be used? Number of items is a common choice, as in the example of 'number of guests per waiter'. However, the productivity may in this example depend upon the demand: how popular the restaurant is and how many customers visit it. The waiter can do very little about these aspects and the productivity measure is then to some extent inappropriate, since output does not fully depend upon input. Time units could be an alternative way of measuring input, where idle time caused by lack of customers is specifically taken out of the productivity assessment. Too much focus on a waiter's time productivity may, however, lead to poor attention to customers and perhaps as a result of this customers will skip the dessert because they don't feel welcome. A better productivity measurement unit may then be value created in terms of sales or value added, measured in monetary units (e.g. 'sales per waiter' or 'value added per waiter'). There are many more measurement units that can be used in productivity measures than the three examples (i.e. number of items, time units, monetary units) discussed above. The relevance of a particular choice can only be assessed in relation to the purpose of the productivity analysis.

Efficiency

If performance is to be assessed in terms of goal fulfilment, then the choice of measurement units and the evaluation of input as well as output items will be vital in order to get a valid assessment. *An assessment of output in relation to input is defined as an efficiency measure if the variables have been measured in terms of goal fulfilment.* Efficiency is thus defined as a specific class of productivity measures, which may be called 'goal productivity', describing how well a process is able to achieve its ultimate goal. Productivity measures may or may not indicate efficiency. For example, labour productivity measured in terms of 'number of customers per waiter' or 'minutes a waiter spends per guest', as discussed above, may coincide with efficiency measures in a fast food restaurant, but not necessarily in a fine dining restaurant.

Efficiency is, to use the terminology of Siegel (1976), a special member of the productivity 'family of ratios of output to input' where performance is assessed in terms of goal achievement. Measurement units should consequently measure the amount of goal achievement, which may be quite clear in theory but less so in practical applications. More particularly: output should be evaluated in terms of how it contributes to the ultimate goal of the process; input should be evaluated in terms of how it would have contributed to the ultimate goal of the process if the input had been used in the most efficient alternative way (its opportunity cost). In economic theory, *utils* (see Reekie and Crook, 1975) would be the appropriate measurement unit under the assumption that utility maximization is the goal of rational activity. In practice, the assessment of efficiency may be difficult for many types of activities. A lot of public services have as their ultimate goal the creation of well-being for their customers, in terms of *health* (hospitals), *happiness* (day-care centres) or *understanding* (schools, broadcasting), for example. To find a valid and reliable measurement unit to measure the output of such activities may well be impossible.

It is important to understand these difficulties and to accept that reliable efficiency measures may be impossible to achieve for many activities. This implies that the concept of efficiency is inappropriate in a performance analysis of such activities. However, productivity measures such as the number of patients per surgeon or the number of children per teacher can be used (and are being used). It is then important to distinguish clearly between productivity and efficiency and to be aware of the fact that a productivity measure may have nothing to do with (or may even counteract) the achievement of the ultimate goal of an activity.

In business activities things are a lot easier if the ultimate goal is to maximize the market value of a firm, because it then follows that the goal is to maximize the present value of discounted market revenue from output minus discounted market prices for input resources. This implies that efficiency for a business activity is measured by the ratio of output to input as long as both the output and the input variables are measured in terms of market prices. Labour efficiency could thus, to return to the example above, be measured (e.g. as value added divided by salary).

MULTIDIMENSIONAL ASSESSMENTS

Various productivity measures, including efficiency measures, are bound to give a variety of answers to a one-dimensional question such as whether performance is 'good' or 'bad'. The correct method is of course to analyse each measure in its own right and extract the information value that is specific to each productivity measure. However, given the number of possible ratios, it is easy to understand that there is a need to condense several measurements into a single measure. A number of fairly similar methods respond to this need, including the Törnqvist index (Törnqvist, 1936), the Malmquist index (Malmquist, 1953), technical and price efficiency (Farrell, 1957), data envelopment analysis (DEA) (Charnes *et al.*, 1978), hyperbolic graph efficiency and the Russell input measure of technical efficiency (Färe *et al.*, 1985) and free disposal hull efficiency (Tulkens, 1990).

These methods are all based on production functions where output is a function of input. But whereas traditional production functions are estimated with parametric statistical methods that describe the expected performance of a 'normally good' production unit, the DEA method is based on a description of the performances of the best production units in each class. Thus DEA uses the production units that are 'best in its class' as reference material, a method very much in line with the basic ideas underlying the concept of benchmarking (Camp, 1989; Spendolini, 1992). This does not involve statistical estimations of parameters and the DEA method is thus based on a non-parametric assessment of production possibilities.

The basic idea of the DEA method is to assign to each production unit one single performance measure between 0.0 and 1.0 (or 0 to 100 per cent). Figure 11.1 illustrates how this is done in a hypothetical example, where six production units (*A*, *B*, *C*, *D*, *E*, *F*) are plotted on a diagram where the vertical axis (the *y*-axis) represents the amount of salary (in pence) that is spent on each pound of value added. The horizontal *x*-axis represents the amount of capital cost in pence for each pound of value added. These values are calculated by the ratio 'total salaries' to 'total value added' and 'total capital cost' to 'total value added' respectively. Labour-intensive production units will be in the north-west-corner (i.e. they will have high salary cost but low capital cost, whereas the capital intensive production units will be in the south-east-corner. Thus, in Figure 11.1 *A* and *E* are labour-intensive, whereas *D* and *F* are capital-intensive. Production units close to the point of origin have low cost (salary + capital cost) and are therefore comparatively efficient. Thus in Figure 11.1 *B* and *C* are efficient whereas *E* is inefficient, relatively speaking.

DEA creates an efficiency frontier that allows each production unit to be compared against a production unit of similar type. A labour-intensive firm, such as *E*, will be compared against the 'best' of the labour-intensive firms (i.e. *A* and *B*) whereas a capital intensive firm, such as *F*, will be compared against *C* and *D*. The measurement of efficiency, which will range between 0 and 100 per cent is achieved by calculating (e.g. for firm *F*) the ratio OF^*/OF where F^* describes how *F* should have been performing had it been efficient. Thus F^* is the real *F* projected on to the efficiency frontier (i.e. *A–B–C–D*). F^* does not exist in the real world but is constructed as a linear combination of 'peers' on the efficiency frontier (i.e. F^* is a linear combination of *C* and *D*).

The DEA efficiency measure is thus based on a comparison between, on the one hand, the specific production unit and, on the other hand, a fictitious production unit that is a linear combination of a number of 'best-in-class' production units. Since

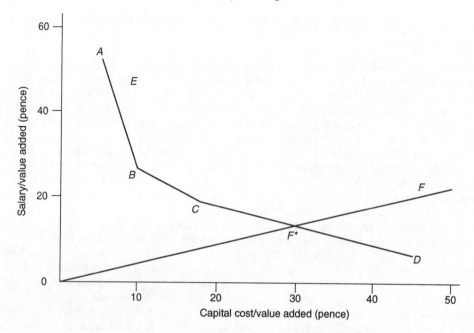

Figure 11.1. Plot of five production units in terms of labour and capital intensity

Note: The line *A–B–C–D* represents the efficiency frontier.

linearity is assumed, linear programming may be used. Linear programming implies that the number of production units must be larger than the number of variables. Thus, provided there is a large sample of production units, the number of output variables as well as input variables is limited only by computerized calculation capacity. Thus, DEA seems to respond very well to the need for a single measure of multidimensional assessment by comparing any number of production units in terms of any number of output variables and any number of input variables. The result of this comparison is expressed by one simple performance measure ranging from 0.0 to 1.0.

The DEA model can, as in Figure 11.1, be explained by a diagram in the simple case of one output variable and not more than two input variables (see Figure 11.2 for such a diagram based on a performance assessment of 16 restaurants). A more general formulation in terms of linear programming is:

$$\min E_1 \tag{1}$$

$$\text{s.t. } O_{m1} < \sum_{j=1}^{N} \lambda_j O_{mj} \qquad m = 1, 2, \ldots, M \tag{2}$$

$$I_{k1} > \sum_{j=1}^{N} \lambda_j I_{kj} \qquad k = 1, 2, \ldots, K \tag{3}$$

where E_1 is performance measure for production unit 1; O_{m1} is output variables of production unit 1 (there are M output variables); I_{k1} is input variables for production unit 1 (there are K input variables).

The production unit being assessed (1) is one out of N production units ($j = 1$, 2. . ., N). By computation of weights λ_j a reference unit is calculated as a linear combination of N production units (certain λ_j may, of course, be equal to 0). These weights are calculated to make the output variables of the reference unit greater than each of the M output variables of unit 1 according to (2). Then the smallest value of E_1 is searched that will keep the value of all K input variables for unit 1 (multiplied by E_1) greater than the corresponding input variable for the reference unit according to (3). This LP problem will be solved N times – one time for each production unit. Since it is required that $N > K$, this implies that the number of production units must be greater than the number of variables in a DEA model.

The description above is simplified and incomplete since a thorough discussion is beyond the scope of this chapter. It refers to the case of input saving and constant returns to scale (Odeck, 1993). For more thorough descriptions and discussions of DEA, see Charnes *et al.* (1978), Färe *et al.* (1985), Bjurek (1994) or Sjögren (1995).

Although technicalities may make DEA look difficult, in practice this is a method that is very easy to handle. Once it has been decided which units (e.g. restaurants) to use and which output and input variables are relevant to the analysis, all that has to be done is to produce a data file, including output and input variables for the units to be compared, and run a computer program. The computer program (e.g. Thanassoulis, 1994) runs easily on a normal PC and provides the results in less than three seconds.

RESEARCH QUESTIONS

The ability of DEA to include several output as well as input variables does not eliminate the need for discussion of the validity and relevance of performance assessments. On the contrary, the above discussion regarding the choice of items as well as the choice of measurement units for both output and input variables is just as vital when a large number of variables are going to be used. Thus, DEA assesses labour productivity if a number of labour-related input variables are selected. If the selected input variables describe all or most of the resources being used in the production of output, then DEA measures total productivity. If variables are measured in units commensurate with the ultimate goal of the activity, then DEA measures efficiency.

The previous discussion suggests a number of questions worthy of empirical investigation:

1. Do partial efficiency measures give performance assessments that are different from partial productivity measures?
2. Do different partial productivity measures (such as labour productivity and capital productivity) give different assessments of productivity?
3. Is DEA able to condense several different productivity measures into one measure that does not contradict any of the partial productivity measures?
4. Does a DEA efficiency measure give a performance measure that is different from a DEA productivity measure?

5. Is DEA able to condense productivity and efficiency into one performance measure by including a large number of variables measured in various measurement units?

The previous discussion assumes that the answers to all five questions are in the affirmative. In the following sections, a sample of restaurants is used to illustrate various measures and assessments of productivity and efficiency. The five questions are then discussed with reference to data from the sample.

DATA

From the yellow pages of the telephone directory of Gothenburg, a city on the Swedish west coast with approximately 500,000 inhabitants, the population of restaurants, defined as places where one can sit down and eat hot food, was estimated to be 363. From this population, a random sample of 73 (20 per cent) was drawn and second-year university students were assigned to make a case study of one restaurant each. The study included a preset questionnaire with questions about pricing policy, staffing and profit and loss statements. Response rates were high for most questions except those regarding the profit and loss statement, where only 63 per cent of the restaurants were prepared to answer. Thus the field sample consisted of 46 restaurants ranging from small fast-food places to a large luxury restaurant with 500 seats. The restaurants were categorized into five types based primarily on three variables – opening hours, service provided and average check – using the following definitions.

- *'Fine dining'* restaurants open during lunch hours and evenings on weekdays and Saturdays and/or Sundays. The average bill amounted to more than £15 (taken at the rate of £1.00 = 10 Swedish kronor).
- *'Family'* restaurants with opening hours as above but an average bill of under £15.
- *'Lunch'* restaurants not open during evenings but with table service (waiters).
- *'Self-service'* restaurants not open during evenings and not having table service.
- *'Fast-food'* restaurants not having table service but open more than eight hours on weekdays.

There were 16 family restaurants in our sample and they represent a sub-sample that is more homogenous than the sample of 46.

Six variables were used to assess various ways of measuring productivity and efficiency. Two of these were output variables and four were input variables.

- NGD: 'number of guests per day' is an output variable describing the average number of guests per day during the last month.
- MVA: 'monthly value added' is an output variable describing the monetary value added (sales – food cost) during the previous month.
- FTEE: 'number of full-time equivalent employees' is an input variable describing the average number of full-time employees during the previous month (two half-time employees count as one employee).
- SAL: 'salary per month' is an input variable describing the amount of salaries paid in the previous month including a salary for a working owner if there is one.

Table 11.1. Some statistics for the sample of 46 restaurants regarding two output variables (NGD and MVA) and four input variables (FTEE, SAL, NSR and MFC)

Variable	*N*	Min.	Max.	Mean	s.d.
NGD	46	30.0	960	236.956	200.2372
MVA (£)	46	850	260,000	22362.82	38080.92
FTEE	46	1	60	7.54347	10.09005
SAL (£)	46	625	160,000	12557.28	23663.22
NSR	46	4	500	112.00	85.62035
MFC (£)	46	290.0	80,000	7344.130	12587.80

Note: The exchange rate is £1 = 10 Swedish kronor.

- NSR: 'number of seats in the restaurant'. This input variable describes the size (i.e. the capital component) of the restaurant during the previous month.
- MFC: 'monthly fixed cost' (excluding labour cost) is an input variable describing the capital component in monetary terms.

Thus, one output variable (NGD) and two input variables (FTEE and NSR) were measured in terms of 'number of units' and there were also one output variable (MVA) and two input variables (SAL and MFC) that were measured in monetary terms. Table 11.1 gives an overview of the sample.

RESULTS

To bring out the points raised previously, performance measures for the five types of restaurants described above are assessed. These restaurant types have different strategies and characteristics, which are illustrated by the information contained in various performance measures.

Productivity and efficiency key ratios

It was argued above that there is a difference between productivity and efficiency. It has also been argued that efficiency for a profit-oriented business firm should be based on measures in terms of market values. Using the six variables described above, straightforward performance measures in terms of key ratios for capital as well as labour resources can be calculated. Furthermore, both productivity and efficiency measures can be calculated. Table 11.2 presents a comparison between labour productivity and labour efficiency as well as a comparison between capital productivity and capital efficiency.

Several discrepancies are worth noting. Self-service restaurants were, for example, the most labour productive type of restaurant but the least labour efficient. Family restaurants were less productive than fast-food restaurants in terms of both labour and capital but, at the same time, they were more efficient than fast-food restaurants in terms of labour as well as capital. However, it is also worth noting that fine dining

Table 11.2. Productivity and efficiency measures in terms of labour as well as capital for five types of restaurants

Restaurant (N)		Productivity		Efficiency	
		Labour productivity NGD/FTE (s.d.)	Capital productivity NGD/NSR (s.d.)	Labour efficiency MVA/SAL (s.d.)	Capital efficiency MVA/MFC (s.d.)
Fine dining	(4)	7.5 (5.26)	0.7 (0.4)	1.9 (0.2)	2.6 (0.9)
Family	(16)	41.4 (18.8)	2.4 (1.3)	2.1 (0.7)	4.5 (2.9)
Lunch	(10)	65.0 (41.9)	2.6 (1.8)	2.3 (0.9)	5.0 (3.9)
Self-service	(10)	69.5 (32.1)	2.6 (1.2)	1.8 (0.5)	3.6 (1.1)
Fast-food	(6)	47.7 (10.6)	4.9 (5.3)	1.7 (0.2)	4.0 (3.3)
All types	(46)	50.5 (31.8)	2.7 (2.4)	2.0 (0.7)	4.2 (2.8)

restaurants were the least productive and one of the least efficient groups of restaurants in terms of both labour and capital. Statistically speaking, it should be noted that standard deviations were considerable and only few differences are statistically significant. One conclusion that can be drawn from Table 11.2 is that productivity measures and efficiency measures do not point in the same direction. One cannot say that they point in opposite directions, but empirical evidence does not contradict the statement that partial efficiency measures give performance assessments that are different from partial productivity measures, as was suggested in research question 1.

Research question 2 suggested that partial productivity measures, such as labour productivity and capital productivity, give different assessments. Data in Table 11.2 do not support this, since there seems to be almost the same ranking of restaurants in terms of labour productivity as in terms of capital productivity. The only exception is fast-food restaurants, which have the highest capital productivity (measured as 'daily seat turnover') but only the third highest labour productivity. The explanation behind this is probably the long opening hours of fast-food restaurants, which of course means that capital resources, such as seats, are used productively during a day, but that staff are needed during unproductive hours as well. There is also quite a coherent ranking among restaurants in terms of both labour and capital efficiency. Data in Table 11.2 suggest that a distinction between productivity and efficiency seems to be more fundamental than a distinction between performance measures based on labour or capital variables. The choice of measurement units seems to have a stronger effect on performance measures than the choice of items.

Multidimensional performance measures

To illustrate a non-parametric as well as a parametric estimation of a production function, only the sub-sample of 'family restaurants' is used, since this represents a more homogeneous sample that better illustrates the point than the whole, rather dispersed, sample would. Figure 11.2 gives a picture of efficiency for the 16 family restaurants.

The vertical axis describes how much out of every pound of value added is used on salaries and the horizontal axis describes how much out of every pound of value added is spent on fixed capital cost. Out of the 16 restaurants, named *A* to *P*, those that are

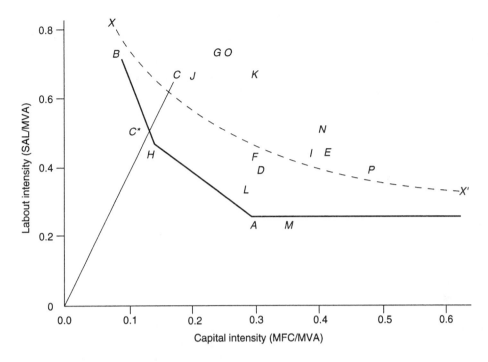

Figure 11.2. Plot of 16 family restaurants in terms of labour and capital intensity

Note: The line X–X' is a log-linear estimation of the production function (SAL/MVA) = 0.34(MFC/MVA)$^{-0.28}$ (R^2=0.17), i.e. MVA = 2.3SAL$^{0.78}$ MFC$^{0.22}$ (in a Cobb–Douglas form). The line B–H–A represents the efficiency frontier.

close to the point of origin (such as H and A) use little money for salary and fixed cost and should be rather profitable. On the other hand, restaurants far out along the axes (such as G, O and K) may use more money for the sum (salary + fixed cost) than the monetary measure of value added and would, in that case, be unprofitable restaurants.

Both lines (X–X' and B–H–A) allow for 'benchmarking', i.e. comparison against a standard. They both also allow for a comparison between firms with different characteristics in terms of size and in terms of labour/capital intensity. This is so because both lines establish a standard that applies to the whole range, from extremely labour-intensive to extremely capital-intensive restaurants.

Primarily, X–X' describes an 'expected output' against which each restaurant can compare itself based on values of labour and capital input and which the restaurant can surpass, achieve or fail to achieve. Performance could be measured in terms of the difference between 'actual output' and 'expected output', which could be a positive value (better than expected, i.e. below the line X–X') or a negative value (below expectations, i.e. above the line X–X').

The line B–H–A, on the other hand, indicates the best performance in each class of labour/capital intensity (in this example) and is not surpassed by any restaurant. Each restaurant will be compared to the best restaurants in its class and achieve a measure between 0 and 1 (or 0 and 100 per cent), indicating how far it is from the production frontier. This measure is calculated as the ratio OC^*/OC for the family restaurant C in our example (see Figure 11.2), where O is the point of origin and C^* is a hypothetical restaurant made up to some extent by restaurant B and to some extent by restaurant H.

The DEA calculates these ratios of B and H that together make up C^* using the linear program formulation discussed above. The output of restaurant C is £310 (value added) and the input is £200 (salaries) and £49 (fixed cost).

$$\min E_c \tag{4}$$

$$\text{s.t. } 310 < \sum_{j=A}^{P} \lambda_j\, O_j \text{ (only one output variable, i.e. MVA)} \tag{5}$$

$$200\, E_c > \sum_{j=A}^{P} \lambda_j\, I_{1j} \text{ (the input variable SAL)} \tag{6a}$$

$$49\, E_c > \sum_{j=A}^{P} \lambda_j\, I_{2j} \text{ (the input variable MFC)} \tag{6b}$$

Where E_c is performance measure for production unit C; O_j is output variables (MVA) for the 16 production units ($j = A, B, C, \ldots, P$); I_{1j} is input variables (SAL) for the 16 production units ($j = A, B, C, \ldots, P$); I_{2j} is input variables (MFC) for the 16 production units ($j = A, B, C \ldots, P$).

The solution to this LP problem is that $\lambda_B = 0.112$, $\lambda_H = 7.56$, $\lambda_j = 0$ for all other j. Thus C is compared to C^*, which is a linear combination of $0.112\ B + 7.56\ H$. Since the salaries of restaurants B and H are £48 and £20 respectively, this means that (6a) becomes $200\ E_c > 0.112 \times 48 + 7.56 \times 20$; i.e. $200\ E_c > 156.6$ and $E_c > 0.783$, which equals 78 per cent. The list below shows the efficiency scores as the output from a DEA computer program (Thanassoulis, 1994) for the 16 family restaurants that were plotted in Figure 11.2.

61.01 *N*	61.18 *G*	61.91 *O*	62.86 *K*
63.51 *P*	63.71 *E*	65.28 *I*	71.07 *J*
77.84 *F*	78.28 *C*	79.95 *D*	87.30 *M*
95.49 *L*	100.00 *A*	100.00 *B*	100.00 *H*

There are three 100 per cent restaurants that are 'best in class' (A, B and H), described as the *frontier restaurants* (see Figure 11.2). Restaurant C is 78 per cent efficient, which means that the ratio OC^*/OC (see Figure 11.2) is equal to 0.78.

The major advantage of the use of DEA is that a performance measure can be based on any number of variables. But DEA does not eliminate the important distinction between efficiency and productivity. On the contrary, since there are no computational difficulties it becomes more important to assess the relevancy of the measures with regard to the objective of the analysis. To illustrate this point, Table 11.3 is based on two DEA runs using the whole ($N = 46$) sample. In one run, the productivity measure is based on one output variable ('number of guests per day') and two input variables ('number of seats' and 'number of staff'). In the second computer run, the efficiency measure is based on 'monthly value added' as output variable and

Table 11.3. Productivity and efficiency calculated by DEA and averaged for five types of restaurants

Restaurant type	N	Average productivity DEA measure (s.d.) (%)	Average efficiency DEA measure (s.d.) (%)
Fine dining	4	19 (17)	79 (18)
Family restaurant	16	54 (20)	72 (15)
Lunch restaurant	10	67 (25)	74 (19)
Self-service	10	79 (17)	69 (14)
Fast-food	6	72 (27)	64 (15)

'monthly salaries' as well as 'monthly fixed costs' as input variables. Based on these two runs, the average performance measure was calculated for each type of restaurant to illustrate the difference between productivity and efficiency measurements.

This illustrates well the fact that, in terms of productivity, quick-service restaurants such as self-service and fast-food restaurants are doing better than the other types of restaurants, whereas in terms of efficiency (i.e. in terms of goal fulfilment, which in this case means in terms of profitability) the picture is much more even. Full-service restaurant types, such as fine dining and family restaurants, not only come out much better in terms of efficiency than in terms of productivity, but also seem to be more efficient than quick-service restaurants.

The theoretical distinction between efficiency and productivity is a major point in this chapter. However, certain practical considerations may sometimes overwhelm theoretical considerations. One such practical consideration is the importance of an unanimous acceptance of selected performance measures in a benchmarking campaign. The first crucial step in a benchmarking process involves 'determining what to benchmark', which 'includes the identification of specific individuals and groups that will use the benchmarking information' (Spendolini, 1992). Needless to say, these parties may have quite a few suggestions for relevant variables to use in a performance assessment. A restrictive selection is of course advisable, but diplomacy is also advisable, since a general agreement of the relevance of selected measures by all parties involved must be of vital importance for successful cooperation.

This is where the DEA method offers a practical opportunity (and a theoretical temptation), since any number of variables can be included in the process (provided the number of production units is greater than the number of variables), to create one simple, easy-to grasp, performance measure. In order to investigate how an 'all-embracing' DEA measure conforms with other proposed productivity and efficiency measures, all six variables will be used in a DEA run, i.e. two output variables and four input variables. If this 'all-embracing' DEA measure gives different indications from more theoretically relevant DEA measures there are reasons to raise a red flag for such a model.

On the other hand, if a large 'all-embracing' DEA model is able not only to include more variables and thus increase the political and/or technical relevance of the model, but also successfully to condense a complicated picture of a large number of relevant variables into one measure that conforms with, and gives similar indications as, partial measures, then DEA may be a very useful instrument for performance measurements of complex activities. Table 11.4 is based on calculations similar to the ones used for Table 11.3 and the results in Table 11.4 should be compared to the results presented in Table 11.3.

Table 11.4. A DEA model based on six (two output and four input) variables with results averaged for five types of restaurants

Restaurant type	N	An 'all-embracing' DEA measure (s.d.) (%)
Fine dining	4	91 (7)
Family restaurant	16	85 (16)
Lunch restaurant	10	87 (18)
Self-service	10	87 (15)
Fast-food	6	82 (17)

Several characteristics of DEA models are illustrated by the results in Tables 11.3 and 11.4:

1 More extensive DEA models tend to have higher performance measures. Whereas the best average productivity measure is 79 per cent and the best average efficiency measure is also 79 per cent (see Table 11.3), the *lowest* 'all-embracing' average measure is 82 per cent and the *highest* average measure is 91 per cent.
2 More extensive DEA models tend to have more even results and a narrower span between the 'best and the worst'. The span in average measures by the 'all-embracing' model (see Table 11.4) is 9 per cent (82 to 91 per cent), whereas the span in terms of average productivity is 53 per cent (19 to 72 per cent) and in terms of average efficiency is 15 per cent (64 to 79 per cent). This characteristic of more extensive DEA models is also evident from the standard deviations, which tend to be smaller for more extensive models.
3 More extensive DEA models tend to 'bring out the best' of each production unit. Thus, the three top restaurant types in Table 11.4 include the top restaurant type in terms of productivity and the two top restaurants in terms of efficiency. All restaurant types in Table 11.4 have higher measures than in Table 11.4.

Thus, one may say that more extensive DEA models are 'kinder' DEA models. They make production units 'look as good as possible'. This may be an advantage from a political/psychological point of view since competing units will not be too far from the target, even though DEA gives a reliable indication of whether a unit is on target or not. In terms of the precision of performance assessments, it may, however, be considered a disadvantage if differences in productivity and efficiency are cancelled out. The assessment will lose clarity and validity as DEA models grow in number of variables and, even though production units 'look better', the information value decreases.

In terms of validity (i.e. what is being measured), more extensive models seem to be more embracing but less clear. They measure both productivity and efficiency. In terms of reliability (i.e. how reliable the results are), large models seem to be able to give a reliable concentrated measure of several aspects. Table 11.5 is based on the large sample of 46 and presents correlation coefficients for all productivity and efficiency measures that have been discussed in this chapter.

The results seem to support several points raised previously. The first three columns show that partial productivity measures (labour productivity and capital productivity) do not correlate significantly with partial efficiency measures. The measures contain

Table 11.5. Correlations among various measurements of productivity and efficiency

	NGD/FTEE	NGD/NSR	DEA-p[a]	MVA/SAL	MVA/MFC	DEA-e[b]	DEA-all[c]
Labour productivity NGD/FTEE	1.00000 0 46	0.15623 0.2998 46	0.83341 0.0001 46	0.19693 0.1896 46	0.12272 0.4165 46	0.03790 0.8026 46	0.51426 0.0003 46
Capital productivity NGD/NSR	0.15623 0.2998 46	1.00000 0 46	0.60291 0.0001 46	0.008435 0.9561 46	0.25329 0.0894 46	0.11922 0.4300 46	0.34761 0.0179 46
DEA-p[a] NGD, FTEE, NSR	0.83341 0.0001 46	0.60291 0.0001 46	1.0000 0 46	0.19100 0.2035 46	0.29292 0.0482 46	0.08667 0.5668 46	0.56871 0.0001 46
Labour efficiency MVA/SAL	0.19693 0.1896 46	0.00835 0.9561 46	0.19100 0.2035 46	1.00000 0 46	0.70057 0.0001 46	0.59552 0.0001 46	0.606854 0.0001 46
Capital efficiency MVA/MFC	0.12272 0.4165 46	0.25329 0.0894 46	0.29292 0.0482 46	0.70057 0.0001 46	1.00000 0 46	0.62527 0.0001 46	0.556174 0.0001 46
DEA-e[b] MVA, SAL, MFC	0.03790 0.8026 46	0.11922 0.4300 46	0.08667 0.5668 46	0.59552 0.0001 46	0.62527 0.0001 46	1.00000 0 46	0.66628 0.0001 46
'All-embracing' DEA NGD, MVA, FTEE, NSR, SAL, MFC	0.51426 0.0003 46	0.34761 0.0179 46	0.56871 0.0001 46	0.60685 0.0001 46	0.55174 0.0001 46	0.66628 0.0001 46	1.00000 0 46

Notes: Values are Pearson correlation coefficients; prob > $|R|$ under H_0: $\rho = 0$; number of observations. [a] DEA productivity model; [b] DEA efficiency model; [c] all-embracing DEA.

different information and each has an information value *per se*. This is in line with research question 1 and the proposition that partial *efficiency* measures give performance assessments that are different from partial *productivity* measures.

The first three columns also show that partial productivity measures do not necessarily correlate. Labour productivity does not, for example, correlate significantly with capital productivity. They consequently give significantly different assessments of productivity or, in other words, they both contain unique information value. This supports the proposition behind research question 2 that different partial productivity measures (such as labour productivity and capital productivity) give different assessments of productivity.

The first three columns further show that a DEA model, set up to measure productivity, is able to capture most of the information value contained in partial productivity measures. There is a clear, significant correlation (0.83 and 0.60), which supports the proposition, made in research question 3, that DEA is able to condense several different productivity measures into one measure which does not contradict any of the partial productivity measures. The same is true for a DEA efficiency model with regard to partial efficiency measures, which is brought out by columns four and five and row six in Table 11.5.

A comparison between a DEA productivity model and a DEA efficiency model (column three and row six in Table 11.5) shows that there is no significant correlation between the two measures. The information contained in each one is different from the other, which is in line with the proposition behind research question 4 that a DEA efficiency measure gives a performance measure that is different from a DEA productivity measure. Thus each model has a unique information value.

Finally, column seven in Table 11.5 illustrates the reliability of measurements by large DEA models. The large model correlates significantly with all other performance measures. Although a 'pure' productivity model better captures productivity measures, a large DEA model seems to give measures that contain almost the same information and, at the same time, also much of the information contained in the efficiency measures. Thus, the results in Table 11.5 support the proposition behind research question 5 that a large DEA model is able to condense productivity and efficiency into one performance measure. Table 11.5 seems to make a strong point for large DEA models since it is obvious that a large part of the information value contained in measurements by partial key ratios and small DEA models is captured by a large DEA model that contains several variables measuring a variety of different items and using various measurement units.

CONCLUSIONS

The objective of this chapter has been to provide an introduction to the DEA technique and to investigate how it performs compared to other traditional key ratios in measuring productivity and efficiency in restaurants. The empirical results make a strong case for a wide and general definition, such as 'productivity is an assessment of output in relation to input variables'. This conclusion is based on variations between the information contained in different ratios and DEA models. Choices of items to be measured and measurement units may produce significant differences in the results of productivity assessments. If a definition of productivity is narrow, a lot of information will be lost compared to a definition that comprises all types of assessments. Thus it makes sense to keep a conceptual definition of productivity in general. At the same time, it is necessary to be aware of the fact that, in order to be operational, productivity must be defined in terms of items as well as measurement units and that these definitions make all the difference for the results. Such operational productivity measures may be called partial productivity measures. Efficiency can be regarded as a special class of productivity measures where the choice of measurement unit is related to the ultimate goal of the activity that is being appraised. Efficiency is thus a measure of 'goal productivity'.

Another conclusion is that a clear distinction between productivity measures and efficiency measures should be maintained using DEA, just as when using other performance measures. The empirical results show that these two types of measurements do not give the same indications, they do not correlate, and the choice of an appropriate measure should be a conscientious choice related to the purpose of the analysis. It should thus be underlined that both measures, productivity as well as efficiency, contain valuable and complementary information. The fact that the two measures do not correlate shows that they are complementary and that one measure contains information that is not contained in the other.

A third conclusion that can be drawn from the empirical tests is that the inclusion of a large number of variables in a DEA model does not seem to distort the results but rather to dilute the value of the results. The more variables that are included, the higher the measures for most firms, and the smaller the variations between firms seem to be. The variation that remains does, however, correlate with productivity measures as well as efficiency measures, in our sample which of course makes a strong point for a large 'all-embracing' DEA model. From a psychological/political point of view, this may be useful because, first of all, if more suggested variables can be included, this may favour the acceptance of a 'benchmarking' programme by all parties involved. Second, since measurements generally are higher and 'gaps' smaller when more variables are added, 'losers' may be less discouraged and more prone to compete for better results. Third, if a DEA model based on many variables generally gives indications that correlate with other, more traditional, measures, those DEA indications will, to a large extent, instil more confidence.

REFERENCES

Bjurek, H. (1994) 'Essays on efficiency and productivity change with applications to public service production'. *Ekonomiska Studier 52*. Göteborg: School of Economics.

Camp, R.D. (1989) *Benchmarking: the Search for Industry Best Practices that Lead to Superior Performance*. Milwaukee: Quality Press.

Charnes, A., Cooper, W.W. and Rhodes, E. (1978) 'Measuring the efficiency of decision making units'. *European Journal of Operational Research*, 2(6), 429–44.

Davis, H.S. (1955) *Productivity Accounting*. Philadelphia: University of Pennsylvania Press.

de Ron, A. (1994) *The Transformation Factor*. Eindhoven: University of Technology.

Färe, R., Grosskopf, S. and Lovell, C.A.K. (1985) *The Measurement of Efficiency of Production*. Dordrecht: Kluwer-Nijhoff.

226 Productivity Management

Farrell, M. J. (1957) 'The measurement of productive efficiency'. *Journal of the Royal Statistical Society A,* **120**, 253–81.

Griliches, Z. (ed.) (1992) *Output Measurement in the Service Sectors.* Chicago: University of Chicago Press.

Johns, N. and Wheeler, K. (1991) 'Productivity and performance measurement and monitoring'. In R. Teare and A. Boer (eds), *Strategic Hospitality Management.* London: Cassell.

Kendrick, J. and Creamer, D. (1965) 'Summary and evaluation of recent work in measuring the productivity of federal agencies'. *Management Science,* **12**(4), 120–34.

Malmquist, S. (1953) 'Index numbers and indifferent surfaces'. *Trabajos de Estadistica,* **4**, 209–42.

Odeck, J. (1993) 'Measuring productivity growth and efficiency with data envelopment analysis'. *Ekonomiska Studier 44.* Göteborg: School of Economics.

Organization for European Economic Co-operation (1950) *Terminology of Productivity.* Brussels: OEEC.

Parsons, L.J. (1994) 'Productivity and relative efficiency: past and future?' In G.L. Lilien *et al.* (eds), *Research Traditions in Marketing.* New York: Kluwer.

Reekie, W.D. (1975) *Managerial Economics.* Chippenham: Philip Allan.

Ross, J.E. (1977) *Managing Productivity.* Reston, VA: Reston.

Siegel, I.H. (1976) 'Measurement of company productivity'. In *Improving Productivity through Industry and Company Measurement.* Washington, DC: National Center for Productivity and Quality of Working Life.

Sjögren, S. (1995) 'A DEA approach to measuring efficiency in road-rail terminals'. Mimeograph, School of Economics, Göteborg.

Spendolini, M.J. (1992) *The Benchmarking Book.* New York: Amacom.

Sumanth, D.J. (1979) 'Productivity measurement and evaluation models for manufacturing companies'. PhD thesis, Illinois Institute of Technology.

Thanassoulis, E. (1994) 'Warwick DEA user manual'. Mimeograph, Warwick University.

Törnqvist, L. (1936) 'The Bank of Finland's consumption price index'. *Bank of Finland Monthly Bulletin,* **10**, 1–8.

Tulkens, H. (1990) 'The measurement of productive efficiency by FDH frontiers'. *Documents de travail.* Louvain-la-Neuve: CORE Publications.

TWELVE

Productivity and the new service paradigm, or 'servicity' and the 'neo-service paradigm'?

Peter L. Jones and Mike Hall

INTRODUCTION

Productivity is clearly a major operational issue in the hospitality industry. In recent years there have been a number of studies that have examined this phenomenon (for instance Ball *et al.*, 1986; Prais *et al.*, 1989; Witt and Witt, 1989). Some of these studies have largely applied established theories of economic productivity and techniques of productivity measurement (Prais *et al.*, 1989), whereas others have attempted to redefine productivity or refine its measurement in order to address characteristics of the industry that make conventional approaches difficult to apply. For instance, Witt and Witt (1989) identify three major problems with productivity measurement in services in general and the hotel sector in particular: the 'definition problem', which relates largely to the intangibility of the output; the 'measurement problem', which refers to which units of measurement are appropriate; and the *'ceteris paribus* problem', which makes comparing one hotel with another, or even the same hotel over time, difficult to do. Ball *et al.* (1986) reports that measuring inputs was also problematic. These studies report specific productivity ratios for hotels, based on their own work and six other earlier studies. In particular they advocate the concept of the 'full-time equivalent employee' as one way of addressing the problem of input measurement. Clark (1994) also discusses this problem, this time in the context of the food service industry. He rejects monetary measurement units and solely time-based ratios, proposing instead the concept of meals per hour per chef.

Jones and Lockwood (1994) have proposed that a general understanding of operations management in the hospitality industry is facilitated by a clear differentiation between different levels of activity. The present chapter builds on this model by exploring the nature of productivity at two of these levels: the industry (i.e. macro economic) level and the operating unit level. The present analysis explains how the ideas presented here about productivity have evolved and how they may be applied to the hospitality industry. Like many of the studies referred to above, this chapter starts from the viewpoint that productivity as applied to the hospitality industry is highly problematic. However, the explanation of why this is so radically different from previous work. At the heart of the argument is the idea that productivity itself needs to be reconsidered as an appropriate concept for the hospitality industry, at least for the hotel sector. Indeed, it may be the case that productivity is actually a meaningless concept in this context. The present authors go so far as to propose an alternative – 'servicity'. However, before defining and explaining this term, this chapter makes a detailed analysis of the productivity concept in order to explain its useful strengths and its weaknesses in terms of the hospitality industry.

HOSPITALITY PRODUCTIVITY: THE PRESENT POSITION

As briefly discussed above, the problems associated with productivity improvement and productivity measurement in the hospitality industry have been clearly identified in previous studies. Most of these studies have sought to suggest ways in which these problems can be overcome. In the present chapter we argue that these proposed solutions to the problems may not be the appropriate way to address the fundamental issue. Put simply, the issue is that productivity is a construct of manufacturing industry. This construct has also been applied to service industries, albeit modified to take into account the differences between making products and delivering service. However, this has for the most part only been possible because some services have elements of manufacturing in them. This is especially true of food service. For example, Levitt (1976) talks explicitly about the 'industrialization' or 'production-lining' of service. He cites in particular the fast-food industry. But although this has a service element, a fast-food operation is also clearly manufacturing a product. In general, the concept of productivity can be applied relatively more easily to the food service sector of the hospitality industry than to the hotel sector. This is because food service operations process mainly materials and customers, rather than information. An accommodation operation, on the other hand, processes mainly customers, with some information and materials processing.

The present authors therefore propose that it is not helpful to think of hospitality provision simply in terms of 'manufacturing' and 'service'. Nor indeed is it sufficient to consider them in terms of a manufacturing–service continuum as proposed by Sasser *et al.* (1978). Both manufacturing and service operations process some combination of three principal elements: materials, information and people (usually customers). Uncontroversially, an operation that predominantly processes materials is considered a factory and thus firmly based in the manufacturing sector. Businesses that have direct contact with customers tend to be lumped together as 'services' even though they may engage in very different types of operation. These processes usually focus upon one of the three principal elements. When such operations concentrate in large part upon materials processing (as in fast food, or information processing) it is likely that productivity as a concept is comparatively unproblematic. However, for people-processing operations, such as hotels, this conception of productivity is likely to be inappropriate, if not downright misleading.

Despite such reservations, productivity has to date been considered at two broad levels within the hospitality industry. At the macro level, productivity considers the industry as a whole or component sectors within the industry. This enables policy-makers and economists to compare one industry with another and to evaluate productivity improvements (or not) over time. Smith (1989) suggests that productivity in British hotels declined by 1.2 per cent per annum between 1971 and 1986. Likewise, a study of hotel productivity by Prais *et al.* (1989) had as its objective 'to obtain measures of average productivity differences between countries'. Witt and Witt (1989) also consider the productivity performance of the sector as a whole. Studies have been carried out at the organizational level, in which the productivity of the firm is the focus. Here the focus of interest is usually the relative efficiency of one firm when compared with another, or the efficiency of the firm over time. Recent trends in 'downsizing' or business process re-engineering are examples of productivity improvement strategies at this level. An example of research into productivity at this level is the study by Ball and Johnson (1989) of a fast-food chain. Another common goal of productivity measurement is the comparison of operating units within a chain or affiliated group. For example, in the hospitality industry, it is common for hotel general managers to be set targets that are *de facto* productivity measures, such as labour cost percentage. Research into unit level productivity in the hotel sector has been carried out by Ball *et al.* (1986) and in the food service sector by Clark (1994).

The specific problems of productivity measurement have been noted at both macro and unit levels of the hospitality industry. These stem from the key characteristics of service identified by Sasser *et al.* (1978) nearly twenty years ago. These characteristics – *simultaneity, perishability, intangibility,* and *heterogeneity* – possess complex inter-relationships. Simultaneity refers to the fact that the customer must be present for the service to be provided, so that production and consumption are approximately simultaneous. This makes the production activity difficult to schedule, leading to peaks and troughs, and hence to relatively unproductive slack time. This simultaneity of the service process also means that service products have little or no shelf life, i.e. they are highly (perhaps ultimately) perishable. This leads to the frequently cited cliché that a hotel room not sold today cannot be sold tomorrow. The inability to hold stock hinders the management of fluctuating demand, and prevents buffering, which in the manufacturing sector would be one way out of the scheduling problem identified above. The fact that service is intangible also presents problems in terms of measurement; if it is not possible to quantify output, it is difficult to measure productivity as the ratio of input to output. Hence the comment is made in the Prais *et al.* (1989) study that 'a large element of judgement is unavoidable if broadly equivalent samples of hotels are to be identified'. Witt and Witt (1989) cite Packer, who 'illustrates how, where the product is intangible, researchers have begun to incorporate subjective assessments'. Finally, the intangible nature of service leads customers to react to the service experience in their own individual ways, i.e. heterogeneously. Again the measurement of output is almost impossible if each customer purchases in effect a unique 'experience'. As Ball and Johnson (1989) explain, 'any attempt to increase productivity. . .would very likely impinge upon customers' perceptions of service offered'. In summary, intangibility and heterogeneity present problems of productivity measurement; and simultaneity and perishability present problems of productivity management and improvement.

So far in the present analysis nothing has been discussed that has not been examined in more detail in other studies. However, the central problem of service 'productivity' is actually hidden by describing and analysing it in this way. This whole discussion, and much of the past research into hospitality, has been based on a 'manufacturing paradigm', and there are grounds for believing that this is an unsuitable paradigm for the hospitality industry.

PARADIGMS DISCUSSED

A paradigm is essentially a general pattern of thought or philosophy. The concept was originally developed to encompass scientific world views such as the globe (as opposed to the flat earth). A paradigm is defined by Kuhn (1970) as

> that constellation of values, beliefs and perceptions of empirical reality, which, together with a body of theory based on the foregoing, is used by a group of [individuals], . . . applying a distinctive methodology, to interpret the nature of some aspect of the universe that we inhabit.

The history of the world is full of examples of paradigms that have been refuted or replaced by new paradigms. In the natural sciences, for example the once-held paradigm of the divine creation of the natural world has largely been replaced with one of evolution. In social sciences, the scientific school of management has been challenged by the human relations school of thought. The idea of paradigm shift has been applied to services by Gummesson (1994). He briefly defines a paradigm as 'values and procedures that control our thinking and behaviour'. Gummesson also identifies a number of paradigms that apply to organizations and business operations: a 'manufacturing paradigm based on goods'; a 'bureaucratic-legal paradigm' found mainly in the public services, and a 'service paradigm' derived largely from marketing and modern quality management. He concludes that there is a general shift away from the manufacturing paradigm towards the service paradigm.

The present authors explore Gummesson's paradigmatic perspective further by examining the hospitality industry at the two levels referred to above: industry level and operating unit level. At the industry level, a paradigm based in economics and the social sciences is relevant. This paradigm has been termed 'Fordism' but, as Gummesson points out, is essentially the same as the 'manufacturing paradigm' outlined above. It can be argued that it is this paradigm that has shaped all previous studies of hospitality productivity. The present authors offer a discussion of two new emerging paradigms: 'neo-Fordism' and the 'service paradigm'. The conclusion is that these do not effectively distinguish between services and manufacturing and they are therefore in effect the same paradigm. The present chapter also offers a similar analysis of productivity at the operating unit level. In the context of a general, unchallenged Fordist view, it is proposed that operations and production management specialists have implicitly established a productivity paradigm that is inherently manufacturing based. The present authors believe that the so-called 'service paradigm' is not so different from the manufacturing model and that the currently accepted productivity concept applies to both. A new paradigm, called the 'neo-service paradigm', is therefore proposed, which offers a more appropriate way of considering the hospitality industry and hence the notion of hospitality productivity, which may be replaced by a new concept, here termed 'servicity'.

MACRO LEVEL ANALYSIS

The manufacturing paradigm

The authors believe that most, if not all, current thinking about productivity stems from a consideration of manufacturing industries in their Fordist stage of development. This paradigm has been developed most notably by the 'regulation' school of theorists, including Aglietta (1976), Benassy *et al.* (1977), Boyer (1979), Coriat (1979), Mazier (1982) and Lipietz (1984). Fordism originated in America during the 1920s and 1930s and became dominant during the 1950s and 1960s. It views production and consumption in terms of semi-skilled workers, control along Taylorist scientific principles, a hierarchy of management and standardized goods produced on production lines. Industrial conflict and motivation of the workforce is managed, according to this paradigm, by mass collective bargaining. The typical Fordist bargain is one in which high pay – often related to high and rising productivity – is exchanged for (and may provide consolation for) intense, highly fragmented, deskilled and alienating labour. As the name suggests, the classic example of Fordist industry is car manufacturing, and the main emphasis is on the mass production and sale of as many identical units as possible. Inherent in this paradigm is the classic concept of productivity as a measurable ratio between tangible inputs and outputs.

The Taylorist approach to manufacturing and the so-called 'scientific school of management' have been heavily criticized. Yet at the time they were a genuine attempt to improve organizational effectiveness, not only for shareholders and management, but also for the workers, since efficient production was believed to bring benefits to all. Indeed, from an operations perspective, the drive to mass production makes perfect sense. An ideal operation is one in which 'a single kind of product [is made] at a continuous rate and as if the inputs flowed continuously at a steady rate and with specified quality' (Thompson, 1967). In reality very few operations have precisely these properties, except, perhaps, the continuous automated conversion of petrochemicals.

The Fordist paradigm owes its dominance to its successful use, both as a socio-politico-economic system and more narrowly as a form of organization in manufacturing industry. Thus the 'Fordist organization' has been the stereotypical business unit since World War II, despite a gradual and continuing decline in most Western economies of manufacturing-based activity and a significant increase in service organizations. The vast majority of service firms have adopted Fordist principles and structures because they had no other model to which to turn. Thus concepts and methods associated with the manufacturing paradigm have tended to be applied across *all* industry sectors, including the hospitality industry, largely without any thought as to whether or not these were appropriately served by a paradigm based on *materials processing* operations.

The service paradigm

In the 1980s the Fordist or manufacturing-biased view of the world began to be questioned, and one group of theorists has proposed an alternative paradigm based on socio-economic analysis, known as 'post-Fordism' (Nolan and O'Donnel, 1987; Amin, 1994). Another group, working largely in the business and operations management arena, has developed ideas that lead to a 'new service paradigm' (Heskett, 1990; Gronroos, 1994; Gummesson, 1994).

Post-Fordism remains based in manufacturing but rejects many of the values, concepts and models associated with the earlier paradigm. It involves a shift towards a customer-oriented view of production. The post-Fordist argument is that modern industries have highly flexible production processes and use information technology to enhance integrated production, marketing, sales and after-sales service functions. In such industries the customer is able to shape the production process through communications systems related to advanced, flexible manufacturing operations. Thus the car industry is now transforming itself as customers are able to specify customized features for their vehicles at the point of sale. In other words cars can be ordered in the same way that dishes from a menu can be ordered in a restaurant. Handy (1994) cites a number of examples of this: 'in Ford's new Atlanta plant, each car needs only 17 hours of direct labour. Clever workers with clever machines have put an end to the mass organization'; likewise 'the *New York Times* commented that Microsoft's only factory asset was the imagination of its workers'. In short, post-Fordism is concerned with the integration of planning, design, production and retailing, a process that makes the distinction between manufacturing and service less pronounced.

In addition to this shift in the manufacturing paradigm, a new paradigm has emerged, related specifically to service industries. The studies on which the 'new service paradigm' was based have emphasized the difference between service and manufacturing. Heskett (1990), for example, suggests that service organizations differ from their manufacturing counterparts in five ways. These are as follows:

- integration of marketing, operations and human resource management;
- the management of people working simultaneously and often in interactive mode in geographically far-flung networks connected by a communications system;
- maintenance of a knowledge of customer needs and the way they are being met;
- 'real-time' nature of service production and delivery;
- customers having direct access to most members of organization.

Likewise, Grönroos (1994) identifies five key facets of service management, similar to Heskett's. These are:

- an overall management perspective;
- customer-driven or market-driven;
- a holistic perspective emphasizing cross-functional collaboration;
- quality is integral not separate;
- personnel development and commitment is a prerequisite for success.

However, three of Heskett's characteristics, and all of Grönroos's, are also compatible with the post-Fordist view of manufacturing. Thus distinctions between manufacturing and service approaches do not really exist if post-Fordism, rather than Fordism, becomes the dominant paradigm. The 'integration of marketing, operations and human resource management' is as valid for the post-Fordist manufacturer as for any service firm. Likewise, 'the management of people working simultaneously and often in interactive mode in geographically far-flung networks connected by a communications system' and 'maintenance of a knowledge of customer needs and the way they are being met' do not distinguish service from post-Fordist manufacture.

In many respects, therefore, post-Fordism and the service paradigm are very similar. However, neither takes into account the notion developed earlier that 'services' are not a homogeneous group in operational terms. Neither Heskett nor Grönroos differentiates adequately between materials-processing, information-processing and customer-processing service operations. It is not surprising, therefore, within both the neo-Fordist paradigm and the new service paradigm, that productivity as a concept survives largely unchanged. It can still be the relationship of tangible inputs and outputs, albeit with some modifications made (as in the studies cited above) and with some concerns expressed. Grönroos (1994) writes that

> voices have been raised that service management overemphasizes [quality and customer satisfaction so that] productivity and profitability issues may suffer. . . .If the service management perspective is applied so that the firm loses track of the importance of productivity and profitability, this criticism is of course valid.

He goes on to say that 'productivity [in services] is measured in an unsophisticated way [and] the influence of scientific management can be seen here'. He concludes that 'how to measure productivity in a service organization is more or less an unsolved problem'. Following a similar discussion, Gummesson (1994) concludes that 'there is an obvious need for basic research and *conceptualization of service productivity*' (italics added). It should be clear from previous discussion that this chapter proposes that such clarification will come about when 'service' is replaced by the idea of customer processing operations.

However, two of Heskett's (1990) characteristics really do distinguish service from manufacture, even the neo-Fordist view of manufacture, and may make it possible to conceptualize service productivity. These factors are the 'real-time' nature of production and delivery and the 'direct access [customers have] to most of the members of the organization'. Both of these would seem to relate to the concept of a customer processing operation, at the heart of which is the 'service encounter'. It is this encounter that should form the basis of a paradigm that is here referred to as the 'neo-service paradigm'. Before we discuss this concept, the three paradigms outlined above are considered at the operating unit level of the hospitality industry.

OPERATING UNIT LEVEL ANALYSIS

The manufacturing paradigm

Productivity has been considered and analysed in a number of texts dealing with the hospitality industry (e.g. Merricks and Jones, 1986; Mill, 1989; Ball, 1994). These analyses and much of the research to date have been based implicitly upon the manufacturing paradigm, since the service paradigm was not yet fully developed to enable authors or researchers to do anything other than apply existing theories and models. Typically, therefore, productivity is discussed in input/output terms, operations are modelled as 'hard systems', and measurement is expressed in quantifiable units. For instance, Merricks and Jones (1986) write:

> The major problem facing catering managers in their attempt to improve productivity is the inexact and diverse nature of the product/service [sic] being sold. . . .The industry has traditionally ignored or overcome this problem by adding together total inputs and outputs and comparing the two aggregates.

Similarly, the study by Prais *et al.* (1989) was designed as one of a set of four studies, of which the other three were in manufacturing: metal components, kitchen cabinets and clothing. Likewise, the Ball *et al.* (1986) study discusses in turn issues of measurement of hotel outputs, measurement of hotel inputs and ratios of hotel productivity. As they say, 'features [which] are complex and inherent in hotels have frequently been perceived as deterrents to productivity measurement rather than hurdles which can often be surmounted'.

The service paradigm

Levitt's (1976) work, which looked at the 'industrialization' and 'production-lining' of service, exemplifies how close 'services' are to manufacturing. Based on his analysis, attempts have been made to adapt existing theories of productivity to fit the service paradigm. For example, Jones (1988) emphasizes the idea of outcomes, as well as outputs, in terms of the relationship between quality, capacity and productivity in services. In some cases, attempts have also been made to apply service productivity ideas to the hospitality industry. Jones (1990) proposes a link between service delivery systems and productivity strategies in the hospitality industry. This development of theory within the service paradigm was satisfactory because for food service operations such analysis was not excessively dysfunctional. However, these studies, and others, tended to ignore hotels and accommodation provision that did not so easily fit with the ideas proposed.

THE 'NEO-SERVICE PARADIGM'

So far it has been argued that productivity is inherently based in the manufacturing paradigm. The present authors have shown how this paradigm has undergone a shift away from Fordism towards post-Fordism and compared the latter with the service paradigm, to show that there are substantial similarities. It is now argued that a paradigm that truly distinguishes between materials processing operations and customer processing operations is needed, along with a new way of thinking about productivity.

According to the argument so far, the defining feature of customer service is the direct involvement of the consumer with the service provider, which may be called the 'service encounter'. This concept is not new (Czepiel *et al.*, 1985) but it appears to have failed significantly to influence thinking about productivity. The neo-service paradigm has this concept of the service encounter at its heart. To be successful, such encounters effect a transfer from server to consumer. Hairdressing services transfer the skill of the hairdresser to the person of the customer; taxi services transfer the utility of the car to someone without one; education transfers knowledge from the teacher to the learner. This transfer is engaged in for some purpose of the consumer, which on occasions he or she is unaware of until the interaction takes place. Often the transference has both tangible and intangible elements, described as a 'service bundle'. The latter has been modelled (originally by service marketers) in a number of different ways (e.g. Shostack, 1977; Grönroos, 1980; Blois, 1983).

However, a key feature of this paradigm is the theory that the whole service encounter is greater than the sum of the individual parts of the bundle. This is one of the reasons why consumers may move away from using services that have been depersonalized altogether back towards less efficient but more 'friendly' service provision. In the United States service has been 'industrialized' for twenty years (along lines advocated by Levitt and others and discussed above). It is noticeable that, since the 1980s, many US service firms have had to reintroduce non-automated delivery for customers prepared to pay a premium price for 'service'. For instance, it is not uncommon to find petrol filling stations with a row of self-service pumps plus a row of attended pumps. It is therefore proposed here that the encounter itself adds value to the value of the tangibles and/or intangibles transferred during the encounter. This can be modelled as shown in equation (1):

$$V^s = v^e + v^t \qquad (1)$$

where V^s is the total value of the service; v^e is the value of the service encounter; v^t is the value of the tangibles and/or intangibles transferred.

The customer processing part of an operation, or the service encounter between server and consumer, is the essence of the service aspect of any industry. It has a number of features. First, it is as much an outcome of the 'work' of the consumer as of the server. It acknowledges that, in paying for the service, customers are generally paying for something that they themselves have helped to produce. Second, the quality of the encounter is determined by the 'felicity' of the interpersonal interaction between server and consumer. This term 'felicity' is used in its sense of aptness and suitability of style, although its meaning of 'bliss' may not be entirely inappropriate for some service provision. Such felicity is an outcome of the many-faceted interpersonal 'chemistry' of the parties involved. Third, the concept of heterogeneity applies to the encounter. Each one is slightly different and many may be radically different from each other, according to the personalities of the participants. Fourth, the felicitous encounter is a whole, integrated experience. Although service provision can be broken down into a series of tasks, each encounter must be considered as a complete interaction involving a minimum of social routines, such as greetings, the

establishment of trust, mutual respect, farewells and perhaps others. Finally, encounters may add value for the customer because they assist in the making of choices,
enable adaptation and customization, and facilitate recognition of the service
available. These features of service, notably felicity, completeness, heterogeneity and
added value, mean that the scope for standardizing the service encounter and
subjecting it to a rigorous division of labour is extremely limited.

It is now possible to examine the problem of productivity and how it might be
conceived within the neo-service paradigm. Over and above the tangibles and/or
intangibles transferred during the service encounter is the felicity of the encounter
itself. It is clear that 'productivity', from the very term itself (i.e. *product* ivity) can
measure tangibles. However, by the same token, a new quantity – *servicity* – is needed
in order to measure intangibles of the encounter, as well as tangibles. Unlike
productivity, servicity cannot be thought of in physical quantities. But this does not
mean that it cannot be defined and measured. Consumers in a market economy can
and do pay more for felicitousness, which contributes to the added value of an
encounter, as in the filling station example quoted above. Indeed, tipping is an
example of a payment frequently found in the hospitality industry, which recognizes
and rewards the felicity added by individuals to the service encounter. If such felicity
can be measured by the 'price' added, then this would provide a measure of servicity
as the value added to a service transaction by personal interaction. In other words,
servicity can be defined as the ratio of physical input with value output:

$$S = v^e : l \tag{2}$$

where S is servicity; v^e is the value of the service encounter; l is labour input.

Although it may be possible to measure the value of the service encounter in the
examples cited above (tipping and petrol filling stations), in reality this is likely to
prove very difficult. v^e is very much a 'soft' measure. Indeed, the idea of presenting
servicity as a ratio may well be an example of how this new paradigm continues to be
influenced by theoretical considerations derived from the pervasive Fordist model.

If servicity is not, after all, appropriately expressed the ratio shown in equation (2),
how might it be expressed? Heskett's most recent work (1990) on the service value
chain suggests that the key features of effective service operation are employee
satisfaction, employee retention, customer satisfaction and customer loyalty. This
emerging theory is consistent with the neo-service paradigm. Hence, it may be more
appropriate to express servicity as a model, rather than as an equation, especially at an
operational level. Such a model might, for example, show the relationship(s) between
the kind of variables Heskett identifies. On this basis, a system of benchmarking,
profiling, may be the most appropriate method to measure and improve servicity.
Certainly there is emerging evidence from one study (Heilbron, 1995) that benchmarking works as an operational tool in a major retail fashion chain in the UK. This
study has shown that measurements of customer satisfaction, repeat business,
employee satisfaction, staff retention and sales are all possible through records related
to the chain's own debit cards. More importantly, comparisons between outlets show
that for those where these measures are high, sales and profits are also high, and vice
versa. Although they are very much more difficult to design than simple measures of
input or output, the use of employee and customer satisfaction surveys also enables
relatively sophisticated analysis, which may in turn enable appropriate action to be
taken to improve performance.

This discussion of the difference between productivity and servicity can also be considered at a more strategic level, in terms of their overall intent. At the heart of productivity, consistent with Fordian analysis, is the idea of producing 'more for less'. In achieving this, it has often been the case that employees have had to pay a high price, by engaging in highly routinized, demotivating tasks. On the other hand, servicity seeks to produce 'more from better'. Inherent in the servicity concept is the idea of a win/win scenario, in which customer satisfaction increases employee satisfaction, which in turn increases customer satisfaction.

CONCLUSION

When this chapter was first conceived it was thought that it could present an argument that fits the existing 'productivity' concept into the emerging service paradigm. Such an argument develops as follows. First, the underpinning theory of service productivity should be based not on an understanding of the relationship between capital or labour and output, but on elements of the service value chain such as employee satisfaction, perceived quality, customer satisfaction and loyalty. Second, the input/output model should be replaced by the new concept (in this context) of an input/*outcome* model. An earlier paper by Jones (1988) identifies the distinction between outputs and outcomes and shows that the latter are more appropriate than the former to the service concept. Third, measurement should shift from being a snapshot at a given moment in time into longitudinal measurement over possibly long periods of time.

However, the more the service paradigm is investigated, the more it is apparent that this paradigm could also be applied to modern manufacturing. Closer inspection reveals few major conceptual differences between post-Fordism and the service paradigm. It is, however, possible to hold values and attitudes that suggest there really is a difference, centred on the provider–consumer interface. Such a standpoint depends upon differentiating between different types of service operations on the basis of their major throughput (i.e. material, information or people). Hence this chapter proposes a 'neo-service paradigm', centred on customer-processing operations, a theory of the service encounter and a model of productivity retitled 'servicity'. It is likely that the concepts of simultaneity, intangibility, perishability and heterogeneity are consistent with this 'neo-service' view of the world, since inherently they centre on the service encounter. To these has been added the concept of 'felicity', the basis of the value added to a service transaction at the customer interface.

Although this discussion of the neo-service paradigm is based upon values, includes some theory and provides some models, it is far from complete. Many more ideas will need to be generated and discussed before such a paradigm is fully developed. Along the way, it is likely that it will be changed, adapted, attacked, rejected and improved. This is in the nature of paradigms. The academic study of service industries, and in particular hospitality, is relatively new. The thoughts and perceptions of those engaged in it tend to have been extensively shaped by their experience of the industry – of what is, rather than what might be. This has tended to result in highly pragmatic research with applied outcomes, but with comparatively little theoretical underpinning or philosophical debate about what is meant by 'service' and 'hospitality'. Two key features of the argument presented by the present authors are the suggestion that a total rethink of theory may have some worth and the emphasis placed on values and attitudes. Discussing productivity in the context of a paradigm, as has been done here, emphasizes that theories and models are not value-free and that thinking about values is an essential part of the development of hospitality research.

REFERENCES

Amin, A. (1994) *Post-Fordism*. Oxford: Blackwell.

Aglietta, J. (1976) *A Theory of Capitalist Regulation: the US Experience*. London: New Left Books.

Ball, S. (1994) 'Improving labour productivity'. In P. Jones (ed.), *The Management of Foodservice Operations*, pp. 188–203. London: Cassell.

Ball, S.D. and Johnson, K. (1989) 'Productivity management within fast food chains – a case study of Wimpy International'. *International Journal of Hospitality Management*, 8(4), 265–9.

Ball, S.D., Johnson, K. and Slattery, P. (1986) 'Labour productivity in hotels: an empirical analysis'. *International Journal of Hospitality Management*, 5(3), 141–7.

Benassy, J.P. *et al.* (1977) 'Approches de l'inflation: l'example francais'. Rapport CORDES-CEPREMAP.

Blois, K. (1983) 'Service marketing – assertion or asset'. *Service Industries Journal*, 3(2), 113–20.

Boyer, R. (1979) 'Wage formation in historical perspective: the French experience'. *Cambridge Journal of Economics*, 3(2), 337–79.

Clark, J.R. (1994) 'Relationship between productivity and catering technology in the hotel and catering industry'. MPhil thesis, Sheffield Hallam University.

Coriat, B. (1979) *L'atelier et le chronom vitre*. Paris: Bourgois.

Czepiel, J.A., Solomon, M. and Surprenant, C.S. (1985) *The Service Encounter*. Lexington, MA: Lexington Books.

Grönroos, C. (1980) 'An applied service marketing theory'. Working Paper No. 57, Swedish School of Economics and Business Administration, Helsinki.

Grönroos, C. (1994) 'From scientific management to service management'. *International Journal of Service Industry Management*, 5(1), 5–20.

Gummesson, E. (1994) 'Service management: an evaluation and the future'. *International Journal of Service Industry Management*, 5(1), 77–96.

Handy, C. (1994) *The Empty Raincoat*. London: Hutchinson.

Heilbron, B. (1995) Private communication to the author, based on MPhil research study at the University of Brighton.

Heskett, J. (1990) *Service Breakthrough*. New York: The Free Press.

Jones, P. (1988) 'Quality, capacity and productivity in service industries'. *International Journal of Hospitality Management*, 7(2), 104–12.

Jones, P. (1990) 'Managing foodservice productivity in the long term: strategy, structure and performance'. *International Journal of Hospitality Management*, 9(2), 143–54.

Jones, P. and Lockwood, A. (1994) 'Hospitality operating systems'. Proceedings of the New Visions for Hospitality Operations Management Conference, Chelmsford.

Kuhn, T.S. (1970) *The Structure of Scientific Revolutions*. Chicago: University of Chicago Press.

Levitt, T. (1976) 'The industrialization of service'. *Harvard Business Review*, 54(5), 63–74.

Lipietz, A. (1984) quoted in M. De Vroey 'A regulation approach interpretation of the contemporary crisis'. *Capital and Class*, **23**, 45–66.

Mazier, J. (1982) 'Growth and crisis – a Marxist interpretation'. In A. Boltho (ed.), *The European Economy: Growth and Crisis*. Oxford: Oxford University Press.

Merricks, P. and Jones, P. (1986) *The Management of Catering Operations*. Eastbourne: Holt Rinehart Winston.

Mill, R.C. (1989) *Managing for Productivity in the Hospitality Industry*. New York: Van Nostrand Reinhold.

Nolan, P. and O'Donnell, K. (1987) 'Taming the market economy? A critical assessment of the GLC experiment in restructuring labour'. *Cambridge Journal of Economics*, **11**, 452–70.

Prais, S.J., Jarvis, V. and Wagner, K. (1989) 'Productivity and vocational skills in services in Britain and Germany: hotels'. *National Institute Economic Review*, November, 52–73.

Sasser, W.D., Olsen, R.P. and Wyckoff, D.D. (1978) *Management of Service Operations*. New York: Allyn and Bacon.

Scofield, M. (1992) 'The emerging paradigm in service management'. Mimeo Universidad de Navarra.

Shostack, G.L. (1977) 'Breaking free from product marketing'. *Journal of Marketing*, **41**(2), 37–47.

Tompson, J.D. (1967) *Organization in Action*. New York: McGraw-Hill.

Witt, C.A. and Witt, S.F. (1989) 'Why productivity in the hotel sector is low'. *Journal of Contemporary Hospitality Management*, **1**(2), 28–34.

INDEX

acceptable quality level 117–8
asset design 10, 121, 133, 137

benchmarking 16, 209
BS 5750/ISO 9000 26, 28, 29, 30, 35, 125, 131
budgeting 125, 126, 133, 136
Burger King 170

central analysis (cognitive maps) 123–4, 125
communication 14, 15, 16, 103, 120
competitive advantage 29, 47, 51, 201
continuous quality improvement (CQI) 23, 24, 25, 118–19
contractive strategies 4, 105, 106, 174
cook-chill (*sous vide*) 12, 105
cost control 68, 201
CREST factors 12–13
cultural fit 33, 35
customer expectations 173, 177, 189
customer satisfaction 7, 59, 154, 155, 157, 197

data envelopment analysis 209ff.
  defined 213–15
  limited vs extensive 222
  sample results 218–21
Disneyworld 104, 120
domain analysis (cognitive maps) 123–5, 127

effectiveness 96, 200, 201–2, 207
efficiency 3, 209, 211, 217
  partial 215
employee turnover 188
  causal model 72–74
  cost 69–71
  culture 79–83

empowerment 107, 108
EPOS technology 196
expansive strategies 4, 105, 106, 174

facilities management 105
forecasting 203
Forte Hotels 11, 104, 105, 106

Gardner Merchant 106

Harvester Restaurants 106, 111
Hilton Hotels 104
Holiday Inns 104, 106
HOST scheme 63
Hotel & Catering Training Company (HCTC) 141, 142, 147, 148, 150, 153
human resource management 58, 59, 96ff.
  definitions 98–101
Hyatt Hotels 106

incentives 34, 106, 107
inefficiencies 10
information technology 11, 136
inputs (defining) 168, 188, 194, 197, 201
Inter-Continental Hotels 107, 108
Investors in People 31, 110

job satisfaction 78, 80, 81, 82, 83, 84, 180

Little Chefs 120
long-haul markets 5

management information system (MIS) 196
management style 59, 206
manufacturing industry 2, 3, 7, 62
  paradigm 230, 231, 233
  vs service industries 228

market structure 50
McDonald's 58, 59, 104, 110, 170, 176
motivation 32, 34, 56, 133, 155, 206
multi-skilling 119, 120, 132

National Society for Quality through Teamwork (NSQT) 27
National Vocational Qualifications (NVQ) 64,
  110, 121, 124, 125, 129, 130

organizational
  commitment 80, 82, 84
  culture 100, 121, 206
  development 174
  downsizing 19, 69
  objectives 14–15, 100
  strategy 39, 51, 174
  structure 11, 23, 29, 34, 35, 133, 134, 135,
    137
outputs (defining) 169, 188, 194, 197, 201

Pareto rule 10
partial productivity 3, 197–9, 211, 215
participation 14, 15
path analysis (cognitive maps) 123, 126
performance 48–9, 52
productivity
  corporate 103
  definitions 20, 38, 57, 115, 150, 176, 187,
    194–5, 210–11
  determinants 204, 205
  improvement 9
  index 201
  levels 102
  management techniques 116, 149
  measurement 7, 8, 34, 38, 144, 145, 146,
    147, 151, 152, 160, 161, 194ff., 209ff.
    activity-related 202
    interpretation 203
    key ratios 210, 217
    revenue-related 202, 203
    total factor 197–8
  pyramid 64
  ratio 2, 4, 20, 58, 143, 167, 170, 172, 196,
    197, 198, 200
  spiral 199–200

profitability 2–3, 28, 33, 96

quality 20, 62, 97–8, 124, 130, 144, 170, 200
  circles 12, 27–28, 31, 32, 33
  control 7, 171
  management system 5, 20, 25, 31

Queen's Moat House Hotels 106

recognition 24, 34
  systems 24–26
restaurant sector 6

Scandic Crown Hotels 105, 111
scientific management xi, 55
senior management 14, 23, 28, 30, 39, 104, 176
service
  characteristics 97, 116–17, 229
  delivery system 180
  interaction 6–7
  paradigm 230, 232–3, 234–5
  product portfolio 39
  'servicity' 236
Sheraton Hotels 107, 108
smaller hotels 116–20, 122, 136, 142

TGI Friday's 104, 105, 106, 108, 109, 111, 120
top-line factors 4–6, 201
total quality management (TQM) 21, 28, 30,
  104, 118–19
training 12, 13, 24, 26, 62, 64, 103, 106, 108,
  125, 136, 159, 189, 206
Tussauds Group 6

value added 145, 195–6
  by service activities 235–6
variability 203
variation 203
visitor management 7

Wendy's 179
Wimpy International 166ff.
work design 11, 12, 103
work flexibility 106, 109, 119, 120
work study 55, 56
workgroup design 11